Frederick J. Jobson

**Australia**

With notes by the way, on Egypt, Ceylon, Bombay and the Holy Land - Vol. 1

Frederick J. Jobson

**Australia**
*With notes by the way, on Egypt, Ceylon, Bombay and the Holy Land - Vol. 1*

ISBN/EAN: 9783337228330

Printed in Europe, USA, Canada, Australia, Japan

Cover: Foto ©Andreas Hilbeck / pixelio.de

More available books at **www.hansebooks.com**

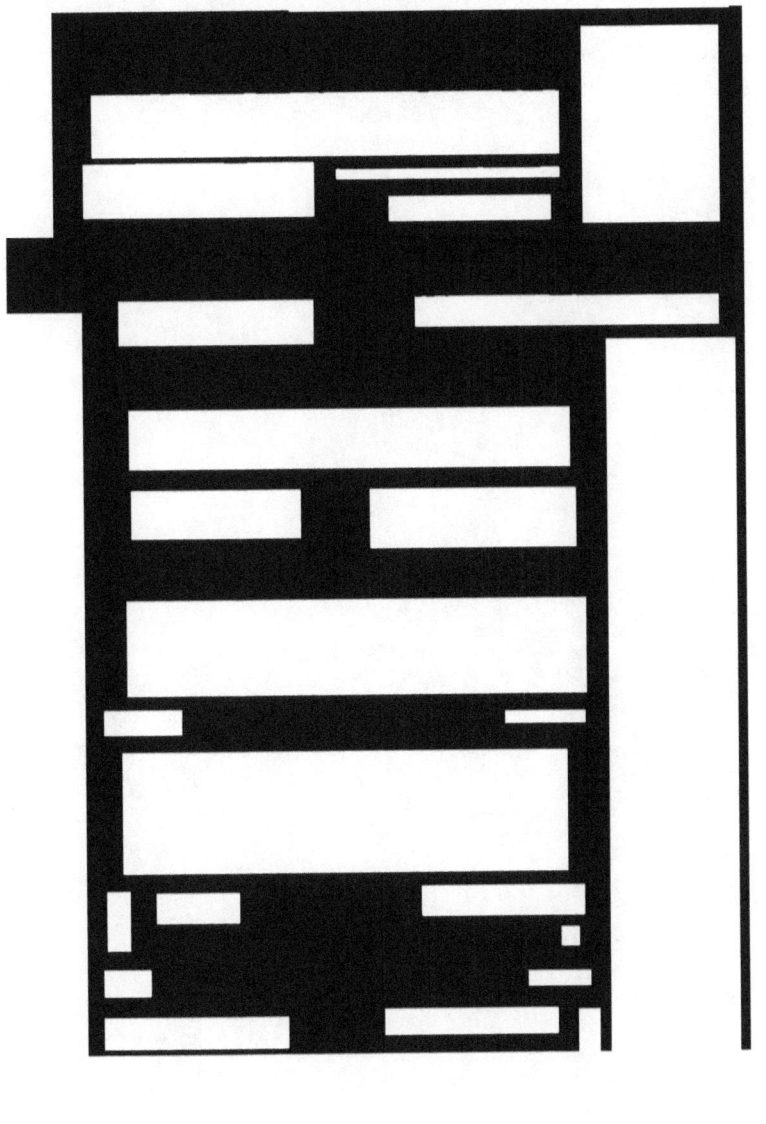

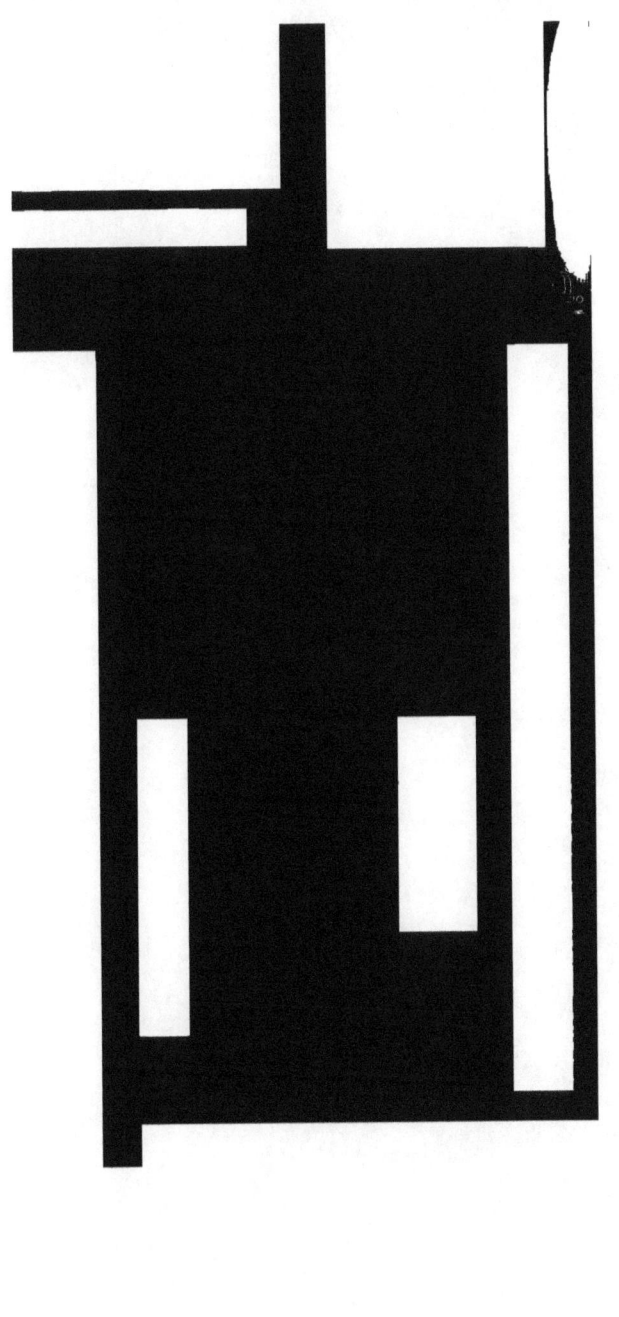

# PREFACE TO THE SECOND EDITION.

A LARGE impression of this volume having been disposed of within a few weeks, the author has taken the advantage of a new issue to revise his book, and to make some additions to it.

The events which have recently transpired in the Australasian Colonies, and which have been reported since the first edition of this book was published, show the rapid change and advancement of British dependencies in that part of the globe. Not only has the "Native-King" disturbance in New Zealand been allayed by the timely measures of its newly-appointed Governor, Sir George Grey, but gold has been discovered in the southern portion of that double island; and the yield is so abundant as to attract thousands to it, across the surrounding seas. Since then, too, the results of the Exploring Expeditions in Australia Proper have been made known, and the character of the interior of that great "South Land" is ascertained. The "Land Bills,"—the reconstruction of the Upper Houses of Legislation,—and other important measures, have also been considerably advanced.

Indeed, since this book was written, it may almost be said that a new history belongs to that part of the world. The writer has, therefore, in his revision, availed himself of the most recent information, and has incorporated it. Encouraged by the favour with which the first issue of his volume has been received by the public and the press, he sends forth this second edition with the hope that it will not meet a less generous reception.

47, CITY-ROAD, LONDON.

# CONTENTS.

## VOYAGE OUT.

### CHAPTER I.

PAGE

INTRODUCTION—Voyage from Southampton to Gibraltar—"The Rock"—The Town—The Market—The Mediterranean—Malta—The Harbour of Alexandria  3

### CHAPTER II.

Egypt—Alexandria—Railway, and View of the Country—Land of Goshen—Cairo and its Wonders—The Suburbs—Ancient Christian Remains—The Nilometer—The Pasha's Naval Architect, and his Methodist Recollections—The "Petrified Forest" and "Tombs of the Caliphs"—Dervish Worship—Heliopolis—Nile Boat and Voyage—The Pyramids and the Sphynx—The Pasha's Palace and his Soldiers—Tombs of the Mamelukes and of Mehemet Ali—Moslem Worship—View of Cairo from the Citadel—Departure—The Desert Railway—Suez, and Embarkation on the Red Sea . . . . . 21

### CHAPTER III.

Passage down the Red Sea—Aden—Monsoons—Ceylon—Rich Scenery—Native Schools—Matura—Animal and Vegetable Life—Buddhist Temples—Dress of the

|  | PAGE |
|---|---|

Singhalese—Dondra Head—Methodism in Ceylon—Constellation of the "Cross"—Morotto—Preaching to the Singhalese—Mr. Gogerly—Colombo—Kandy—Buddhu's Foot and Tooth—Opening of a Wesleyan Chapel for the Singhalese—Their Liberality and Devotion—Farewell—Re-embarkation . . 56

## AUSTRALIA AND TASMANIA.

### CHAPTER IV.

The Indian Ocean—Albatrosses—Southern Constellations—Cape Leeuwin—King George's Sound—Aborigines and Wild Flowers—Convicts—Voyage from Albany to Port Phillip—Melbourne—Ballarat and "the Diggings"—Geelong—Notes on Melbourne, Ballarat, and Geelong, and on Methodism in the Colony of Victoria . . . . . . 91

### CHAPTER V.

Tasmania—River Tamar—Launceston—Stories of the Old Convicts—Last Night of the Year 1860—Coach Journey from Launceston on New Year's Day, 1861—Beautiful Scenery—Reaping on New Year's Day—Arrival at Horton College—Sunday-School Children and New Year's Festival—Coach Journey renewed—Tales of Sportsmen—New Face of Nature, Trees, Birds, and Insects—Arrival at Hobart-Town—Notes on Tasmania—Return to Launceston—Re-passage of Bass' Straits, to Melbourne . . . 119

CONTENTS. xi

## CHAPTER VI.

PAGE

Voyage from Melbourne to Sydney—Port Jackson—Reception at Sydney—Opening of the Australasian Conference—Paramatta—Return to Sydney—University—Bible Society Meeting—Beautiful Suburbs and Neighbourhood of Sydney—The last Native—Again to Paramatta—Richmond—Bullock-Drays and Loads of Wool—Splendid View of Sydney and its Harbour—Botany Bay—House of Legislation—Notes on Sydney and New South Wales—The Australasian Conference, and Methodism on the other side of the Globe . . . . . . 138

## CHAPTER VII.

Departure from Sydney—Return to Melbourne—House of Legislation—Meetings with Friends and Ministers—Opening of New Church at Collingwood—Passage to South Australia—Extreme Heat on Arrival—Visit to Kapunda in a Mining Region—Sabbath Services—Plains and City of Adelaide—Farewell Breakfast—Notes on South Australia—Western Australia—General Views of the Island-Continent—The Aborigines . . . . . 180

# RETURN HOME.

## CHAPTER VIII.

Voyage back from Australia to Ceylon—Visits to other Buddhist Temples—Interior and Fort revisited—Farewell to Ceylon—Voyage to Bombay—Caves of

Elephanta—Ramble through Bombay—The Parsees—Voyage from Bombay to Aden—Voyage up the Red Sea—Scene of the Israelites' Passage—Arrival at Suez—At Cairo—Loss of Luggage—Arrival at Alexandria—Luggage not found . . . . 213

## CHAPTER IX.

Departure for the Holy Land—Jaffa—Pilgrims returning from the Holy City—Associations of "Joppa"—Journey to Ramleh—Night at the Latin Convent—Scriptural Sites in the Journey from Ramleh—Watchhouses—First Sight of Jerusalem—Church of the Holy Sepulchre—Sacred Places—View from St. Stephen's Gate—Valley of Jehoshaphat—The Mount of Olives—Zion Gate—The Jews' Quarter—Mount Zion—Ancient and Modern City—Walls and Streets—Bethany—Church of the Ascension—Sepulchre of the Holy Virgin—Other Sepulchres—Tophet—Aceldama—Jews' Wailing Place—Solomon's Bridge—Second Visit to the Church of the Holy Sepulchre . 229

## CHAPTER X.

Journey to Bethlehem—Rachel's Tomb—Salesmen in Bethlehem—Church of the Nativity—Tombs and Shrines—The Plains of Bethlehem—The Garden of Gethsemane—Ancient Olives—Pentecost, and a Sacrament with Christian Jews, in Jerusalem—Room of the Passover—Pool of Bethesda—View from the Mount of Olives to the Dead Sea and the Mountains of Moab—Journey to Bethel—Gibeah—Mizpeh—Ramah—The Mosque of Omar and the Tower of Hippicus—Farewell to Jerusalem—Journey back to Jaffa—Voyage Home . . . . . 261

# Part First.

## VOYAGE OUT.

# VOYAGE OUT.

## CHAPTER I.

INTRODUCTION—Voyage from Southampton to Gibraltar—"The Rock" —The Town—The Market—The Mediterranean—Malta—The Harbour of Alexandria.

THERE is a current observation among readers, that books of travel are becoming vexatiously numerous; and that people who pass over old or oft-trod journeying routes should be content to see all the sights for themselves, and say nothing of what they have seen, except in conversation with their family and friends at home. The only readable volumes of travel, now-a-days, according to this opinion, are those of Du Chaillu, who has so lately presented us with his marvellous pictures of the gorilla,—of Livingstone, who devotes a life to the real exploration of Africa, with a view to its real civilization,—or of some other explorer of regions hitherto unknown, of which it is highly desirable we should have a true knowledge, such as voyagers in search of the North-West Passage, or civilian companions of the march into China. The present writer respectfully demurs to these sweeping opinions. He suggests, for the reader's favourable consideration, that, so long as a traveller along the very oldest highways of the world takes up no unreasonable time in relating his story, and does not swell it full of borrowed details, but gives it in earnest,—because he was in earnest in going to see what he has seen,—his book must have such a degree of readable freshness as should be sufficient to interest every reader who is not incurably fastidious. Every eye has its own point of sight from which it regards scenes and objects; and it is by comparing the different views of different travellers that a true knowledge of foreign countries and their inhabitants is to be gained.

The author of this volume has endeavoured to give, in as brief and succinct a form as possible, his own views of the countries through which he has passed, being mindful of the exhortation by the Rajah of Travancore to a Christian Missionary, in the sixteenth century: " Friend, be not tedious: remember, life is short ! " His aim has not been to write a large book; but to reproduce, for the benefit of others, the impressions made upon his mind by what he saw and learned. For this purpose he has chosen what, perhaps, is not the most inviting form of published writing,—that of the journal-register;—and has transcribed from his note-book the fragmentary jottings made by the way. He hopes, however, that advantage will be found in this form of recital: it will give the best transcript of the impressions as they were made on the mind.

It is the writer's conviction that the British Colonies, at our antipodes, are but very partially understood and valued: he will be glad if his own brief and imperfect representations shall serve, in any degree, to render them better known and appreciated. This volume might have been swollen considerably, had he written at length and to the full, on this great topic; but he has striven to confine his record to matters least familiar to English readers. A like consideration of proportionate claim has governed the selection of engraved illustration for this volume. The author sketched his way in pictures, as well as noted it in writing,—not only for practice in Art, to which he had been attached from childhood,— but also to have the forms and associations of what he saw more distinctly and ineffaceably imprinted on his mind. So it would not have been difficult to have crowded the volume with sketches from his portfolio, and to have made it a picture-book; but he has, from motives of economy, selected only one of his sketches for publication.

The reader may as well be informed, at once, who the author is, and what was the cause of his transit to the other side of the globe. He is a Wesleyan Minister who, by the appointment of his brethren, went forth as their Representative to attend the Australasian Methodist Conference which, in January, 1861, assembled at Sydney. His wife, though of delicate frame, resolved to accompany him, and to share in his adventures and perils. His appointment was made, without previous notice or intimation, far on in August, 1860. Within a month afterwards, we sailed in one of the Peninsular and Oriental Company's steam-ships; and, after lingering in Egypt and Ceylon, on our way, we reached Australia before the end of the year. In the Australian Colonies, I visited the principal cities and towns, and ministered in them; and I mingled with all classes of colonial society, finding among them a large number of individuals to whom I had previously administered the word of life in different parts of the United Kingdom. We returned home before the end of June, 1861; and the following record, in journal form, will enable the reader to retrace our passage from place to place; to learn the sources whence information was obtained, and the circumstances under which the impressions described were produced:—while persons contemplating travel in the same direction may ascertain what can be done within a given period of time.

At noon of Thursday, September 20th, 1860, we went on board the steamer, "Ripon," at Southampton, accompanied by our friends,—Rev. John Scott, Rev. Dr. and Mrs. Hoole, Rev. Dr. Osborn, Rev. William Arthur, M.A., and J. Robinson Kay, Esq., of Summerseat, Lancashire. These friends remained with us till the vessel started; and then left us for a point of land from whence the last sight of us could be had, and from whence they might beckon us "farewell." We were soon out of view, and were passing between the Isle of Wight and the Hampshire coast. Seriousness, but not sadness, possessed us; for we were going on the service of God, and knew that, under His protection, we were as safe at sea as on land.

Our cabin was at the "poop," opposite the cabin of the Captain, and was a convenient one; but it was continuously tremulous, through the perpetual movement and rattling of the chain on the helm-wheel. The after-deck was appropriated to the seats and promenade of passengers. Forward, the ship was occupied by cabins of officers, in the middle,—and by live-stock for provision, at the sides: at the bow, was the crew's sleeping-place. Round the saloon, were passengers' cabins,—first class, aft,—and second class, next the engine-room, which, of course, was in the middle of the ship. Under these, were holds for bullion and luggage. We had about three hundred souls on board. Our ship was well-provisioned; the Captain and officers did all they could to render the voyage pleasant;—entering freely into the conversation, games, and pastimes of the passengers. Being English men and women, we, of course, availed ourselves, at intervals, of our privilege of grumbling; but the accommodation was as good as could be reasonably expected in a floating habitation; and the supplies were abundant. Passengers of both sexes were not sparing of bitter-beer, any more than of wine and spirits, especially they who were returning to the thirsty plains of India; and the daily scene at table in the saloon was that of a brilliant assembly at a banquet.

We were awakened every morning at four by the violent scrubbing of the decks; at six the steward brought us coffee or tea; at nine the passengers met for breakfast; at twelve for lunch; at four for dinner; at six for tea; and at nine, as many as were disposed so to indulge themselves, gathered at the tables for grog. The deck and the saloon, especially towards evening, became scenes of animation and amusement; and much ingenuity was exercised to pass away time until half-past ten, when lights were extinguished for the night. Such were the main features of our home on the deep; and such our daily routine of sea-life: in the midst of it, there was considerable time left to the thoughtful and serious for reading and reflection.

When we went into the saloon for dinner, on the day

of departure, we had the first full view of our fellow-passengers. Many of them were military officers, their wives and daughters,—and others young civilians,—going out to India, China, and the Mauritius. There were also a few colonists returning, by the Overland Route, to Australia. We had witnessed most affecting scenes between some of them and their friends, at parting; and sorrowful affection still lingered upon their countenances, although two hours had passed away; but, by degrees, most of them became lively and talkative. At half-past four, P.M., we sailed by the "Needles," and the wind and the sea became rough, so that many passengers took early to their berths; but, though the vessel pitched considerably, we continued on deck till after nine.

*Frid., Sep. 21.*—No land in sight all day. Weather boisterous; so that the ship plunged and rolled continuously, and we could do little but accommodate ourselves to its motion.

*Sat., Sep. 22.*—Rough sea and wet weather; but contrived to read Dr. Maury's "Physical Geography of the Sea." Retired to bed at half-past ten; and had a pretty good night, considering that we were now in the turbulent Bay of Biscay.

*Sun., Sep. 23.*—In the morning, read the Liturgy and preached on Divine Providence to an attentive audience assembled in the saloon. Being requested to hold another religious service in the evening, I read the Evening Prayers of the Church of England, and explained the nature and necessity of Religion, from the thirteenth chapter of the First Epistle to the Corinthians. Several thanked me for the day's services; and some conversed with me on the subjects of discourse. I found we had with us, on board, both men and women who feared God and worked righteousness. The weather cleared up about noon; and in the evening we quitted the Bay of Biscay, and saw on our left the coast of Spain.

*Mon., Sep.* 24.—A fine day. Passed the entrance of the Tagus, with Lisbon in the distance. We could see palace-like houses crowning the hill above the city, with vessels crowding up the river. In the evening our ship rode gallantly along; the night was calm and fine, and the moon threw her soft, silvery light over the sea.

*Tues., Sep.* 25.—A bright, cheerful morning: nearly all the passengers were on deck for an early walk, and then at breakfast by nine. The thermometer rose to seventy. In the afternoon saw the Spanish mountains, and then Cape St. Vincent. Later in the evening, we were within sight of Cadiz, and passed, at a distance, the little town of Palos, whence Columbus set sail for the discovery of America. We then sailed by Trafalgar Bay; and soon, through the hazy, lingering light of the setting sun, Gibraltar might be discerned in the distance, with its bold, massive outline like a huge lion couchant in the midst of the sea, keeping constant guard for Great Britain at her main portal to the East. A strong current from the west favoured us, and we drove rapidly forward, that we might gain the bay before gun-fire. The brilliant light of Europa Point appeared amidst the increasing darkness. "The Rock ahead!" thundered the gruff, husky voice of the watch at the bow. Our pace immediately slackened. "Stop her!" cried our thin, wiry Captain, from the paddle-box. The steam fumed and screeched; the chain-cable rattled and shook the vessel; and then fell for the night. The officer of *pratique* appeared in a boat, came on board, made his inquiries, and, at once, pronounced egress and access free between the appointed hours of sunrise and sunset. Our Missionary at Gibraltar (Rev. R. Webster) was soon on board, and arranged to receive us at the quay of the New Mole by seven the next morning; after which, we and our fellow-passengers retired to our berths for the night.

*Wed., Sep.* 26.—Rose early, to look at the grand Rock. At seven, drove with Mr. Webster to the Mission-House; and found attached to it a spacious chapel, with school and reading-rooms, in good condition, but not in the most eligible situation. We were glad to find that the Mission was prosperous, and that on the Sabbath morning, when the Methodist military attend, as many as five hundred persons assemble in the chapel for Divine worship; and that on the Sabbath evening, when the military are absent, there is a good congregation. After breakfast, we drove through the town, viewing its narrow, thronged streets, small shops, motley crowds of inhabitants and visitors, and went round the North Point, from whence, on the neutral ground, the best and fullest view of Gibraltar can be obtained. As we returned, we saw the fish and r ovision markets, public buildings and gardens, and as much of the military defences and establishments as our time would allow.

GIBRALTAR, as seen from the bay on the west, is about two and a half miles long, and slopes rapidly upwards from near the water to the ridge of the mountain-rock, which is from 1,300 to 1,400 feet high.

It is broader and bolder at the north end than at the south; but throughout, as viewed at a distance, it appears hoary with age, and browned by the sun. The pent-up town and line of military works skirt the base of the rock along the western side; and fortifications and batteries bristle, tier above tier, from the long bastion by the water's edge to the very summit; while innumerable holes from interior galleries and caverns, with cannons' mouths pointing towards the sea, may be seen at all heights, and in all directions. The eastern side of the Rock is almost as perpendicular as a built-up wall; and appears like a huge stone-mountain cut straight down through the middle, with no shore, or ledge at the foot; but falling precipitously, and plomb at its side, from the narrow ridge at the top into the transparent blue water below; so that on the east side the natural form of the fortress is its own defence. On all others ides it is strongly fortified; and it is not difficult to believe what is affirmed by military officers in charge of it, that the Rock is impregnable. There are extensive galleries in different directions, excavated within by engineering skill; and from all these, at intervals of a few yards, port-holes are broken through to the exterior, having artillery so directed within them that, at any moment, an approaching enemy might be fired upon and destroyed. The Rock appears dotted all over with these military perforations; and at the north end, where it is united to the Spanish continent by a narrow isthmus of low sand, there is a sort of tramway, all undermined, so that an army coming towards it by land could at once be blown up, with the road itself. The gates are equally prepared for resistance and destruction; sentinels appear at every turn; and everywhere strict military vigilance seems to be constantly maintained. Altogether, perhaps, Gibraltar is the strongest and most formidable fortress possessed by any nation. Its situation, at the extreme tongue-end of the Spanish coast, at the entrance of the Mediterranean from the Atlantic, and almost within gun-shot of the coast of Africa, is the most advantageous possible. We do not wonder that Spaniards and Moors, who have more than once witnessed its burning fury, and felt its destructive power, should speak of it, and of its projecting battery, by such ominous names as,— "The Mouth of Fire," and "The Devil's Tongue." Some of the gates are ancient, and have upon them heraldic representations of renowned sovereigns, such as the Emperor Charles V., and King Philip II.; but by far the most interesting relic of former times is the venerable Moorish Castle, standing about midway up the ascent of the north-west shoulder of the Rock, on the western side. It is nine hundred years old; and has been successively in the possession of Saracens and Christians, Africans and Europeans; and is still noble in decay. It is large, contains spacious apartments, and a lofty tower rises above its square, massive quadrangle. It is of deep yellow tinge, and bears upon its surface, on all sides, unmistakeable proofs of furious siege.

In the middle part of the western side of Gibraltar is the Almeida,—supplying to the resident, and to the visitor, as enchanting a place for promenade as can possibly be found in Europe, or, perhaps, in the world. It is an open space, extending from the sea-wall to the base of the steeper part of the Rock, which has here been levelled for the soldiers' parade-ground. It is skirted with walks and ornamental gardens, with alcoves, and seats in sheltered and attractive nooks. The grounds are planted and laid out with ingenious taste. Aloes, cactuses, figs, olives, orange-trees, and all kinds of semi-tropical fruits and odoriferous plants, cluster together upon it in rich profusion; while in one part are the graves and monuments of Trafalgar heroes, and in another stands the bust of Wellington, which, the inscription records, was brought from Lepida.

The public buildings of Gibraltar are not large or impressive, except the military establishments. The Governor resides in an old Franciscan convent; the cathedral is a miserable imitation of Moorish architecture, mingled with Italian; and the Exchange, courthouse, &c., are without any architectural merit whatever. The streets are narrow and irregular; the houses and shops low and small, and huddled together in all imaginable shapes and colours at the foot of the arid precipices of the Rock; while ships of war, and groups of small craft, lie under the sea-wall batteries in front. The Protestant Bishopric has been restored to Gibraltar, so it is now dignified with the name of "city;" and the diocese of the Bishop extends all round those parts of the Mediterranean where there are any Protestant Christians. The natives of Gibraltar are principally Roman Catholics; and are spoken of contemptuously by the other residents as "Rock Scorpions." About one half of the inhabitants are said to be natives, and the other half is composed of Spaniards, Moors, Jews, Italians, Ionians, and British. There are some 5,000 British soldiers at Gibraltar, in ordinary times.

The scenes in the streets and markets, composed of this mixed assemblage of inhabitants from various countries, are diversified and picturesque. Spanish peasants are seen, bringing provisions from the neighbouring country, on their large, powerful mules, which are showily arrayed in crimson and yellow trappings. Each peasant looks as haughty as if he were a hidalgo; and his swarthy, stalwart frame is encased in velvet breeches and a tight, embroidered jacket, and is surmounted with a slouched black hat of conical shape. In his broad crimson sash lurks the dangerous knife, too readily employed as the arbiter of quarrel. In contrast to the excitable Spaniards, and with dignified and imperturbable looks, stand their old hereditary enemies, the Moors from the opposite coast of Barbary;—their ebony faces overshadowed by huge white turbans, their bodies robed in loose flowing dresses of blue and crimson, and their feet resting in yellow upturned pointed slippers. These are provision merchants, who have brought over, in small craft, fowls, eggs, meat, and fruit. Among these glide Jews, with their long flowing beards and greasy clothing, ever looking askance, as if all around were leagued in hostility towards them. Then there are coarsely clad Spanish women from the country, also with their provisions; and Spanish ladies, arrayed in graceful black lace mantillas, and closely-drawn veils,—from under which they dart piercing glances,—as we read, in the old stories; and having in their hands the coquettish fan, which is made to express in its position and wavings all the varied feelings of the bearers. Among these are English mammas and their rosy children, and nurses, and English soldiers in bright scarlet uniforms; while, above the noise and jargon of the many tongues, may be heard the military band, playing "God save the Queen," or "Rule, Britannia." When we were there, the British volunteers for Garibaldi were in the streets, on their way to join the patriot hero in Sicily; and by their gay coloured dresses, and swaggering demeanour, they gave increased enlivenment and interest to the scene.

The Rock itself is unproductive, but provisions from the neighbouring coasts are abundant. There is a large supply of fish daily; and we purchased in the fruit-market four pounds of grapes, half a hundred walnuts, and two pounds of apples,—all for fifteen pence! Many native women and children are employed in the manufacture of cigars. Poverty and crime, it is reported, are not great at Gibraltar, though immorality is said to prevail. Convicts may be seen at public works in blue cotton clothing, attended in batches by a guard, who bears a staff. The climate of Gibraltar is soft, balmy, and exhilarating; and yet we were informed that epidemics have, at different periods, swept off large numbers of the inhabitants. Monkeys, which abounded a few years ago, are no longer tenants of the Rock. As our steamer glided away from it, I sketched the back of the fortress, in its deep precipitous fall, with the Spanish scenery adjoining.

*Thurs., Sep. 27.*—Clear, bright day. The sierras, or Spanish mountains, still seen on the left. Had an interesting conversation with a Professor of Learning from India, on Hinduism and the religious systems of the East,—on the late Mutiny, the Oxford Perverts, the writings of Macaulay, &c., &c.

*Frid., Sep. 28.*—On deck at six. Sun's glare very great. Passed Algiers. Huge fishes, sporting and darting through the clear blue water.

*Sat., Sep.* 29.—Weather still warmer. Morning very sultry; and, in the day, a hot breeze from the African coast. In the evening we passed, at a distance, the Bay of Tunis, and the site of desolate Carthage.

*Sun., Sep.* 30.—Rose at half-past six. Climate fine and warm. Religious service in the saloon at half-past ten: good attendance. Preached on Abraham's call to go to a strange country; and applied the subject to the passengers on their voyage to distant lands. Several wept at the remembrance of home, and the mention of the uncertain future in a new land. The large saloon was filled with passengers, officers, and crew in their dark blue Sunday clothing; the "Union Jack" was spread on the cushion, under the Bible and the Prayer-Book; and it was affecting to hear the deep murmur of earnest responses during the reading of the Liturgy. I was impressed with the reflection that to me had been practically committed the ministerial charge of so many souls! By two, P.M., we sighted Malta; and, steaming past the island of Gozo, we reached the harbour of Valetta by four in the afternoon.

The scene from our vessel was as busy and as brilliant as could well be conceived. We had passed, on our left, the massive forts of Ricasoli and St. Elmo, and had beheld, between these, the jagged shores and indented fortifications on both sides of the "great harbour;" and now we were in the quarantine harbour, with forts Mancel and Tigué on our right, and with the clean, beautiful city of Valetta, the capital of the island, immediately before us. The basin, all around, was covered with life and activity; ponderous tiers of batteries lined the shores; and the stately houses of the city, as pure and unstained as if they had that day been fresh excavated from Bath-stone quarries, rose, story above story, on the elevated ground in front; their clear outlines and flat roofs cutting sharply against the rich blue sky, while their bright forms and flowered balconies were reflected in the liquid mirror beneath. Crowds of picturesque boats, of all shapes and colours, were putting off from the quay, and crossing the harbour, to convey passengers ashore; while from antique canoe-like skiffs, of native construction, tawny men and boys, of half African mould, and all but naked, were plunging into the deep bay, and exhibiting their extraordinary feats of diving after silver coin thrown from our vessel.

We went on shore as soon as possible; and climbing the successive streets of "cursed stairs," we pushed our way through hosts of touters and beggars, who hung most tenaciously upon our skirts, until we reached the summit of the steep ascent; when, crossing the busy Strada Reale, we found the chief object of attraction to us,—the celebrated cathedral of St. John. The exterior of the church greatly disappointed us. It has a common flat *façade*, with two plain turrets containing the famous bells of Rhodes; and is built closely against, on both sides. But on pushing aside the heavy curtain which screens the entrance-portal, a scene of gorgeousness and solemn grandeur presents itself. The church is of Italian style, large and spacious, with a high vault in the middle, and with arched aisles at the sides. At the further end is the high altar, on an elevated platform, and with its stately seats for ecclesiastical dignitaries. All this is covered and enriched with marbles, historic paintings, and tapestries, and with bronze figures of sombre hue, while the pavement of the whole church is one vast escutcheon, composed of monumental marble slabs for the chivalrous Knights of St. John, richly inlaid with heraldic devices in mosaic, and with inscriptions, in black, red, and deep yellow colours. Upon the floor were seen kneeling Maltese men and women,—the latter appearing half nun-like in their black mantilla coverings. Suspended from the walls are the trophies and insignia of celebrated conquests, and the rusty keys of memorable cities, such as Rhodes, Jerusalem, and Acre. The solemn chant of the priests, accompanied by the deep tones of the organ, which roll and echo through the lofty vaults and remote recesses of the church,—everywhere redolent with perfumed incense,—give a sort of dreamy enchantment to the scene; which in its sombre hues, after the glaring sunlight without, and the clamorous sounds and offensive stenches encountered in the way, makes the visit to St. John's a treat indescribably pleasurable. We worshipped silently among the congregation, after our own Protestant manner,—praying for the Roman Catholic devotees around us; and, as it was the Lord's day, we left the Grand Palace of the Knights, and the other sights of the city, to be viewed on our return. With grief we saw not a few of our fellow-passengers openly casting off religious restraint, and publicly trafficking in lace and filagree-work of gold and silver. Their conduct could not fail to be injurious, not only to themselves, but also to the credit of Protestant Christianity. On returning to our ship, the descending streets, thronged with Maltese men, women, and priests,—Arab merchants in their long flowing garments,—red-coated British soldiers, and rollicking English Jack-Tars,—presented a stream of picturesque variety. The shops were open as on ordinary days of the week, exhibiting in full view their various articles for sale; and through public purchases and pleasure-taking, the city, throughout, was utterly devoid of the serenity belonging to the day of the Lord. At ten, P.M., we heaved anchor, and steamed out of the harbour, nearly leaving behind some young military officers, who had been carousing at the *cafés*, and who had to make their way to us, after we had started, by hard rowing from the shore. Darkness was thickening upon us as we left; but we could discern, as we passed, frowning upon us in gloomy grandeur, the massive granite fort of St. Elmo, in which lies the body of the gallant Sir Ralph Abercrombie.

*Mon., Oct.* 1.—Rose early. Weather close and oppressive; but a refreshing breeze sprung up in the day. Passed several vessels in full sail, and spoke with some, all being anxious to learn more of the events of Italy; but they could not tell us more than that Garibaldi had gained some advantage over the Pope's troops.

*Tues., Oct.* 2.—Had a refreshing bath in sea-water, some hours before breakfast. During the day an Arab pilot came on board to take charge of our ship, and conduct her between outlying sunken rocks into the harbour of Alexandria. Towards evening the ship's fire-bell rang, to prove that all the crew were ready for an emergency. This alarmed some of the passengers who had been left unapprised of the object.

*Wed., Oct.* 3.—Passengers early on deck, and busy with luggage, to be ready for landing. All hilarity among them, being the last day and night to be spent on board before reaching Egypt. The sun set gloriously in the evening, flooding the whole scene with vermilion and gold, while opposite rose the moon as from a furnace of molten metal.

*Thurs., Oct. 4.*—By half-past eight, A.M., Alexandria in sight. A long, horizontal line of sand-banks—the Pasha's palace and lighthouse on the left—innumerable windmills, having half sails, and dumpy forms, on the right. Arab pilot, now in full charge of the steamer, seen with glass in hand on the bridge in midships, excited and highly pretentious. On drawing near to Alexandria, several barge-like boats approached us on both sides, swarming with Arabs, Egyptians, and Nubians, dressed in all sorts of clothing, and some with scarcely any clothing at all. Clambering up the sides of our vessel, they crowded the deck, but did not seem at all eager for exertion, until one of the officers roused them to it by masterful words and attitudes. The hurry and confusion which followed can scarcely be imagined. Luggage was tumbled over the ship in all directions; and woe betide the portmanteau that was not strong! The Arabs shouted, screamed, and gesticulated in the most frantic manner. We stood by our luggage until it was removed to the tender on which passengers were going ashore. The harbour was crowded with ships of various nations; and among them were several French frigates, which had recently brought soldiers to suppress the insurrection and massacres in Syria. On landing we were beset by all kinds of eager aspirants for leading and conveying us into the city; but, selecting the most honest-looking dragoman (as we thought) from among the crowd, we made our way with him to the Orient Hotel, paying some five shillings expenses from leaving the steamer to settlement in our inn.

# CHAPTER II.

EGYPT—Alexandria—Railway, and View of the Country—Land of Goshen—Cairo and its Wonders—The Suburbs—Ancient Christian Remains—The Nilometer—The Pasha's Naval Architect, and his Methodist Recollections—The "Petrified Forest" and "Tombs of the Caliphs"—Dervish Worship—Heliopolis—Nile Boat and Voyage—The Pyramids and the Sphynx—The Pasha's Palace and his Soldiers—Tombs of the Mamelukes and of Mehemet Ali—Moslem Worship—View of Cairo from the Citadel—Departure—The Desert Railway—Suez, and Embarkation on the Red Sea.

---

Our drive through the narrow, irregular streets of Alexandria was an introduction to Eastern life. It impressed us with a feeling of ancientness, as well as of novelty. Our first sight of camels and veiled women seemed a realization of Scripture scenes and patriarchal times. But soon, the vision of merchants lounging on cushions, and smoking long pipes,—half-naked and embrowned water-carriers, with their swollen goat-skin burthens,—women, glancing eagerly out of the large wrappers with which they were enveloped to the eyes, and attended by glossy negroes in loose white dresses and crimson turbans,—ebony grooms in petticoat trousers, leading high-mettled Arabian horses with richly embroidered saddles,—sleek asses, with carpet saddles and mercurial boy-drivers,—and strings of lofty camels, with their rolling eyes and slow, swaying motion of their large heads and long necks,—transported us to the enchanting and bizarre associations of "The Arabian

Nights," and awoke within us the memory of young dreams full of the pageantry of Oriental romance.

In the oblong square before our hotel the *élite* of the inhabitants out of a population of 80,000—Turks, Albanians, Syrians, Greeks, Jews, Copts, Arabs, Nubians, Armenians, and Franks—promenaded, in stately and motley show, from four to six in the evening. We found the famed Alexandria, in which royal magnificence and academic learning once out-rivalled Rome itself, to have "bequeathed to the modern city only its ruins and its name." The old foundations cannot even be traced, the present city having shrunk within the ancient girdle considerably. Fragments of fallen columns lie widely scattered, and mounds remain half hidden by drifting sand; but there is no record of the buildings to which they formerly belonged. We drove, of course, to the obelisk named "Cleopatra's Needle," which was brought by one of the Cæsars from Heliopolis to adorn a temple, though tradition falsely ascribes the removal to Egypt's sumptuous Queen. It is covered with hieroglyphics, familiar in their forms to English eyes, by miniature models of this very obelisk, and is some seventy feet high. Its prostrate fellow column, given to England by Mehemet Ali, remains, as every one knows, still on Egyptian soil. We next visited "Pompey's Pillar," a well-proportioned column nearly one hundred feet high. These gigantic fragments of polished syenite are nearly all that remains of the architectural splendour which distinguished the capital of the Ptolemies. They stand, the one at the northern, the other at the southern extremity of the modern city, as if in monumental mockery of fallen greatness. We visited the Pasha's palace, with its half-European, half-Turkish furniture and adornment; then walked through the long bazaars; and, after a solemn stroll in the evening through unlighted streets, we retired to rest, but had little sleep, for the constant howling and yelping of quarrelsome dogs, and incessant calls of watchmen around the square.

*Frid., Oct. 5.*—Breakfasted at half-past seven, and left for the train to Cairo at nine. The railway station, at the south-east extremity of Alexandria, is a large structure, with its ticket-offices and waiting-rooms, in Continental rather than English style. The carriages are English, bearing the name-plates of "Wright and Son, Birmingham;" but we felt it odd to have the carriage door opened for us, and to be attended on our journey, by railway guards in turbans. An attendant very courteously deposited for us, in a net overhead within our carriage, an earthen bottle fresh filled with water from the Nile, and adjusted the Venetian windows so as to screen us, as far as could be, from the drifting sand and sun's blazing heat,—evidently relying on our English generosity for some remuneration. Our course lay through the cultivated land of the Delta, and, having passed by the villa-like houses of the suburbs, and burial places crowded with Egyptian tombs and graves, we were soon among fields, where natives were at work, making sluices, and raising water by their bucket-wheels, to irrigate the land. Several villages, chiefly composed of dark mud dwellings, lay by the railroad, with here and there a stone mosque and minaret; and then we swept by clumps of trees, and now and then a picturesque and solitary palm.

We felt at once that we had reached the Egypt of our dreams. The palm tree,—that familiar type of Eastern scenery,—the foliage of Scripture illustrations, which were so dear among the pictures of our childhood, associated with the figures of Patriarchs, Prophets, Apostles, and Christ,—was before us at every stage. We thought of Joseph and his brethren and Pharaoh, of Jacob and Moses, and of the Virgin and her persecuted Infant. It is true that on the way we saw much to disturb the pleasantness of our reveries. Upon the sandy embankments we saw strings of camels and asses, attended by men, women, and boys, who were generally very meanly and scantily clad, and who were often filthy in the extreme. Now and then, astride a nimble-footed donkey, might be seen a fat, shaky Turk, clothed in rich, flowing robes, and his red-slippered feet dangling within six inches of the ground. At intervals we passed an Egyptian family of the better class travelling with the Eastern ass, most strikingly after the style and manner in which Italian painters represent Joseph, Mary, and the young child Jesus in the flight into Egypt. But, in most cases, the low, degraded appearance of the groups of natives which we passed could scarcely be exceeded by that of the savage inhabitants of the interior. Neither men nor women had sufficient covering for decency; while boys and girls, up to ten or twelve years of age, were entirely nude, and were often clotted and bedaubed with sand and mud, like so many mere wild animals. "Surely," we said, as we dashed along in the train over the level land, past group after group of dirty, shameless men and women, "the Scripture prophecy concerning this country is literally fulfilled, and Egypt has become the basest of kingdoms; for in it cleanliness has scarcely any existence, and nakedness no shame!"

Parts of the country, with its overflowings of water, resembled the fens of Lincolnshire; the style of ploughing and labour was of the most primitive kind, and we saw, in our way, many striking illustrations of Scripture in the manners and customs of the people. The hot climate seemed to have tamed and subdued both beasts and men. Buffaloes were resting in the water, with their nostrils out only; the cattle employed in husbandry and as beasts of burthen went lazily along; and both labourers and travellers, whom we passed, moved leisurely. Half way to Cairo we stayed for refreshment, at the station provided by the Pasha; and partook of a semi-English repast. Soon afterwards, we crossed the Nile, and were in the Land of Goshen, where verdure and trees were abundant.

By half-past three, P.M., we had our first sight of the Pyramids, with their long familiar forms mellowed to the view by a rosy hue which rested upon them in the distance. The sky was a soft purple rather than a bright blue, and it bathed all things in its warm, sombre light, and harmonized them delightfully. The country, as we advanced, became increasingly green and luxuriant, near to us; but beyond we could see the hot, steaming desert, quivering in parts with reflected light. The mosques and minarets of Cairo appeared before us, with the Mokattam mountain range behind. At half-past four in the afternoon we reached the famous Egyptian capital of Saracenic times—the most wondrous city in the dear old stories of the "Thousand and One Nights" —and drove at once to Shepherd's Hotel, where, from notice previously sent by Indian passengers who preceded us, we found a good double-bedded room awaiting our arrival. After dinner and a short walk in the suburbs, we retired to rest; but through the tattered state of the bed curtains, we were preyed upon by musquitoes until covered all over with the effects of their bites. It seemed that night as if all the tormenting insects of Cairo had been summoned to a luscious feast upon English flesh; for they came through the open windows, and preyed upon me to the full.

*Sat., Oct.* 6.—After breakfast went to the door of the hotel to engage donkeys for the day, and found a swarm of boys with asses. On sight of me, the lads all vociferously solicited engagement, in the loudest and most amusing manner. "You want good donkey?" one inquired. Another shouted, "Mine the best donkey!" and another, "Mine a stallion donkey!" Then the names of their several steeds would be sounded out loudly, and all together. One exclaiming, "Have my Snooks!" another, "Have Jenny Lind!" and another, "Have Garibaldi!" These youths are sharp, eager aspirants for employment, and have picked up as much English as enables them to be guides to travellers: they are dragomen in embryo. Their complexions are a light reddish bronze; they are dressed mostly in dark blue blouses, or tunics; have bare legs, feet, and arms, and wear upon their heads either a red cap with a black tassel, or a gay-coloured handkerchief picturesquely folded around the temples. The donkeys are of various sizes. Some are large white Meccas, nearly as high as our mules; but the greater number are smaller than European asses, and are darker in colour. Nearly all of them are arrayed in red saddles with high pommels, and they are owned by proprietors who employ the boys for small daily wages to hire them to travellers, at sixpence per hour, or one and sixpence for the day. I selected from the fair of donkeys a large white Mecca one for myself, and a darker, smaller one for my wife. Mounted on these, we set forth on a ride into the city, our exultant drivers walking behind, and waving their sticks in triumph. Sudden strokes on the haunches of our beasts startled both them and us, and we wen trotting on at a smart ambling pace, by what would be called the boulevard of a continental city, until we reached the Frank part of the new European Bazaar. This was thronged with persons of all ranks and costumes, who were threading their way in carriages, on horseback, on asses, or on foot, as best they could. We had to be careful on our saddles; for if our donkeys saw an opening, they suddenly started for it; and, if we had not been upon our guard, they might soon have slipped us off behind, and let us lie, amidst the laughing crowd, on the ground.

Keeping our seats, we pursued our way through a labyrinth of narrow streets and lanes to the Turkish bazaar, attended by our donkey-drivers, who, in addition to the sharp strokes inflicted upon our steeds behind, loudly vociferated to all around to make way for us, as if we were the most important personages in Cairo! The scene, as we went along, was a perfect masquerade. It was an ever-shifting drama of Eastern life, acted immediately before you,—being of all forms, and of all colours. There were ladies in dark and white veils; some riding like puffed up balloons, on asses led by fat, shining eunuchs; and others on foot, with their respective guardians. They were clothed in a hood-like mantle of black, yellow, or white, and no part of their person was seen but their dark eyes, rimmed with khol, gleaming lustrously out from two holes in the front of their head-dress, and which head-dress is divided in the middle, from the forehead to the chin, by a string of yellow ornaments like coins. Under their bulged external covering they wear loose trousers,—yellow, pink, or white,—and on their feet small turned-up shoes with sharp points. The women ride astride on the asses, and the stout, black eunuchs who lead the asses are showily, and in some instances sumptuously, arrayed in long blue robes. They strut along by the side of their charge with conscious importance. The females of the lower classes were seen moving among the crowd; some bearing pitchers of antique form upon their heads, remarkably upright in their bearing, and their scanty dresses falling down upon their bare legs, revealing too fully the outline and symmetry of their forms. These were loosely clad in dark blue cotton shirt-like dresses; and their faces were only partly covered. Others were more scantily clothed, and had their naked infants—with sore eyes covered with preying insects—astride on their shoulders, or on their hips. Among these were old women, who, under the fierce heat of the Egyptian sun, had been burnt and dried until their skins had become shrivelled and hippopotamus-like, and they were truly hideous. Strings of calm, dignified camels, laden heavily on either side with panniers, strode dreamily along; and on their tawny scabbed humps you would see dark Nubians or sallow Egyptians, nodding at the tread of the beasts that bare them. Then came half-naked water-carriers, with blown-out goat-skins, dripping from the Nile, holding in the one hand the mouth of the skin, and in the other a can into which to pour forth the water for sale. Then you would see Franks of different European nations, and here and there a portly well-dressed Englishman on a donkey, and wearing a wide-awake hat turbaned with a roll of white muslin about the crown, to avert from his head the rays of the sun. He looks round and speaks as if master of the drama, and as if the whole scene had been made up purposely for him. On each side of the narrow streets are small cupboard-like shops, stored with shawls and gay articles; and on the tailor-like boards in front—some one or two feet from the ground—sit crosslegged, calm, imperturbable Turks, in rich turbans and long, flowing robes, smoking their long pipes, looking exactly as if they were sitting for portraits, and as if they had been sitting there undisturbed for half a century; for they have no movement whatever except in their eyelids. The streets are narrow enough below, but they decrease in breadth above by storied projections,—after the manner of the old houses which remain in Coventry, Tewkesbury, Shrewsbury, and such of our towns as were famous in the Wars of the Roses,—until they all but meet overhead, and only a narrow zig-zag stripe of blue sky at top is discernible. As you proceed you will see masons busily building in turbans; with carpenters and other artisans, all petticoated and turbaned. Then you come upon the disgusting sight of Dervishes, all naked except at the loins, with matted hair and filthy skin, asking alms, with their bag; but they give way for the four-wheeled carriage with its gaudy trappings, containing a Turkish lady of rank, and preceded by a dark runner, dressed in crimson and blue, bearing his silver-tipped wand, and warning the crowd of the approach of his window-screened mistress. On the box with the coachman, or slung behind, are the guardian eunuchs, with faces like polished ebony, fat and plump, and richly clothed. Scattered among these, in greasy dresses, are sordid, sharp-featured, sly-looking Jews, from various nations; jaunty, rakish Greeks, with finely moulded forms and picturesque costumes; and dark, turbaned Copts, claiming to be descendants of the ancient Egyptians, and wearing crosses on their wrists and other parts of their bodies. Some of them are shouting "backsheesh!" at the top of their voices: indeed, this is the common cry heard by Englishmen wherever you go in Egypt.

Before we reached the Turkish Bazaar itself, the narrowing streets seemed literally choked with the motley crowd passing and repassing through them. The scene, as viewed from our saddles, was strange and picturesque in the extreme. It seemed like a sea of population, with the white turbans, bobbing up and down, amidst rising and subsiding waves. Again and again we were jammed tightly up in the living mass, when our driver could not open space for us in front, however loudly he might scream, nor move our donkeys an inch forward, however smartly he might belabour them behind. All we could do was to exercise patience, and attend to the warning of our youngsters, who repeatedly cautioned us to have a care over our pockets and jewelry, for there were Arab sharpers in the crowd. By movements at intervals, we pushed our way slowly forwards, alighting at different stages to examine richly ornamented mosques, marble fountains, and baths. Leaving our asses at the pole-barrier next the street, we went into the mosque of Sultan Kalaóon, or the "Mosque of the Madhouse," as it is commonly called, and found it to be a large, solemn structure, supported by huge ponderous columns, and surmounted by arches of the Saracenic or horseshoe form. Taking off our shoes, as required on entering upon the "holy ground" of Mahommedan worship, we passed through the doorway of the screen into the inner compartment, where stood the tomb of the founder,—and beyond it the circular niche for prayer curiously inlaid with mother-of-pearl and mosaic work, and divided into compartments by rows of small, dumpy columns. The spandrils of the arches and the windows above are adorned with light, elegant tracery; and on the whole the effect is gorgeous and impressive. On resuming our ride, we soon reached the veritable Turkish Bazaar, which we entered on the right by a narrow, shady, lane-like passage, where it was all but impossible for two donkeys on meeting to pass one another. We saw, as we rode leisurely along in these dusky passages, all redolent with aromatics and musk, the small, cupboard-like shops at the sides, richly stored with clothing and jewelry; and their owners sitting on the low dais in front, in dreamy repose, with slippers by their side, smoking their pipes, or sipping tiny cups of hot coffee, as if careless and independent of business altogether. We then rode through other bazaars, stopping at the several departments of manufacture and sale, to examine different articles of silk, cotton, and woollen dresses, and handling the curiously wrought slippers, gold embroidered jackets, ornate and elegantly fashioned pipes, and firelocks inlaid with ivory or gold. We gazed upon magicians, snake-charmers, mountebanks, and story-tellers, with their encircling crowds of wonderers, as we passed along on our patient steeds; and returned to our hotel another way, by unpaved streets of the narrowest dimensions, where—from the projecting lattices above—occupants of opposite houses might hold *tête-à-tête* conversations, and look into each other's apartments without difficulty; and where the only opening for light was from a narrow strip of sky, like a wave of blue ribbon, overhead. The lattice-work in front of some of the projecting windows of the upper stories is very beautiful: and some houses, in their lower stories, have circular and horse-shoe headed doorways, with ornamental hoodmoulds covering delicate interlaced stonework, and enclosing sentences in Arabic characters from the Koran. On looking through the doorways of some superior dwellings, we could see large open courts surrounded by spacious suites of apartments for the different sexes; while in front of the entrance were seated black, swabby eunuchs, in their purple, green, and scarlet dresses, lounging on cushions, and waited on by slaves, as if they were the major-domos of these mansions. Most of the streets, however, through which we passed, were lined at the sides by the darkest and dirtiest hovels imaginable, from which emerged half-naked men and women; and at length we had to hasten the paces of our beasts from a part occupied by females, who, without veil or covering of any kind to hide their painted, saucy faces, made it plain, by their looks and gestures, what they were.

After taking rest at our inn, we rode some four miles north of the city, to the celebrated Gardens and Palace of Shoobra. The road was broad, and lay through an arched avenue of acacia and sycamore trees, which shaded us effectually from the sun, and rendered our ride cool and pleasant. We found the gardens pretty, and fragrant with the scent of roses and geraniums, but too formal and Dutch-like in their arrangement and radiating lines to satisfy English eyes. We plucked lemons and oranges, by leave of the native gardeners, and found them truly refreshing after our protracted ride. We were then admitted to the palace-fountains provided by Mehemet Ali for the ladies of his hareem. It is a large quadrangular bason of water, surrounded by a covered corridor, the mason-work of which is of Carrara marble, fancifully sculptured and adorned by Italian workmen. On each side, within the corridor, and projecting into the large bason, are sumptuous seats; and at each angle of the building is a superb room with divans, fitted up in Turkish and European styles combined; while in different parts stand and hang large, brilliant glass chandeliers. To this spacious marble fountain of, perhaps, one hundred yards long on each side, and four feet deep, the Pasha's wives come at their pleasure to bathe and to sport themselves, attended by their watchful keepers, the eunuchs, who have the sole guardianship of the place during its possession by the ladies, and who alone have the privilege at such times of entering within its precincts. On going, we met the Pasha's brother on the road, and in returning we passed, in their several carriages, the Pasha's sister and the Pasha's child, with its English governess. The road was thronged with natives, their asses, and their camels; and at every few yards on our way, both in going and returning, we met richly dressed merchants of the city, who had their villas and gardens in the neighbourhood, some of them in carriages, preceded by outrunners, but mostly on slender, prancing steeds, richly caparisoned.

In the evening, after dinner, we went to the English Church clergyman's, (Rev. Mr. Lieder's,) attended by a man with a lanthorn, which all persons are required to have with them in the streets of Cairo, after nightfall. We here found Miss Daniell, whom we had known in England, and who, with Mrs. Lieder, her friend, most readily gave us useful information, and showed us all the courteous and considerate attention we could desire during our stay in Egypt.

*Sun., Oct. 7.*—Went to the English Church, in Rev. Mr. Lieder's house: heard a converted Jew preach a good gospel sermon, from Rev. i. 5, to a congregation of about thirty persons, chiefly English; and afterwards partook of the Lord's Supper with about a dozen communicants. In the evening we had a "church in the house," being too much indisposed by eastern sickness to leave our room; and the night that followed was one of considerable suffering.

*Mon., Oct. 8.*—Mrs. Jobson and self rose in the morning in great weakness. During the day, however, we felt sufficiently restored to visit the Protestant burial-ground, and read the names and inscriptions on the grave-stones of many from our own land; and we afterwards drove to the Mosque of Omar, the Roman Camp, and Old Cairo. The mosque is said to be the oldest in Egypt, and to have been built on the model of the temple at Mecca. The Roman Camp is, in reality, a ruined fortress; and within its enclosure lies a Coptic village. Here the Copts show you a building which, they say, was occupied by the Holy Family while in Egypt. The inside of it we could not see, the key being missing. Napoleon III. recently sent from his army a guardian for this "holy place;" but the Coptic priest who had the charge of it, preferring to remain its custodian, hid the keys. It was only a mean-looking building externally. Another spot shown by the Copts, and much revered by them, is one on which some cruel martyrdoms of the early Christians were made under Diocletian. They also show you an upper room, at the head of a broad flight of stairs, which they aver to have been the banquet-hall of Marc Antony and Cleopatra. To me, the really impressive remnant of antiquity shown here was an old Coptic Christian church in an upper story, and which is declared by the Copts to be as much as fifteen hundred years old. This is an exaggeration; but it is evident that the church is very old, and it probably stands where believers in Christ assembled for worship almost as far back as the beginning of Christianity. The church is very primitive in its plan and form. Lengthwise it is divided into four compartments, each of which has now an altar at the east end; and now, as in early times, the females, the novitiates, and the young, have their several places assigned to them in these different compartments. The church is supported in its upper walls by marble pillars, originally white, but now grey with age. It is covered by four open, circular roofs of primitive construction. The pulpit is also of white marble. Within the latticed screen of the chancel is the reading-desk, from whence the Scriptures are daily read; and there is another similar reading-desk in the nave on this side of the screen. The church, in its fittings and ornaments of altars, gilt pictures, and suspended lamps, displays signs of departure from primitive simplicity. Nevertheless it is a marvel that here, where Roman paganism sought by its iron power to crush Christianity in its infancy, and where Mahommedanism has for so many years raged with fanatical fury, a church should still exist, where Christ is professed and worshipped, and where His Gospels are read daily. Surely some great design of Divine Providence must be connected with this fact,—the true emblem for which is the bush unconsumed in the flame. In the large, spacious passage to this building a Christian schoolmaster was instructing a number of gabbling children, who with himself were seated cross-legged upon the floor. From the upper story of the church there is a good view of the Nile and its fertile borders, with Old Cairo immediately on the right, and with the dusky Pyramids beyond.

From the Roman Camp we went down to Old Cairo, which we found as narrow and dirty in its streets as the lowest parts of New Cairo, and as much thronged with inhabitants and traders of various classes. On reaching the river side, we had a full view of the Isle of Roda, which, opposite Old Cairo, stretches its banks lengthwise in the middle of the river for good part of a mile. Roda is a most lovely island, and has been carefully planted with trees, shrubs, and flowers, by British horticulturists, employed by the Pasha. It was at this island that the " goodly child " Moses is said to have been discovered by Pharaoh's daughter, when she came down to bathe. It might be so. There are still flags growing at the borders of the island ; but the weight of water rushing past it, with the turbulent eddies in front, where the two currents meet, would make it, if then as now, a most dangerous place for the ark of bulrushes and its precious contents. We went in a boat over the deep, hurrying water, to see at the head of the island what has probably been on it, in one form or other, from the time of the old Pharaohs—the Nilometer. This is well know to be a graduated upright pillar, or shaft, placed in a chamber, while the water rises, through under channels, to a height equal to what it is outside the island. During the season the rise of the Nile is published by criers daily in the streets of Cairo; and taxes are levied by Government upon the land accordingly. But it is said that the height of the waters at the Nilometer is by some means made to correspond more with the state of the exchequer than with the river itself. When we were there, the river was higher than it had been known to be for many seasons, and consequently we could see little of the Nilometer-chamber and its pillar, which were nearly covered by the abundance of water that had flowed into the enclosure.

*Tues., Oct. 9.*—We could not leave our room for sickness till the latter part of the day, when the Pasha's chief engineer, who boarded at our hotel, proposed to drive us down to Boulak, the port of Cairo, where he would introduce us to an interesting character—the Pasha's naval architect. We accepted his proposal; and on reaching the house of the architect were surprised to see, on his book-shelves, Adam Clarke's Commentary, Wesley's and Watson's Works; and the Reports and Notices of our Wesleyan Missionary Society. We were wondering at the unexpected sight, when the master of the dwelling entered, and was introduced to us by the engineer as "Hassan-ain-Effendi." He was a finely-framed man, with large round head and face of true Egyptian, or red olive, complexion, and in full dress, of red cap, embroidered tight jacket, baggy breeches, broad sash, &c. He very courteously bade us be seated; and when I told him that I was a Methodist Minister, on my way to a Conference in Australia, he became greatly excited, and related to us how, when in England for education in his profession, under the patronage of Mohammed Ali, he had seen much of the Wesleyans at Sheerness and Rochester, and in London; that he had received favours from them both in social entertainment and religious instruction; had heard their most talented preachers, such as Watson, Bunting, and Newton; and that he felt as if he could never repay the debt of gratitude he owed the Methodists for what they had done for him. He further stated that he continued to read their publications, and thus explained what had so greatly surprised us in the books on his shelves. He expressed his great delight at our visit; and said that he had seen me on a former day in the city, and was strongly moved "by a mysterious impulse" to step forward, and introduce himself; but refrained from doing so, lest he should be deemed by one who knew nothing of him as a mere touter, seeking to make gain of a traveller. The friend who had brought us said he knew nothing of this, nor that I was a Methodist Minister; but simply thought that we should be gratified by intercourse with an intelligent and accomplished Egyptian. We mutually rejoiced in our acquaintance, thus strangely brought about; and, not willing to enjoy his pleasure alone, he went and brought to us his beautiful wife. After the ceremonies of introduction, she gradually unveiled herself, and became very free and conversable. His youthful son, the true image of his honest-faced father, was also brought to us. We conversed on various subjects; and arranged with him rides and walks for sight-seeing in the city and its neighbourhood. He told us of wonderful deliverances he had received under persevering persecutions from men who, as he described, had "the wayward minds of children with the despotic power of lions and tigers;" and he thankfully ascribed his deliverances to God.

*Wed., Oct. 10.*—In the house all day; and in bed most of it, from continued exhaustion.

*Thurs., Oct. 11.*—Somewhat stronger; and rode on donkeys several miles out of Cairo, to see the "Petrified Forest." We wound through the narrow, unpaved streets of the crowded city, and, leaving it at the huge, massive "Gate of Victory," we found ourselves in the sandy desert, without a tree, or a bush, or a single habitation to break its dead, monotonous aspect. Immediately outside the gate was a crowded burial-ground, covered with Egyptian graves and tombs, and without a particle of verdure to relieve its loose, sandy soil. We rode on under the scorching sun, meeting in our way companies of dark Bedouins, with their camels and firelocks, looking fiercely and savagely upon us, as though they were going to take advantage of our helpless condition. We smiled, and nodded good-will towards them, and they passed on with their burdened beasts to the gate of the city. By the time we reached the "Petrified Forest" we were much exhausted by the heat that fell directly upon our weak frames from the sun overhead, and which was reflected from the burning sand. We were disappointed with the "Forest," as it is erroneously called: for though there are pieces of petrified wood—of as much, in some instances, as one or two feet in length—strewing an elevated part of the desert for miles in extent, yet there are no stems of petrified trees *standing*, as we had been led to expect. After some rest on the heated ground, we returned over the bald, bare desert, having the Mokattam range of mountains on our left; and seeing in our way, as the only things to break the monotonous scene of parched sand, the whitened bones of camels and asses that had fallen there, and been left to bleach in the sun.

We rode up to those wonderful monuments of the past, erroneously called "Tombs of Caliphs;" and read in those massive and highly-ornamented structures, with their dilapidated walls, minarets, and domes, a humiliating lesson on human vanity. Whom those gigantic tombs, with all their Saracenic arches and enrichments, were founded to represent, none can now tell with certainty; though their builders, of not more than five or six hundred years since, reared them as proud memorials of their own families and names! We found in them most wretched, half-naked men and women, who literally "had their dwellings among the tombs," and who, like all others of their class in Egypt, clamoured hard for "backsheesh." Our donkey-drivers, on returning to the city, plied us equally hard for "backsheesh;" telling us that their eighteenpence a day for each donkey had all to be given to their masters; and that, if we gave them nothing, they would go altogether unpaid. We did not believe this. But it seemed hard to be enjoying so much ourselves, and not to gratify at a small cost poor lads who had been civil and constant throughout; so I invariably gave them something for themselves at the end of our days' rides.

On reaching Cairo we found that the mail-bags had arrived by Marseilles and Alexandria from England; and we were cheered with letters and news dispatched for us a fortnight after we left Southampton. In the night the Bombay and India passengers came to Cairo, and with great noise and clamour took possession of bed-rooms within our hotel. On former nights, the several republics of dogs in the streets made noise enough in their wolf-like barking and howling at one another; but on this night one would have supposed that every foot of street in Cairo was crowded with disturbed and angry dogs: so loud and violent was the noise which they made.

*Frid., Oct.* 12.—Still weak and incapable of much exertion; but drove with Hassan-ain-Effendi, to the College of the Dervishes, to witness their strange ceremonies. The building—or convent, as it may be called—stands upon the bank of the Nile. We entered next the river, through a quadrangular court-yard, in which, on high, long benches, under over-shadowing trees, were spread hairy mats for the recluses. We entered the Mosque, and saw in the middle of the floor from twenty to thirty wild-looking men, standing in a circle round their leader, or fugle-man, in various costumes. On one side of them were musicians with their tom-toms, cymbals, trumpets, and other instruments of which we knew not the names. At the sound of the music, their leader, a noble-looking man in a rich dress, began to move, and to say, with a gentle voice, " Allah ! " " Allah ! " The men in the circle followed him in his movements, and said, almost in a whisper, " Allah ! " " Allah ! " The leader then, instead of walking round and nodding, as it were, to each of his brethren, stood in the centre, as a position-master and time-keeper for them all, and increased his motions gradually, until the action became quick and violent, and until, by swinging and bending backwards and forwards, his long, dishevelled hair swept the floor, alternately, before and behind. This was accompanied by groans, and sighs, and exclamations of the deepest and wildest kind, and was imitated by the men in the circle. The whole company continued their excitement, until they seemed to become mad with it, and you felt sure they must drop down dead with exhaustion. To our surprise they prolonged these violent motions, which made them sweat and foam terrifically, for a considerable time; and until by their loud exclamations of "Allah!" "Allah!" in connexion with the discordant sounds of the tom-toms, cymbals, and trumpets, the Mosque seemed to become a perfect Pandemonium in sight and sound. Then, in obedience to the change of motion and cries from their leader, they would all suddenly change, and be like him, until nature could endure no more, and they rushed forth from the Mosque into their court-yard, and threw themselves at length upon their mats. Hassan-ain-Effendi led my wife away on his arm, and I followed. The dervishes gazed curiously upon us as we passed by them. We were feeling sad at this strange exhibition of poor deluded human nature, when our friend and guide broke the silence by saying, "They whom you have seen to-day are the Ranters of Mahommedanism! What you have witnessed is not prescribed by the Koran, but is performed under the false idea of higher sanctity and of more meritorious service."

*Sat., Oct.* 13.—Went to Heliopolis—about two hours' ride from Cairo—passed some mosques and tombs, and one of the Pasha's palaces, on the road. Then we rode through the village of Mataréëh, beyond which we saw a well,—the water was raised by oxen,— said to have been the well where Joseph and Mary were refreshed on their flight into Egypt. Adjoining the well is a garden, in the midst of which is an extremely old sycamore, under which, it is also said, the Holy Family reclined. The tree and well are in the direct road from Syria to Egypt; and the traditions of their use by Joseph and the Virgin are very old. We had some difficulty in reaching Heliopolis, because of the inundation of the Nile. There are numerous mounds around, by which we could trace the position and circuit of the city, once so famous for its schools of philosophy; and in a garden stood a solitary obelisk of red granite, said to be one of two which stood at the entrance of the great Temple of the Sun, and at the end of a line of sphynxes. Plato, Herodotus, and, perhaps, Moses, learned here the wisdom of the Egyptians; and here, four thousand years ago, Joseph married the fair Asenath, daughter of Potipherah, priest of On.

*Sun., Oct. 14.*—Went to the Episcopal Church at Cairo in the morning, and heard there a faithful and excellent sermon. In the afternoon, attended the service of the American Missionary, who also preached a good practical sermon from, "Do ye now believe?"

*Mon., Oct. 15.*—Arranged for a Nile-boat with Hassan-ain-Effendi. There was much difficulty in getting it ready, because of the leisurely movements of the natives; and we did not leave Boulak till half-past five in the evening. Our boat was large and commodious. The fore-part was alloted to the Arab sailors, who were seven in number. The after-part contained a saloon with cushions, a bath, and three bed-cabins; and there were pillowed seats on deck by day. Our vessel had but one mast forward, with yard and sail bowed like the wing of a bird. We took a cook with us, and he cooked well; but he looked like a rascal, and was known to be one. Our turbaned captain was a tall, upright, venerable-looking man, with a long, flowing, white beard, and a Turkish robe. The turbid water was abundant in the river, and overflowed its banks in all directions. We floated quietly down with the current until we reached the neighbourhood of old Memphis, and there we anchored for the night.

*Tues., Oct.* 16.—Rose early, and went on deck, when, in excess of our expectations, we beheld before us a multitude of Pyramids; some twelve or more in number. They were the Pyramids of Geezeh, Sakkára, Abooseér, Dashóor, and Memphis; and looked, as they loomed through the maze of the Egyptian atmosphere, with their vague, vast bulk, like antediluvian things, or gigantic tenants of a former world. Yet one could not but remember that busy crowds of toilers—perhaps of God's own chosen people—had piled them up at the bidding of despotic kings, and amidst great suffering; that solemn trains of priests and heralds of pomp and power had stalked around them; and that the oppressive tyrants who had devised their erection had passed away to death,—the pale realm of their imagined Osiris,—in some instances without securing their own interment in the colossal piles called by their names. The crowds had also passed away, and successive crowds of varied visage and speech had struggled for power by their side, and were now hushed in death; but there, before us, were these huge dumb witnesses of the busy deeds of four thousand years, with the mantle of eternal silence upon them, seeming to assert for themselves the office of everlasting guardians of the desert.

We left the vessel for a day's excursion to the Pyramids of Geezeh, and went over the inundated country some mile or more in a small boat to a point of land where we found asses waiting for us; they had been sent there for us in the night, by our own direction. We had now seven or eight miles to ride on embankments, in a circuitous and serpentine route, because of the overflowing waters. On our way we passed by villages of mud buildings and fields of date-palms, and met numerous travellers with their loaded camels and asses; while, on either hand, we saw the residents of those parts treading their painful way upon narrow miry paths, or paddling over submerged fields to their isolated dwellings. In our winding course on the mud-banks the Pyramids were sometimes before us, and sometimes behind us, and sometimes it seemed that, instead of advancing towards them, we were leaving them altogether.

Having crossed the inundated country, we reached the desert, in which we had several miles to ride. The wide expanse of sand was immeasurable. The heat was intense, and seemed to pierce to the very brain. I remained behind to meditate, and the solitude was awful. The silence that reigned there was of eternity rather than time; so that one could imagine that the beat of the pulse could be heard in it. I toiled on after my wife and some friends from Cairo who had accompanied us. The blanched surface of the sandy expanse glared all around under the fiery rays of the noonday sun, until the reflected and glittering heat dazed and pained the eyes exceedingly. Before they arrived at the Pyramids, I overtook my companions; but I was so spent and exhausted, that I could not even look upon the massive wonders I had travelled to see. With trembling limbs, I got down from my worn and jaded ass, and threw myself into the mouth of an old gaping tomb, until I should recover my strength; while my wife, who had borne the heat better than I, kept at bay, by determined looks and threats, a crowd of Arabs, who in their filthy garments thronged near to minister to me. After an hour's rest, we rode round the vast structures, and were followed close by noisy men and boys, who cried incessantly for "backshcesh." Two gentlemen who were with us, and who were strong and expert in limb, climbed the great Pyramid of Cheops with difficulty; but a number of the begging Arabs ran up to the top before them with the agility of cats. We went into the mouth of the descending passage by which this Pyramid is entered; but did not attempt to mount the polished stones at the angle,—not venturing upon a climb up successive shelving heights to an altitude of one hundred and twenty-two feet higher than St. Paul's—and that under the vertical rays of an Egyptian sun.

It was not till we had paced our weary way round the Pyramids, and viewed them at different points and groupings, till we had seen a man dwarfed to an insect in size, at the top of the highest, and, finally, marked that the human stature was little more than half the height of the lower tiers of stones with which they are built, that we realized the vast size of these monster erections. That type of mystery—the Sphynx—raised in us, as it has raised in thousands, dumb wonder. What could we say to it? Carved out of the solid limestone rock, of which the Pyramids are built, and imbedded in the accumulating sand, until its breast and paws, with the temple they enclose, are entirely buried out of sight, it still measured more than one hundred feet from the surface of the plain to the top of its frittered crown. The face is much mutilated, but it still bears the expression of calm and dignified repose, and some of the colouring with which it was originally covered remains. With its broad and sharply-defined Nubian lips, and large, elongated eyes, it seemed to smile sadly, as if at the futile efforts of Caviglia and others, to wrest from this giant child of the desert the yellow sand which it has increasingly gathered within its embrace, during forty centuries.

The great causeway upon which the prepared stones were brought from the quarries of Toorah and Massarah, several miles off, for the outer casement of the Pyramids of Geezeh, on the rock platform here levelled for them, seems to have been a more marvellous work than even the Pyramids themselves. This mountain embankment, made of polished stones and sculptured with ancient figures, broken in some parts, and hidden by the drifted sand in others, may still be traced, stretching its gigantic way across the desert towards the Nile.

I sketched these wonders from their most impressive points, amidst the prying gaze of surrounding Arabs, who eagerly sought to do anything for me that would secure to them money payment. Having obtained coffee, eggs, and cakes, from a village by means of these Arabs, who fetched them through a full mile of the flood, and having sung, "Home, sweet home!" from the side of the great Pyramid, with our faces towards

England, and some verses of a hymn on the immutability of God,—much to the astonishment and apparent delight of the natives,—we distributed among them, through their sheik, what both he and they said would satisfy them; but after we had done so, they still followed and clamoured for "backsheesh." My friend the engineer pointed his gun at them, to frighten them away; but they would not leave us, or cease their entreaties. He then snatched from one of the stoutest of them a heavy staff, with which he belaboured them most unmercifully; but they bore it all in the most servile manner possible, still hoping to gain a few more coppers. I gave them more, thinking I should never see them or the Pyramids again, and being desirous of leaving them contented and happy; but they still begged of me, and even more clamorously than ever. The orb of day was wheeling round to the west, and descending so low, that the shadows of the Pyramids spread themselves over miles of the plain. It was, therefore, time for us to return. We obtained a boat to convey us part of the way; then rode on donkeys some miles to the point where we had left our Arab sailors in the morning waiting for our return. On regaining our vessel, we dined with a good appetite, and slept through the night in our saloon cabin, dreaming wildly and confusedly of our sights and exploits during the day.

*Wed., Oct.* 17.—Floated in our Nile-boat to points of the swollen river from whence we could see other Pyramids—Sakkára, Dashóor, Abooséer, and Memphis. The site on which stood the ancient Memphis of the Pharaohs was overflowed with water, through the high inundation. Moses is said to have been found in the ark at the Isle of Roda, but it was more probably here. We went opposite the vast quarries of Toorah and Massarah, which are on the eastern side of the river, and gazed on their huge blocks and excavations. Upon some of these the names of early and mighty Egyptian kings may be seen inscribed, with a relation of the removal of celebrated slabs and monuments there prepared. We then returned down the Nile, leaving Geezeh on our left, and the Isle of Roda and Old Cairo on our right, passing the Pasha's Palace, which is large, in the form of two squares, and adorned with arches and colonnades. The railway runs into its very court; and when lighted up, after sunset, the building, with its abundance of windows, looks almost like the Crystal Palace by night. Palaces and soldiers are the Pasha's hobbies. He has several palaces in different parts; and he takes with him thirty or forty thousand soldiers wherever he goes. They are principally young men, raised by conscription, kept two or three years, and then sent home without pay. To avoid this service many used in former times to mutilate their hands, and to destroy the sight of their eyes: so that the number of maimed hands and of one-eyed men in Egypt is amazing. Such self-disqualification for military service is now prohibited under severe penalty, and is thereby discouraged. We saw some thirty thousand of the Pasha's soldiers enter Cairo one day, returning with him from his palace in the desert. First came several rows of pioneers, with aprons and axes; then the tom-tom band; then the brass band; and then foot and horse soldiers. The infantry were in soiled cotton uniform, and the cavalry in gay trappings, helmets, and swords. Then came carriages, with cannon and ammunition. This order of things was repeated several times in the march of the Pasha's troops, as they passed before us towards their barracks by his palace at Old Cairo; and it was evidently a show exhibition, got up for effect. Many of these soldiers were thronging the courts of the Pasha's Palace, as we sailed by it on our return from the pyramids, and served to give life and colour to the scene as we approached Boulak. The sun went down that evening in fiery vermilion, and flooded the river, its banks, the palm trees, and the several groups of pyramids, until, by degrees, the whole picture was dyed next in deep crimson, and then in red purple, and changed, lastly, into a colder and more solemn tone. It was a memorable close to a memorable excursion, and can never be forgotten by those who witnessed it. On landing, and driving to our hotel, we found that no news had arrived of the "Candia," the steamer we had been daily expecting would reach Suez to convey us to Ceylon.

*Thurs., Oct.* 18.—Went with Hassan-ain-Effendi to see the tombs of the Mamelukes, and found the royal ladies of the Hareem at the family burial-place of Mehemet Ali, close by. The tombs of the Mamelukes are on an elevated platform, and adorned with pillars, or upright marble slabs at the ends, bearing Arabic inscriptions. After examining them, we went to the celebrated Mosque of Mehemet Ali. It is his family burial-place, and has within it some gorgeous tombs, with embroidered blue and green cloth and velvet coverings. The ladies of the Hareem were still on the premises, having come there to mourn for the princely dead; and their sumptuous carriages, with Nubian attendants, and lounging eunuchs, were waiting for them outside. When following our Turkish guides among the tombs, we heard some laughing voices in the adjoining court. I stepped hastily to the window to see who they were, but there were shouts and gestures of warning to me not to look; and we were afterwards informed that the ladies of the Hareem with their white slaves had been peeping at us from the court-yard, through the mosque windows, and that their keepers were alarmed. Of all the sights of Egypt, nothing was more offensive to me than the huge, turtle-fleshed eunuchs who had the guardianship of higher-class women. It is true that, in mere physique, some of them were large, grand men. But they looked so bloated and dead-eyed, and were so brutally haughty and overbearing, that one could only feel disgust for them. This feeling was deepened by some things that we heard of their conduct towards the ladies of the Hareem,—and which one cannot repeat.

*Frid., Oct.* 19.—At noon rode up to the Mosque at the Citadel, it being the great day of the week for Moslem worship—the Mahommedan Sabbath. We were permitted to enter, on pulling off our shoes at the threshold of such holy ground, and on the payment of "backsheesh" for cloth coverings to our feet. This mosque is a huge structure, standing on a level platform of the rock, high up above all other buildings, at the back of the city. Its plan is a square, with tall, slender minarets at the angles, and with a large court in front surrounded with a corridor, and having a superb fountain in the centre. The whole of this is in Oriental alabaster, except the outer walls. The mosque itself is covered with an immense dome. The interior is sumptuously fitted up with arabesque ornaments, coloured windows, Turkey carpets, and with hundreds of swinging glass lamps in radiating circles. On the right corner, as you enter, is the tomb of Mehemet Ali, the founder, covered and adorned within its screen with the richest colours. The worshippers under the lofty dome were numerous. When I entered, they were seated upon the carpeted floor, without their slippers, and in their white turbans, listening to an Imaum, or priest, who was addressing them from a side gallery-like pulpit. Afterwards the priest came down, approached the central niche at the far side, looking towards Mecca, and prayed, when all prostrated themselves with their foreheads upon the ground, and responded until the murmur of their worship seemed to make the place tremble. The Mahommedans were evidently jealous of our presence, and eyed us askance with fiery glances; but I sketched a plan of their proud building, notwithstanding.

Through the court in front, and stepping a few paces beyond, we reached the spot were Emin Bey desperately leaped on horseback over the parapet some forty feet down, and saved his life at the well known massacre of the Mamelukes. In the front of the mosque, from the projecting platform of the foundation-rock, is a commanding view of Grand Cairo and its surrounding neighbourhood. Immediately below are the massive buildings of the arsenal, with the splendid mosque of Sultan Hassan on the right, and the mosques and tombs of the Mamelukes on the left. Around these is the vast, mingled mass of city streets and buildings, not pressed downwards by the heavy mounds of numerous domes as in the Turkish cities of Europe, but lifted up lightly towards heaven by innumerable lofty minarets, which gleam and glitter, with their golden crescents, like brilliant stars of the early evening. Beyond this, on the one hand, flows from Sakkára in the south, to the point of the Delta in the north, the broad, shining river, fringed on both shores to some distance with rich green verdure, and bordered with palms; and on the other hand, beyond the city walls and gates is the vast, level desert, with the cathedral-like tombs of the Caliphs in its midst. And all this is viewed, not under a glaring light which distracts you, as when looking upon great cities of the west; but under a soft, balmy, mellowing light of creamy transparency, which smooths down all rigid lines, and blends the whole into harmonious dreaminess, such as has been most successfully given in the mysterious colouring of Claude and Turner. Indeed, Egypt, and especially as seen from an elevated stand-point like the Citadel, and under the tints of a golden purple sunset, is the most perfect dreamland that can be visited by the European traveller. It is the true field for imagination, being, with all its picturesque and glittering objects, and its dreamy light, the seat of early fable and history, the birthplace of art and science, and the cradle of philosophy and learning.

*Sun., Oct.* 20.—We left Cairo by rail for Suez, to sail by the "Columbian," as the "Candia" had not arrived. We sat for a time with our backs towards the engine, that we might see the mosques, minarets, and pyramids of the city which had so deeply interested us, as long as possible. They gradually faded from our view, and were at length wholly lost in the red, dusky haze of an Egyptian atmosphere. We turned to the scene immediately around us. Our way was through the great desert, and it seemed a real desecration of the solitude which had dwelt there through successive ages, for our screeching engine to rush furiously over it, dragging a train of hollow-sounding carrriages, with their eager, living contents. But there was nothing to disturb in our course. No animals; no birds; and no wind. There was no danger of our scattered sparks setting fire to grass or corn; for there was not a tuft or a blade of vegetation to be seen. There needed no guardsmen at crossings; no gatekeepers; for there was not a living, moving thing to be seen, except here and there some straggling Bedouins, with their patient, plodding camels, until we reached the midway station, provided by the Pasha for the refreshment of travellers, and where some two or three Europeans were to be seen among the attendants. As we progressed, the hot atmosphere became very oppressive, and trembled over the sandy expanse around like the quivering film over lime-kilns. The delusive mirage now fantastically played its tricks before us, as we rushed along. It expanded into bright, blue lakes, bordered with clustered groves, and glittered at different points with mimic waves. The vision then receded, dissolved, reunited, and combined again with fresh forms, and at length faded away altogether. Near Suez we passed two or three mud villages of the meanest and most desolate kind; and the natives came out of their filthy hovels to gaze upon us, almost naked. We wound round by some dark, rocky mountains, and by four, P.M., we reached Suez, where there is a fortification and a few desolate houses. We dined in the large, quadrangular court of the European hotel, belonging to the Peninsular and Oriental Company, and where they charged an extravagant price for a scanty dinner. In the evening we left, with our luggage, by a small steamer, for the "Columbian," which was some two miles from us. We steered our serpentine course amidst the dangerous shoals at the head of the Red Sea, by floating lights sent out for the occasion, and placed at certain points. Arriving at our ship so late, with a crowd of passengers beyond what the vessel could accommodate with a prospect of anything like comfort, there was no little noise and scuffle on board; but as soon as a cabin had been allotted us by the purser, we went to it, and retired for the night—not to sleep, but to rest ourselves as best we could in our coffin-like berths.

## CHAPTER III.

PASSAGE down the Red Sea—Aden—Monsoons—Ceylon—Rich Scenery—Native Schools—Matura—Animal and Vegetable Life—Buddhist Temples—Dress of the Singhalese—Dondra Head—Methodism in Ceylon—Constellation of the "Cross"—Morotto—Preaching to the Singhalese—Mr. Gogerly—Kandy—Buddha's Foot and Tooth—Opening of a Wesleyan Chapel for the Singhalese—Their Liberality and Devotion—Farewell—Re-embarkation.

*Sun., Oct.* 21.—ROSE early, and on opening our cabin door found men, women, and children, with black and white nurses, lying on the floor of the passages around, and giving a most camp-like appearance to things between the decks. We picked our way to the staircase, and climbed up speedily into the open air, being anxious to escape from the suffocating atmosphere below, and also to look upon the coast scenery of the Red Sea. On deck we found a crowd of passengers complaining of the insufficient accommodation they had had through the night. Some were very loud and boisterous in their complaints, and angrily threatened protests against the Peninsular and Oriental Company for ill-treatment and fraud. One, a military gentleman, going out for command in Ceylon, declared that he would report the whole affair to the "Horse Guards!" This somewhat amused us; and we were ready to ask, if he would not have the Directors of the Company tried by court-martial, and punished at the halberts. In one sense there was reason for complaint, inasmuch as very high fares had been paid, with the expectation of good accommodation; and though soldiers may be willing to "camp out" on hard and scanty beds when on the march, and travellers generally may be willing to "rough it" in the bush, yet when comfortable sleeping room has been purchased at large cost, and is not provided, no wonder that men irritated by nausea and sea-sickness should complain. We did not, however, join the complainants; for though we had not the cabin-comfort paid for and expected, yet we believed the officers of the Company to have done the best they could in the circumstances. The "Candia" had broken down in her way from Aden to Suez, as we afterwards learned, and on her non-arrival at port the "Columbian," one of the Company's steam-ships there for troops and not for passengers, was hastily fitted up to receive us. This was the best that could be done in the emergency; and when men have done their best, it is vain to complain—though with an overcrowded ship, not the most clean, nor best provisioned, the passage down the Red Sea, where some preceding us, with more ample accommodations, had recently died under the intensity of the heat, was not pleasing. By degrees, however, the noise of complainants subsided, frowns relaxed, and gave way to smiles; and our companions on board submitted to their condition, and became agreeable and cheerful. There were no seats provided on deck for the passengers, not even so much as a hen-coop. It seemed to be taken for granted that all would bring with them their own chairs. Most of the old travellers had done so, but novices in the route had expected to find forms or benches awaiting them. They, however, who had nothing but the deck, or the rope-platform at the stern to rest upon, packed themselves up with cushions and rugs, and made the best of their circumstances.

We had passed in the night the part of the Red Sea where the Israelites are supposed to have crossed from Egypt to the wilderness, before the pursuit by Pharaoh and his host; so that in going we were deprived of a sight eagerly desired, and we could only hope to realize it on our return. We could see on our left the Sinaitic range of mountains, red and bald, as if they had passed through fire, and then cooled down again, standing against the blue sky in bold relief, and resting upon a flat shore of yellow sand, which had not a bit of verdure, or a living thing of any kind upon it; but which contrasted finely with the dark indigo colour of the water that margined its long, horizontal line. We could not see the "Mount of God," from whence the Law, with all its dread accompaniments, was given. It was more easterly in the Sinaitic range than could be seen from our line of passage, except under peculiar circumstances of the atmosphere. Some lofty, conical peaks gleamed out in the white heat of the distance, and some affirmed these to be the veritable mountains of Serbal and Sinai; but we could not confidently receive the affirmation.

Notwithstanding the confusion and disquietude of our over-crowded ship we contrived to hold two religious services in the saloon during the day, and they were well attended by the passengers and the crew. A clergyman of the Establishment, proceeding as a missionary to India, took part with me in conducting the services. We had on board the "Columbian" nearly four hundred souls in all. Among the passengers were military officers of rank, returning with their wives and families to their regiments; scions of the nobility, going to Madras for the shooting season; and merchants with their families, returning to Calcutta, Hong-Kong, and other parts of India and China, after a sojourn in their native land to recruit health. Among all classes of passengers on this route we found the Scotch preponderate. Several sea-sick, languishing young ladies, who seemed to have no objections to kindly attentions from young gentlemen, and who could give no better account of their errand to the eastern world than that their brothers and cousins had sent for them to go thither,—ceased, after awhile, to exact compassion, and, like every body else, grew heartily cheerful, and made sport of the very inconveniences and discomforts of which they had at first distressingly complained. The greater number of the crew were dark-coloured Lascars; and it was pleasing on the Sunday to see them in their clean cotton dresses, and gay sashes and turbans: but we felt it odd to see them at meal times taking up their curries with their fingers from open, salver-like dishes, around which they gathered. At sunset the Mahommedans among them might be seen bowing down upon the deck in profound reverence towards Mecca. It seemed strange to behold such devotion in men of their class; and we were ready to inquire, When will British sailors show themselves as devout for the religion of Christ? The Lascars let themselves out for hire in companies, under their elected head-man or captain; and it is amusing to see the strut and swagger of some of these native chiefs, and to hear their loud and shrieking whistle of authority. One of these was our pilot down the Gulf, and seemed a most careful watcher of our course both by day and night.

*Mon., Oct. 22.*—Lost sight of land on both sides.

Increasingly hot. Prayer-meeting at noon. Most of the passengers slept on deck at night, but we kept to our cabin for retirement, though the heat of the atmosphere below was almost suffocating, and the ceaseless plaintive cries of suffering children around us were distressing.

*Tues., Oct.* 23.—Breeze on the open sea, which somewhat tempered the heat, and made it bearable.

*Wed., Oct.* 24.—Heat very oppressive. The fierce rays of the sun penetrated the double awning stretched over us; and, at times, when a breath of wind came upon us from the coast, it was so heated by the desert over which it had come, as to seem like the breath of a furnace. Our drinking-water from the condenser was too hot for use. Much bitter beer was taken by the passengers, but it only seemed to increase their thirst, and they lay faint and languishing from morning to evening. In the afternoon we passed the remarkable rocks of long table form, named the "Two Brothers," which stand up from the sea a considerable height, about halfway down from Suez to Aden, and near to each other. At the close of the day the sun went down in fiery splendour, and made the whole scene appear as if ready to burst forth with flame. The atmosphere of the night was fearful, and one could hardly think of continued life until the morning. The thinnest night-dresses seemed too heavy for coverings; and as for sheets, or quilts, they were discarded by all.

*Thurs., Oct.* 25.—Several islands on the right. Our passage between the coasts narrowed itself quickly; and now we were in the Straits of Bab-el-Mandeb, at the south-eastern neck of the Red Sea. This was known to be the most perilous passage in our course;

and it was no relief to be told that if the ship were to founder upon any of the shoals of that part, and the passengers were to make their way to the coast on either side, death or slavery would be their inevitable doom. Rain fell, so that we could not see our way; and as Arab pilots steer by sight principally, our steamer stopped her engines for a considerable time, and remained stationary. The moistness of the heated atmosphere below steamed as in a scullery; and we had to lie on the cabin floor for as much air as could be obtained.

*Frid., Oct. 26.*—A fresh breeze sprang up, and in some degree moderated the heat. Rain fell copiously, and the weather became rough, and even boisterous. We had passed in the night Mooshedjerah, where the "Alma" was wrecked in 1859. Some of the passengers of that ill-fated vessel were with us, and made us shudder with the recital of their privations and sufferings. Late in the evening the high, conical peaks of Aden frowned upon us; and before midnight we had anchored in the harbour, to remain there, for a fresh supply of coals, until noon of the next day. Solemn darkness shrouded the scene, and the points of light gleaming in different directions on sea and shore, with the wild screaming of unseen natives in unseen boats around, rendered our position mysteriously impressive.

*Sat., Oct. 27.*—On deck early to see the scenery and the natives. The volcanic region of Aden looked grim and grand. It has been aptly described by Sir Charles Napier as "a gigantic cinder;" and consists of high conical scorched hills, without a particle of verdure on any portion of them. One large sugar-loaf mountain is covered with loose shingle as black as coal. A mass of high jagged peaks of lighter colour, broken down in parts, and looking like the shattered crust of an old exploded crater, assumes the form of a walled-up fortification; and this appearance is strengthened by a signal-flag being placed upon it. Between two of these conical elevations are coal-stores for the steamers. The post office, shops, and stores, are near the water's edge, while above and beyond are rugged hills and heaps with buildings and sheds upon them scattered here and there. The British flag, on a mast of great height, is beheld on one of the hills near the shore. Several British ships of war are kept here.

On the narrow roads by the beach, at the foot of the surrounding hills, were seen stalking camels with their burdens, and asses, with boy drivers. Boats of all shapes and sizes were being rowed towards us by wild black men, almost naked, and their heads covered and surrounded with matted and stringed red hair, as bulgy and hive-like in form as the immense head-coverings of the cannibal Fijians. They jabbered and gesticulated most violently: and they leaped into the water and dived down to amazing depths after money thrown to them, notwithstanding the numerous fierce sharks which frequent the harbour. They brought for sale beautiful pieces of coral, broken from the reefs under water, and picturesque baskets with coverlids, tastefully striped and ingeniously interwrought with white, red, and black bamboo. Greasy clad Arab Jews, who stank of dirt, and cleanly respectable-looking Parsees, said to have the best commerce of the place, came on board, with black and white ostrich feathers, Indian-wrought boxes, and tortoiseshell curiosities, and prevailed on passengers to make purchases at prices for their articles far above those of London or Paris. Huge barges, laden with bags of coal for our steamer, were drawn by ropes towards us, surrounded and surmounted with crowds of natives, powdered thickly with coal-dust, and looking, in the distance, like swarms of baboons, or large monkeys. The Arabs all were abjectly civil to us, hoping to receive money recompence for being so; but it is well known that if a European advance beyond the British boundary into their own region, his life is unrelentingly taken by these red-haired descendants of Ishmael. They are exceedingly jealous of the English having any foothold in their arid country, and think it is only by the special favour of the Turkish Sultan we are allowed to enter the bay, or to hold the garrison of Aden; believing him to be the supreme ruler among men. I remained, and sketched Aden, while most of our passengers went on shore, and then set scampering off on hired donkeys to the cantonment, or principal township, some three miles away round the hills behind us. On returning, they told strange things of the bamboo-built houses and bazaars of the town; and seemed to have been much interested with the commanding fortifications of the garrison. Aden is another important link in the chain of British possessions stretching onwards towards India, and has been fitly described as " the Gibraltar of the East." We had finished "coaling" by two o'clock; and as we ran out swiftly to sea, our steamship bore, in passing, upon the outstanding bowsprit of a large ship, and snapped it in a moment, as if it had been a brittle carrot. We saw, as we left the harbour, the Arabian desert on our right, with its bald, rocky mountains and vast plains of sand, all reeking in the white heat. A fine breeze filled our sails and quickened our speed; and we had a most favourable passage out towards the Indian Ocean.

*Sun., Oct.* 28.—A fine morning, and the fishes sporting in " a sea of glass like unto crystal." The vast expanse of water shone like a polished mirror, under the pure blue sky, and seemed, in the language of Byron, to " glass the Almighty's form" all around us! It appeared the shining image of His immensity! We had service in the saloon as usual.

*Mon., Oct.* 29.—Passed Cape Guardafui, and then the Island of Socotra. Sunset was gorgeous.

*Tues., Oct.* 30.—Serene, calm morning, with a bright silvery light. No land anywhere in sight. Flying fishes leaping out of the water, gliding in the air a considerable distance, and then dipping again into the sea.

*Wed., Oct.* 31.—Another calm morning; but clouds gathered in the afternoon, and rain fell in heavy heaps and torrents; so that we could not remain on deck without being wet through. And when driven down into the saloon, it seemed as if a deluge of waters was falling in lumps upon the deck overhead. The weighty falls of rain actually made our steamer stagger again and tremble. It was difficult to conceive how the vacuities produced in the African and Arabian deserts by the swallowing-up heat of the sun could so disturb the atmosphere at such a distance over the sea, and cause such descending torrents of waters.

*Thurs., Nov.* 1.—Monsoons continued. Rains fell very heavily, and hindered us greatly in our course.

*Frid., Nov. 2.*—Fine, fresh morning. Sea calm, and in colour rich ultramarine. Good speed of eleven knots per hour.

*Sat., Nov. 3.*—Monsoons in the morning; but they cleared off by noon, and the remainder of the day was fine.

*Sun., Nov. 4.*—Exceedingly warm. Divine service on deck, under the awning. The scene was deeply impressive, and our singing seemed to ring upon the vast expanse of the Indian Ocean. At noon it was reported that we were two hundred and fifty miles from Point de Galle, in Ceylon.

*Mon., Nov. 5.*—Brisk, fresh morning, but not able to reach Galle to enter the harbour before sunset; so slackened our speed, that we might ride safely for the night outside the dangerously projecting reefs. Awoke in the night, and saw huge black rats in the cabin; so got no more sleep, though I left my berth on the floor, and climbed up into a higher one—having an instinctive horror of rats.

*Tues., Nov. 6.*—Reached Point de Galle by six in the morning. The harbour picturesque and impressive. We made our way round fortified rocks, and amidst coral reefs, to the principal basin of the harbour, from whence we had to land in small boats. The sea was as blue as sapphire, and broke with white foam upon the rocks and strand, and the rich green palm trees bent their lofty forms inwards, and overshadowed the water in every direction; while over them in the distance were numerous blue and purple hills of every variety of form. Several vessels and steamships were lying around us; some with French troops on board, going to China; and in front of us, near the shore, rose out of the water the upper masts of a ship recently foundered there. The

Rev. John Scott, our missionary, came on board. We obtained a boat, and landed in Ceylon by eight. The scene on the pier was strange to us. The natives, who crowded around, were, for the most part, upright, well-made figures of rich bronze colour, with jet black hair, turned up before and behind, and fixed in a coil at the top of the head with large tortoiseshell combs. They were unclad to the loins, where they wore a wrapper of white and coloured cotton, which hung down to their naked feet, like a long petticoat. They had little or no beards, or hair of any kind upon the face; and, with earrings dangling on many of them, they had a very effeminate appearance. In fact, we took them all, at first, to be women! We passed quickly through the Custom-house, and drove up in a cab-like carriage, having Venetian blinds, accommodated at will to the direction of the sun, to " Richmond Hill,"—as the Rev. Joseph Rippon named it,—where our spacious Mission premises stand, surrounded with very striking scenery. Cocoa-nut trees, jungle, and pleasant hills were in our neighbourhood, and richly clothed hills, with the conical mountain of Adam's Peak beyond, were in the distance. We could see heathen temples on several of the elevations around us, and could hear the tom-toms of numerous devil-worshippers. Indeed, on our passage from the beach to the Mission premises we had met several processions of Buddhists, with their dresses and discordant music.

After breakfast went to the Mission school on the hill,—a good building, shaded by verandahs all round. Found there a native minister and a native schoolmaster, with some sixty Singhalese children, who were taught to read and speak English as well as their own language. Heard some of the boys read a lesson on astronomy; then examined them on their conceptions of God, who made the heavens, and on what they knew of the way of salvation. Their understanding of Divine things, as well as their general intelligence, was most gratifying. In the evening preached to a native congregation, through an interpreter, our excellent native minister, Rev. G. E. Goonewardene. The assembly was novel and impressive. The women in their white dresses, the higher class men with combs in their hair, the Dutch burghers, with the solemn darkness open to us from the verandah around, were all Rembrandtic in effect.

*Wed., Nov. 7.*—Went to Matura, driving through the Fort of Galle, which, apart from the barracks and Government buildings, is but a large village of mud streets and squat houses. As we passed through the town, the natives strove to tempt us into purchases of their tortoiseshell ornaments, mock precious stones, and lacquered jewelry. We saw in the streets much variety of race and costume. There were European officials in loose clothing, covering themselves with large cotton umbrellas; there were Singhalese natives, clothed as I have described; and the women, some of them prematurely old and very ugly, in white jackets: there were Moors and Mussulmen in turbans and yellow coverings, carrying japanned paper umbrellas: there were Malabars and Malays, and Buddhist priests with shaven heads and saffron robes; and mingled with these were English soldiers in cotton uniform, and native chiefs in gay, embroidered dresses, and jewelled ornaments. On quitting the town, we skirted along the side of the harbour, passed by the crowded market-places, and entered a splendid avenue of tall cocoa-nut trees, overarching the road, and rendering it pleasantly cool. The natives, like living bronzes, and in their pink, yellow, red, blue, and white costumes, thronged the road, and, blending with the green foliage, formed a gay and pleasing picture. We saw many long snakes in our way, and several cameleons. Sometimes the guano—a large, green lizard, three or four feet long: a pre-adamite looking reptile, but little afraid of man—ran across our way, or dragged up its length on the banks at the roadside. There were beautiful openings of the sea-coast at intervals, with masses of snow-white coral strewing the shore. As we advanced, innumerable insects of various kinds thronged the air, and filled it with a perpetual hum. Among these were large, gorgeous butterflies, and huge dragon-flies, of bright metallic lustre; while ever and anon would come, booming on their short wings, lustrous beetles of rainbow hues. The dark natives were turning their cocoa-nut mills under shady trees, at the sides of the road, or working in the open "paddies" or rice-fields. Long, slender cranes were standing in pools, and buffaloes, like huge black pigs, were luxuriating in deep soft mud. Gay flowers, of bright yellow and deep crimson, on trees, and not on mere bushes, lined the way; and a vast variety of orchids climbed the boles of the palms, and entwined themselves gracefully around them. Trees with roots above ground,—seeming formed of writhing snakes,—were seen at intervals; as also the drooping banyan tree, with its long, rope-like roots descending from its branches. We passed the gigantic figure of "Kustia Raja," an Indian prince, who is said, by tradition, to have first taught the Singhalese the culture of the cocoa-nut. It is carved out of the rock by the wayside. We reached Belligam in the forenoon, when the heat had become very oppressive, when the hum of insects had ceased, and all living things had retired for rest into the shade. At Belligam there is a "Rest-house," provided by the Government for travellers,—as there is at certain distances on all the high roads of Ceylon. In these "Rest-houses" needful refreshment can be had at appointed prices. While the ladies reclined under the shade, and breakfast was being prepared, Mr. Scott and I went forth to see the village, our chapel and school in it, and some Buddhist temples.

The village of Belligam, like other villages of Ceylon, is picturesque and pleasing, with its luxuriant foliage overhanging mud-built dwellings, thatched with the feather-like branches of cocoa-nuts. We went down a lane or street, overshadowed by cocoa-nuts, in which we found our native school and our native chapel. The children were few in the school, for dysentery had thinned them; no uncommon thing in the schools of the island. I sketched the chapel by the roadside. We saw a somewhat rude Buddhist temple, as we passed, with its tall dome covering some pretended relics; but at a distance of some quarter of a mile over the fields, in the direction of Galle, we visited a celebrated temple, and examined it carefully. Ascending by broad steps, we reach a large, elevated court-yard, surrounded by an embattled wall, skirted by cocoa-nuts. As we enter, there is a large Bo, or sacred tree on the left, overshadowing the seat or surrounding platform, built up with its roots, which are above ground. A high, sugar-loaf structure encloses some reported relics of Buddhu, named the Dogeba. Within is a tall, niched flower-altar; and in the middle, on the far side of the court, is the temple—a common Italian-tiled building. You find yourself now in the very " chambers of imagery," gaudily coloured with yellow figures illustrative of the life of Buddhu, and with rude, purgatorial exhibitions of punishments for the unfaithful. Within the inner chamber there reclines at full length the yellow-coloured figure of Buddhu, eighteen cubits, or twenty-seven feet, long, in somewhat rude wooden workmanship. At the sides are vermilion and gold coloured figures of Buddhu and Vishnu, of human stature. Before these are tables, or altars, with flower-offerings upon them, fresh plucked in the day, and placed there by poor, deluded votaries. Some were there at the time, presenting their flowers; and as I stood in the midst within a heathen temple for the first time in my life, a shuddering horror came over me. I felt no patience with the yellow-robed priests about me; they seemed ministers in the very precincts of hell. Adjoining the court are the dwellings of the priests, who constitute a college or ecclesiastical establishment of Buddhu. We silently paced our way back to the "Rest-house," and felt a grateful relief in gazing upon the fine open bay, with its coral strand.

Resumed our drive to Matura at four. There were lovely openings to the sea on our right. Our road was a deep chocolate, darker than the soil, and harmonized pleasantly with the green luxuriant foliage. Sometimes we passed through cuttings of the rocks, and then caught glimpses of well-moulded hills covered with lofty trees and shrubbery, and resembling the " Green Mountains," in the Northern States of America. Again and again, we passed through long avenues of tall cocoa-nut trees, bending over crowds of native pedestrians in their many-coloured costumes. At intervals all along the road, in front of the native huts, were fine plump children playing—boys and girls, full of quirk and fun as Reynolds's Puck. The girls had bracelets of a white shining metal around their wrists and ankles, and sometimes around their loins: otherwise they were perfectly nude. The faces of men and women upon the road were often not so pleasing, owing to their chewing a composition of tobacco with a sort of white paste, wrapped up in a green leaf. Through pressure in the mouth a red liquid is produced, and this gives a bloody appearance to it, and destroys the teeth. In other respects the natives were cleanly and decently clad. We met and saw, towards the end of our day's journey upon the road, several bullock-waggons, vehicles covered with cocoa-nut leaves, after the manner of an English carrier's tilted cart, but lower, narrower, and larger in proportion. They were each drawn by two oxen of small size. In some instances we met a carriage for one or two persons, drawn by one small bullock of surpassing speed. We reached Matura soon after five o'clock; Mr. Eaton having sent us a pony carriage, attended by a native runner in gay costume. Our native minister, Daniel Henry Pereira, received us very hospitably. We were delighted with the fine, spacious Mission premises. But as we sat at our eastern dinner served up in native fashion, in a verandah open to the garden and broad river beyond, with the dim lamps swinging over our heads, and the native servitors gliding in stealthily, out of the dusk, from among the clumps of palm trees, we were a little startled to hear that there were large deadly snakes in the garden beneath our feet, and that in the river at the bottom of it, but a few yards distant, the savage combats of huge alligators, and the snapping of their fell teeth, were often heard! It was a more pleasing subject of reflection, that on these Mission-premises had resided brave pioneers of Christian truth who have since gone to their eternal reward.

*Thurs., Nov.* 8.—We journeyed from Matura to Dondra, along a good road by the sea-side for a few miles, and reached the house of the native missionary. He was from home, among his people; so we drove round to Dondra Head, the extreme south point of Ceylon. A long avenue of cocoa-nut palms conducted us to a line of square pillars, each eight or nine feet high, extending from a Hindu temple, the remains of which are still standing here by the sea. The remains of this temple show that it has been originally for Hindu, and not Buddhist, worship. It has had a central way, with side-aisles formed of upright pillars, and has extended as much as two miles in length. At the upper part, most distant from the sea, there has been a sort of transept, or cross, formed by similar pillars; and beyond this there is still standing in front of the temple ground a curious old gateway, covered with sculptured Hindu figures and ornaments. The rest of the original temple is gone; but a plain modern building has been put up; and at certain festivals Hindu worshippers repair to it from afar, and make much noise and show around it, as a most sacred place. There are mounds and pillars in the court-yard, and in front is a very old stone with an inscription upon it in a learned language, which few can read. The pillars, gate, and stone, are of grey granite. At the left corner of the old court is a Buddhist temple, made up in parts of the figures and fragments taken from the Hindu temple. The scene from the rocks and boulders in the sea, at the extreme south of the island, that is, at Dondra Head, is very beautiful. Coral reefs stretch far into the sea, against which the pure blue water foams and splashes. Palms crown the shores down to the edge of the island, and border it most gracefully; while beyond, inwards, are forest and jungle, grand in colour, and in their vast extent. The natives came out of their huts, and gazed curiously upon me, as I sketched these things; and seemed filled with wonder as they saw their familiar scenery copied and coloured before them. We returned to the native minister's house, who, with his newly-converted sister residing with him, gave us a cheerful welcome. We went into the school-room, just by, and killed there a centipede on the floor. The missionary told us that cobras and the most deadly serpents were numerous in the neighbourhood; that leopards were seen at times in the adjoining jungle, where there were also troops of monkeys, and plenty of paroquets. On the coral shore of the sea before us the turtle is taken in abundance.

We conversed at length upon the state of the Mission in that part, found that it had been injured by extreme jealousy of demon worship on the part of one of our agents; and, after giving counsel on the matter, we returned to Matura. On our way we climbed "Brown's Hill," on the left, and had a fine panorama of the surrounding country and of the sea. Descending, we visited another Buddhist temple, ruder and more modern than the one at Belligam, and which has adjoining a temporary wooden erection for festivals.

Reached Matura as the sun was setting in solemn grandeur behind the large dark trees. We took a boat at the bridge, and were rowed to the garden of the Mission-premises in time for evening service in the chapel. The building could not contain the congregation, composed of English residents, Dutch burghers, and Singhalese; and there were many outside in the verandah and in the street. The audience seemed to enter very heartily into the spirit of worship, notwithstanding the most soaking heat and the musquitoes.

*Fr. d., Nov.* 9.—Returned to Belligam; met there our native Catechist, and conversed with him on his work. He is all but alone as a Christian teacher in the village; and related to me several instances of the cunning of the Buddhist priests to keep the people from him. He preaches in the chapel, teaches daily in the school, and visits the natives in their houses. Some, but not many, treat him with ridicule; and the priests set watchers against the chapel, to see who enter it, and then to injure such in their temporal circumstances. On leaving Belligam we overtook a marriage procession. The bride was borne in one of three palanquins in front, and at some distance behind was the bridegroom. The woman was attended by a crowd of native females gaily dressed; and the man by his male friends, dressed up in blue European-looking coats, gilt buttons, breast belts, and swords. The bridegroom had more ornaments than the others. On the road we also saw natives at work under the trees and elsewhere, breaking up cocoa-nut, drying it in the open air, and pressing out the oil in rude mills turned as on the pivot-cup by oxen or men. We reached Richmond Hill by half-past five, and had a welcome tea-meeting in the school-room at six. This tea-meeting had been spontaneously provided by the natives for Mrs. Jobson and myself, as an expression of their esteem for us and for the churches from which we had come. The room was most tastefully decorated with various flowers and fruits of the island, as well as with emblematic figures and forms suited to the occasion. The company filled the place. Around us, at the upper end, sat native women in clean white and gay coloured dresses, and adorned with ear-rings and bracelets. Beyond them sat native men, with large combs upon their heads; and among them were Dutch burghers, clad in loose European style; while, in the verandah encircling the building, the native children of the schools were crowded, and peered at us with their sharp black eyes. The room was lighted by lamps swung from the rafters of the open roof; and beyond it was the solemn darkness of the forest and the jungle. The tea and cakes were good, and were most courteously handed round by natives who were officers in our Wesleyan Society. We sang and prayed together; and afterwards I addressed them on the social character of Christianity, and on what British Methodists from whom I had come wished them to be, as professing members of the church of Christ in Ceylon. It was a cheerful, happy meeting, and I trust not without profit to any of us. The excitement of the evening prevented sleep, and we lay through the night on our bed at the Mission-house listening to the chirping of numerous lizards from the open roof above us.

*Sat., Nov.* 10.—Took coach for Colombo at five in the morning, amidst profound darkness, and here first saw the beautiful constellation of the Cross in the heavens. For some time we could not see who were our companions in the coach; but as the day opened, we discovered we had before us a native of high class, wearing a full Moslem turban, a crimson vest, and a large signet-ring. Before this, we had found to our annoyance, that he was strongly scented with cocoa-nut oil. By his side sat a dark-looking Dutch burgher, in a sort of settler's loose dress. An Englishman and a native were with the burgher coachman on the box; and a native guard hung on behind, or rode upon the step at the side. The horses were rather small; but, being stallions, were usually restive and ungovernable at starting. Our road throughout was deeply interesting. For good part of seventy miles it was in an avenue of lofty palms, which, at the first, solemnly overshadowed us. As we proceeded, we perceived fires by huts, where the natives were cooking their breakfasts, gleaming out in the distance from among dark cocoa-nut trees. As the day dawned, fine underwood and creepers, and beautiful flowers, and banyan trees with branches returning to the earth and taking root, graced our road on either side. Several times we crossed creeks and rivers on wooden bridges; and saw on the water curious canoes having no iron-work in them, but bound together wholly by cocoa-nut fibres; and yet in these the native fishermen venture far out into the sea. Some of the coves and bays in the coast on our left were very fine; and amidst bold, rocky scenery we came upon a large Buddhist temple with a dome. The shaven priest stood with his broad fan before his eyes, as if he would have us believe him to be a strict observer of the rule,—"not to look upon a woman." The lofty Adam's Peak was seen at a distance on our right. It seemed to be buttressed and upheld by numerous surrounding mountains. We breakfasted at Bentotto, on oyster currie and fish; and there first observed, what we afterwards found to be almost universal, that the telegraph wire was fastened to the living cocoa-nut trees, as its supporters along the road. We turned a little from the sea-shore on leaving Bentotto, passed through Caltura and came to Morotto, a village of twelve thousand inhabitants, who are chiefly carpenters and fishermen. Here I saw our native minister, and engaged to preach in his chapel the next Sunday morning. On our way dancing gay butterflies, and metallic-lustred insects had swarmed around us. Birds of gaudy plumage had chattered and sung among the branches, and many bright green lizards had crawled over the road and up the trees. Indeed, until we approached the noon of day, all nature seemed to teem with life. Our road from Morotto lay through the cinnamon grounds for the space of several miles; but the air was not at this period loaded with the perfume of this renowned laurel so richly as we had been led to expect. After passing under an old venerable banyan-tree, which overarches the entire breadth of the road, and drops its roots into the earth on the other side, we reached Mr. Dalziel's, the police magistrate at Colpetty, two miles from Colombo, the capital and seat of government in Ceylon. We were kindly and hospitably received; and in the evening were surrounded by friends and ministers of different denominations. Sadness had been brought over many minds by the untimely death of a respected clergyman of the neighbourhood, who had that day been killed by the falling of a wall upon him, on his own premises; but we sought to improve the event by serious conversation, and by speaking to each other on the state of religion in the island of Ceylon.

*Sun., Nov.* 11.—Preached at Morotto in the morning to a Singhalese congregation, through an interpreter. Our chapel here is a new structure comparatively; and, with its pointed arches, gables, buttresses, and pinnacles, is as good Gothic as many of the churches and chapels in England. It is seventy-two feet long, forty-two feet wide; and cost some four hundred pounds. The central roof of the nave is supported by rows of lofty columns. Towards its erection the natives had contributed liberally; and one man in humble circumstances was pointed out to me as having at very great sacrifice contributed as much as twenty pounds. The congregation filled the building. The men were in their native costumes, clean and neat, and some of them with high combs in their hair; and the women were dressed in white and flowered cottons, muslins, and silks, with bracelets, necklaces, and earrings. Our native minister here read Wesley's Abridgment of the Liturgy, and the entire congregation responded earnestly. After the singing of a Methodist hymn in an English tune, I preached, by interpretation, on the Mercies of the Lord, and saw several moved with devout feeling under the truth. At the close of the service multitudes gathered round me, looking as if wishful to know whether they might shake hands with me or not. I greeted them fraternally, and delivered to them Christian salutations from my brethren and people in England. The dark, serious faces of the Singhalese men beamed with pleasure, and several of the women laughed out, like children, with joy. Peter Gerhardt de Zylva, our native minister at Morotto, is a good example of what may be expected by the church from Singhalese preachers and pastors, under proper direction and training. He has been labouring with his dark flock for many years; and though it has been divided again and again, and considerable numbers have been given to the charge of other native ministers, yet he has still in his Circuit, of Morotto and the neighbourhood, three hundred and twenty-seven fully accredited church members under his pastoral care. In the surrounding parts, he has several chapels, or preaching bungalows, as well as schools, which he regularly visits; and, perhaps, on the whole, has as flourishing native churches under his care as can be found under any minister of his class in India or in Ceylon. He is somewhat worn by his labours; but his grey hairs are a crown of glory to him in his old age; and he is venerated and beloved as a father by his people. He related to me, as we walked together after the service under the cocoa-nut trees, several deeply-interesting instances of the conversion of Buddhists and Buddhist priests which he had witnessed, and told me of the difficulties and triumphs of his work. I was sorry to learn from him, and from others of our native teachers, that high ecclesiasticism had of late cruelly sought to disturb native converts by the introduction among them of foolish questions on priestly authority, and the validity of the sacraments. In the evening I preached in the large Wesleyan chapel at Colombo to a crowded congregation of different denominations.

*Mon.*, Nov. 12.—Spent the day with the Rev. Daniel John Gogerly, general superintendent of our Missions in that part of Ceylon, and who resides at Colpetty, a suburb of Colombo. He is a "noticeable man, with grey eyes," as Hazlitt, in his boyhood, remarked of Coleridge; and much resembles, both in face and figure, the portraits given us of that "dreamer." But Mr. Gogerly is most successfully active, both in learning and in practical life. He is acknowledged to be the best Singhalese scholar on the island; and, while preaching several times a week to the natives in their own language, and superintending the Singhalese press for the most important books of all kinds, he has most carefully instructed and trained many of the native ministers and catechists employed in the seventeen circuits spread over the south-west parts of Ceylon. He has thoroughly studied the works of Buddhu, and has mastered the system of Buddhism, as far as it can be comprehended with its numerous inconsistencies. He showed me, with evident delight, a complete copy of the works of Buddhu, which had been made for him by an intelligent and learned Buddhist priest, belonging to one of the chief temples; and out of which he refutes the advocates of the atheistical system, from their own standards. He explained the system of Buddhu to me, and showed me its contradictions in scientific teaching, and its impositions upon the deluded Buddhist worshippers. He also showed me his quarterly returns of the missionary work under his care. They are kept in the most exact order; and he is minutely and regularly informed of what the several agents for Methodism are doing in the island. He took me to the Printing Establishment at Colombo; and showed me, on the premises first obtained by our brave pioneer Missionaries,—Clough, Harvard, Squance, and others,—native printers at work in their different departments upon the Singhalese Scriptures and school-books which he was then superintending. He is now seventy years of age, and is anxious that some English minister should be prepared for his place.

Colombo is not in itself attractive, though its zig-zag batteries, ponderous draw-bridges, weather-beaten gates, and picturesque openings towards the rocky headland, and the bay, render it impressive from some points of view. The buildings within the Fort are principally occupied by Government and military officers, and, though of good form and style, are too English for a tropical climate. The natives of various classes, such as the Singhalese, Tamils, Moors, and Malays, have their lowly dwellings immediately outside the walls; while the British whose residences are not provided for them by Government, live in the open suburbs overlooking the bay, among the cocoa-nut shades by the shore in the beautiful hamlet of Colpetty, or in the sweet-scented cinnamon grounds beyond. Their houses, or mansions, (as some of them may be called,) are mostly but one story high, and are widely spread over the ground, with broad verandahs, which extensively overshadow the inner apartments, and screen them from the heat of the sun. They are floored with brick tiles, have their doors and windows framed after the Venetian model, and with the wafted air under the Indian punkah are made deliciously pleasant and cool. Life in these dwellings is cheerful and even sumptuous; and as happy companionship is found in them as in any English home within our own land. So we found it in the tasteful abode of our kind host and hostess, Mr.

and Mrs. Dalziel, and in the evening conversations we held with them and their intelligent neighbours and friends. Mr. Ferguson, the able and energetic proprietor and editor of the principal newspaper at Colombo, gave us much information on the island and its inhabitants; and our friend Mr. Dalziel related to us strange and amusing things witnessed by him in courts and trials, where known Buddhists not unfrequently forswear themselves Christians, in order to be deemed more reliable in evidence they give relating to their own interests. This abuse of Christianity is traceable, in a considerable degree, to the Dutch and Portuguese Governments in Ceylon, which made religion a political engine, rather than a means of moral and spiritual instruction for the people. There is a delightful promenade by the sea shore, between the Fort and Colpetty; and the grounds, lake, and scenery within are charming. Colombo has several streets crossing each other at right angles, and in it there are some good public buildings. We went to the sheds and large fodder-yards of the Government elephants; but we only saw one there, and that was young and small. The others were out at public works. We learned that the number of these animals in the island is much reduced, and that the herds of them which remain are principally in the mountainous regions of the interior, most removed from the presence and reach of man.

*Tues., Nov.* 13.—Rose at half-past three, A.M., and at five left Colombo by coach for Kandy. Our way at first lay through low streets, then over a bridge of boats, then through an avenue of cocoa-nut trees. We passed many bullock-waggons belonging to Government, and a dark, ponderous elephant, working on the road. After a time the country became more hilly, with large, heaved-up rocks clothed in rich verdure. The bullock-waggons were drawn by larger animals, white in colour, brought from the coast of India; and the scenery, as we advanced, became increasingly picturesque and romantic, combining many of the best features of Matlock, in Derbyshire. We breakfasted at Ambepusse, and the hills became sterner and larger as we proceeded. Soon after noontide we entered passes in the mountains, composed of huge rocks, piled up in fantastic forms, the trees wrapping their roots around them. High above the hills there was rich and various verdure; down below were deep, tremendous precipices, with here and there a glimpse of bright pea-green, from the "paddies," or rice fields. Reached Kandy at half-past three, P.M.; was met by the Rev. Mr. Hobbs, Church Missionary, and Superintendent of the Mission to the Tamils; accompanied him to his lovely residence above the lake, where we had the most kind and fraternal entertainment.

*Wed., Nov.* 14.—At seven in the morning went with Mr. Hobbs to Arthur's Seat, to view the scenery of Kandy and the surrounding country. It was exceedingly fine. At the foot of the hill on which we stood is a large, square lake, with the Government magazine for gunpowder in the centre. Beyond it rose the domes of the celebrated temple of Buddhu; and over these the Governor's house, with the streets, churches, and public buildings of the city. Then, around all, were blue, swelling hills, with fine, bold outlines; and all were reflected in the deep, glassy lake below as clearly as Helvellyn and Catchiedecam are reflected in Ulleswater. In the forenoon we went to the temple grounds and grove, and saw the huge impression, in granite, of Buddhu's foot, as copied from the indentation on the summit of Adam's Peak,—the sacred relic for which Buddhists make long pilgrimages from different parts of the east, but which is the object of conflicting claims by the Brahmans as the footprint of Siva, by the Chinese of Foe, by the Mohamedans of Adam, and by the Roman Catholics of St. Thomas, or the Eunuch of Candace, Queen of Ethiopia. We also saw how the emblems of Hindu and devil worship are there mingled together, the priests submitting to almost anything that will bring them gains from the people. Some of the forms, both of the temple and the grove, were antique and picturesque; but it filled the mind with horror to think of the delusions which had there been so long practised on redeemed and immortal beings. At noon we went to the Rev. Mr. O.'s, the elder clergyman at Kandy, and conversed with him on the moral and religious necessities of the place. We also visited a higher class school belonging to his church, conducted by the Rev. Mr. Jones, an Irish evangelical clergyman, and examined the youths in the Scriptures, and in various departments of learning. We found them well instructed, and able to answer, with readiness and accuracy, the various questions proposed to them. In the evening we attended the Church service, and heard an excellent sermon from Mr. O. Afterwards we went again to the temple to see the renowned casket which encloses, as it is said, Buddhu's tooth; but the priests would not admit us; and only said, in answer to our requests, "Come again to-morrow!" We slept at the hotel, to be ready for the coach early in the morning; but we were sadly tormented by musquitoes from the lake near us.

*Thurs., Nov.* 15.—Took coach at five, A.M., for Colombo. As soon as the light broke, we found ourselves surrounded by grand and magnificent scenery. We skirted several coffee plantations, and saw the coffee tree frequently as we went along. We had two coffee planters inside the coach with us, talking incessantly of their possessions. One of them had bought, at an auction on the previous day, some eleven hundred acres of coffee-ground, at forty-three shilllings per acre. We learned from them, as from others, that the scenery higher up, in the interior, is finer and more panoramic than any we had beheld; and that in that higher and mountainous region herds of large wild elephants are found. We reached Colpetty again in the evening, and were in bed there by half-past ten.

*Frid., Nov.* 16.—Rose at six, refreshed by a good night's rêst, and at ten drove with Mr. Gogerly to Papaliano, to open a new chapel there for the natives. It is about six miles from Colombo, and on our road we saw something more of interior Singhalese life, and entered one of our smaller village chapels, used also as a schoolroom. On the road we passed many natives walking, or riding in their bullock-waggons, and going to our opening service. On arriving at Papaliano we found the large, new chapel full, and many not able to gain admittance, though all the children had been sent away to make room for adults. The scene outside, thronged with natives in holiday dresses, and skirted with cocoa-nut trees, was very pleasing. We ascended the steps on which the chapel is raised, and found the interior imposing. Lofty columns, with high pedestals and well moulded capitals, supported the central roof, and all over the spacious area were the crowded natives in their gay and picturesque costumes, with not a white face among them. Here and there might be seen native ministers and catechists from different parts, in half European clothing; and near to the pulpit were a few burghers and their families. The pulpit was a large hexagon, made of brick and plaster, and was surrounded by a wide cedar communion rail. Mr. Gogerly read the abridged form of the Liturgy and the Commandments in Singhalese; and the responses of the people were loud as the sound of many waters. I then ascended the pulpit, to preach to them through interpretation by their own native minister. The sight was novel and affecting. The many colours of women's dresses made them like garden beds of lilies and dahlias, and the trinkets on their necks, arms, and ears, gave a glitter to the scene; while, beyond the women and the better-dressed men, lining the walls, and crowding the doors and windows, were fine, bronze forms, bare down to the loins. All were devout and attentive, and after the sermon plates, neatly covered with white napkins, were handed courteously round among them by native office-bearers, upon which they respectively placed their contributions for the house of God. Some of them had given liberally before, both in labour and money. Several among the poor had devoted as much as two and three months' pay for work to it; and the chapel is a standing memorial both of their generosity and devotion. In this service, also, I saw the stolid, cautious Singhalese tremble and shed tears under the free proclamations of the Gospel to sinners, and at the declarations made of the love and sympathy for them in Christian England. After the service in the chapel, I met the native ministers and catechists present in the school-room opposite, and addressed them in the name of my ministerial brethren at home. Now, as before, grateful mention was made of missionaries formerly among them, such as the Revs. Robert Newstead, R. Spence Hardy, and Dr. Kessen. They gathered closely around me, and brought their wives and little ones near, that I might speak to them also. They gave me fruit and milk, which I enjoyed in their society more than I should have done a sumptuous banquet in the company of nobles and their heirs. We wept at parting; and as I returned to Colombo with Mr. Gogerly, I learned from him that Singhalese women are not the abused and oppressed drudges under their husbands that women are generally in heathen countries. In Ceylon many of them have their due place and influence in the household.

*Sat., Nov.* 17.—Left Colombo by coach at five o'clock in the morning for Galle. In the way found, at the change of horses, our native ministers, their families, and their people, crowding around the coach, with remembrance-tokens for Mrs. Jobson and myself. We prized these the more, inasmuch as they had been charms and amulets worn by the natives before conversion from Heathenism to Christianity. They also brought us, from cottages and huts under the shady palms, bottles of warm tea and of cool cocoa-nut milk; and as we left them on the road and by the wayside, with their children as well as themselves in neat, clean clothing, they significantly smiled and beckoned to us grateful and Christian farewells. The day was fine, the scenery luxuriantly rich, and our progress through the half hundred miles of avenue,—all festooned with gay creepers and tendrils,—was, amidst the throngs and smiles of Christian natives, almost to be likened to a triumphant procession. We reached Galle by half-past three, P.M., and before sleeping at night secured a comfortable cabin for our approaching sail to Australia.

*Sun., Nov.* 18.—Preached in the Dutch Presbyterian church at nine o'clock in the morning to a good and attentive congregation; and, in the evening, to a crowded assembly of all denominations in our own plain, but spacious old chapel.

*Mon., Nov.* 19, *and Tues.*, 20.—Devoted to letters for England.

*Wed., Nov.* 21.—Went on board the "Behar" by twelve at noon. Found her to be a good, new steamship. Sailed by nine in the evening, with pleasant memories of Ceylon, and not wondering that it should be so highly celebrated for its surpassing loveliness.

# Part Second.

## AUSTRALIA AND TASMANIA.

# AUSTRALIA AND TASMANIA.

## CHAPTER IV.

THE Indian Ocean—Albatrosses—Southern Constellations—Cape Leeuwin—King George's Sound—Aborigines and Wild Flowers—Convicts—Voyage from Albany to Port Phillip—Melbourne—Ballarat and "the Diggings"—Geelong—Notes on Melbourne, Ballarat, Geelong, and on Methodism in the Colony of Victoria.

*Thurs., Nov.* 22.—REFRESHING breeze, and fine through the day, but out of all sight of land. Scotchmen still preponderated on board, both among passengers and crew. Our steamship had been built at Greenock for the French; but, being too costly for them, had been given up to the Peninsular and Oriental Company.

*Frid., Nov.* 23.—Another fine and very warm day. The sun set gloriously. We crossed the equinoctial line in the night; and the heat was intense.

*Sat., Nov.* 24.—A bright morning. Ships in sight, going north. Waterspout in the distance. A squall came on; we had a wet night, and the port-holes were closed.

*Sun., Nov.* 25.—Our Captain read prayers, in the forenoon, in a most hurried, slovenly manner, getting through the whole service in twenty minutes. In the evening we had worship in our cabin, for ourselves.

*From Mon., Nov. 26, to Sat., Dec. 1.*—Weather very changeable throughout the week, so that our progress over the Indian Ocean was not very rapid.

*Sun., Dec. 2.*—Read the Liturgy, and preached on "Conscience" in the saloon. Weather fine, but wind still against us. Sensibly cooler.

*From Mon., Dec. 3, to Thurs., 6.*—Weather growing rapidly colder, and wind still against us. Saw several large albatrosses sailing in the wind in our wake, and then wheeling their long, bent wings around us, as if they had been sporting companions of our voyage. Some of them must have been twelve feet from tip to tip of their expanded wings. Whales, too, were seen in the distance towards the south. Night fine, and the stars and constellations of the southern hemisphere shone brilliantly over our heads. The Southern Cross was conspicuous in the jewelled heavens, and we watched it as it rose in an inclined position above the horizon to a perpendicular elevation, and until it declined again. We now understood the reported cry of travelling Arabs in the desert: "It is past midnight; for the Cross begins to bend." We could trace in the firmament some forms familiar to us, but most of the constellations were new, and shone in the deep, blue vault with a piercing brightness, surpassing what can be seen in a European sky. The moon, too, came up at her hour in full-orbed splendour, and looked larger than she seems in England. She shed a bright pathway over the ocean; and the night was magnificent.

*Frid., Dec. 7.*—At eleven in the forenoon sighted Australian land, on the left. For some time it was indefinite in its form and colour, but by one it grew more distinct, though from the peculiar effect of the atmosphere upon it there was difficulty in judging of its elevation and sea-line. Something like the fantastic mirage of the desert seemed to play upon it, and to shape, elevate, and double it by reflexion, until it was hard, even for the officers of our ship, to say what was visionary and what was real. At length the positive was plainly before us, and with our straining eyes we saw a long, low, horizontal, coast line, clothed with a dull, leaden, brown-green scrub; and, where rising to anything like hills in elevation, covered with thick forest trees of the same heavy, monotonous colour. On advancing towards Cape Leeuwin, the south-west angle of this island-continent, the scenery becomes more bold, rocky, and picturesque in front; while over and beyond the coast-ridge may be discerned hills and mountain ranges. Huge boulders of hoary grey stone obtrude through the scrub of the elevated ground by the sea, and group themselves into almost every variety of form, —seeming at times like remnants of baronial castles, or old watch-towers, with fallen walls between,—and then like Druidical remains;—until it is difficult to believe that what is before you is a singularity of natural form, and not the handiwork of man. Our powerful glasses, however, dissolved this charm, and brought to our view the veritable structure of these up-heaved rocks. On nearing Cape Leeuwin the rugged cliffs became more perpendicular and precipitous in their fall, and off-lying islands appeared at some distance in the sea; some of them resembling the rock on which Dumbarton Castle stands in the Clyde. The sunset among all these fantastic forms was gorgeously picturesque, but had more of deep orange than crimson. It was more American than Egyptian in its tinge.

*Sat., Dec.* 8.—After a sail of nearly two hundred miles from Cape Leeuwin, we entered King George's Sound at daybreak, around high rocks and forelands—a circuitous and intricate course, which requires a pilot of the place for safe entrance. Large islands of grim, frowning rock were in our course, and the sea dashed and foamed against them with impetuous fury. When we reached the harbour, we found ourselves in clear, smooth water, of considerable extent. The Adelaide steamer was here, waiting for the mail-boxes for South Australia; and convicts came off in boats, and took them, and the boxes for Western Australia, under guardsmen. As soon as practicable, we went ashore, and stayed at Albany for several hours, while convicts coaled the ship. Here we had our first sight of the aborigines of Australia; and here, at this southern port of Western Australia, we saw the convict system in operation. We wandered from the shore through the scrub, and up the stony hills, picking our way as safely as we could, in the entangled abode of deadly snakes, plucking ferns and wild flowers, many of which were surprisingly beautiful. A company of aborigines, scantily covered with kangaroo skins, clotted with red grease, and bedaubed on forehead, cheek, and limbs, with white pipeclay, followed us,—jabbered their semi-English jargon in our ears,—and, to obtain our white money, gathered for us profuse bunches of flowers, and exhibited their surprising feats of throwing the boomerang and the spear. We were nearly alone with them, but we found no occasion to fear, and engrossed their attention by talk of "white money." One convict, whom we came upon at a secluded spot, when in company with our dark and disgusting attendants, had a tame opossum for sale; and others of his class, whom we passed on our return, were eager to sell us shells, parrots, and cockatoos. We found many Irish at this convict settlement. There is but little cultivated land, we were told, in the country around Albany, and scarcely anything but distant patches of ground between it and Perth (three hundred miles off) which can be employed even as sheep and cattle runs. The situation of Albany, as viewed from our steamship, and encircling the crystal harbour, backed and flanked by bold, rocky hills and heights which are covered with dense dark green foliage, was remarkably picturesque. It reminded us of our own Windermere, as beheld from the middle island, and looking towards Bowness; only there was less variety of colour, and Albany Harbour has a broader water in its basin than Lake Windermere. From King George's Sound we threaded our way back amidst rocky islands, and passed again into the open sea. Steering our way eastward, we had the Australian coast on our left; and beyond a lofty conical hill by the sea-shore, (apparently a spent volcano,) called "Mount Gardinere," we could see high mountains, far back inland, of which we could not learn the names. And now, standing out into the great Southern Ocean, we had to sail some thirteen hundred miles across the great bight of the south coast of Australia to Port Phillip.

Another gorgeous sunset; and the night which followed one cannot easily describe. The stars seemed to be pendant from the sky, and to be scattered so strangely over the heavens that it looked to our English eyes like the sky of another world. We never lost this feeling under starlight, until we returned to Europe, when to gaze again on our northern constellations was like looking on old faces.

*Sun., Dec.* 9.—Beautifully fine, and climate pleasant. Read the Liturgy and preached.

*From Mon., Dec.* 10, *to Thurs.*, 13.—Wind and weather variable; but our passage not altogether slow.

*Frid., Dec.* 14.—Early in the morning arrived at the entrance to the large harbour of Victoria, called "Port Phillip," having seen no land during four preceding days,—nor until we neared the outstretching headland of "Cape Otway," on the Thursday. We now passed two lighthouses on the west side of the entrance to the harbour; and between them rolled majestically the heavy swelling waves from "Bass' Straits," which separate Tasmania from Australia. We rode buoyantly upon them, and shot our way into the smoother water. Day broke with a most gorgeous sunrise. The clouds were dappled crimson. The sky glowed like burnished gold; and when the sun appeared above the coast-hills on our right, the quarantine houses under them, and the lighthouses and coast opposite, with the glancing, rippling waves between, were all bathed in a flood of golden light of the purest and brightest lustre.

A mail-boat came off from the lighthouse side for letters to Geelong; and after it had departed, we again careered through the great inland basin, some forty miles long from the entrance to Hobson's Bay, where we had to land for Melbourne. The crimson and yellow morning light gradually changed to one more silvery, or rather, amber-like, in its liquid transparency. The coast on our left showed miles of flat, arable and pasture-land, with the blue range of "Mount Macedon" behind, and the dingy, boat-building, Blackwall sort of a suburb named "Williamstown" (the port of Melbourne) in front, at the edge of the water. The scenery on the right, stretching far away, was that of brown-green trees and scrub, with several mountain ranges beyond; and with white cottages and broad-eaved villas dotting the coast in front, at "Brighton." Before us appeared the Metropolitan city of the Australian colony of "Victoria," stretching over miles of gentle slope from the shore to the flat hills upon which the main part of it stands. Immediately on our left was Sandridge Pier, with shipping from various parts of the world; and steaming away from thence to the city was the railway-train. It was a wondrous scene to behold; and deeply illustrative of the energy and power of man. Considerably within our own life-time, the whole of what we saw now cultivated and built upon had been a wilderness, peopled only by savages, and known only to here and there an enterprising voyager, who had touched this coast in passing round the Australian shores! Our steamship, which had to proceed to Sydney, anchored at a distance of two miles from the landing-place; but we soon saw our friends approaching in a boat; and we were heartily welcomed to this southern world by the Rev. D. J. Draper, and his ministerial brethren of Melbourne, and were conveyed to the hospitable home of the Hon. Alexander Fraser, a member of the Legislative Council, who also came in the boat to welcome us. His house was at St. Kilda, a pleasant suburb, some two miles beyond the centre of Melbourne.

*Sat., Dec.* 15.—Drove with the Rev. D. J. Draper, Wesleyan minister, and Chairman of the Victoria District, to look round Melbourne. Its large, massive granite buildings, its wide and numerous streets,—its sumptuous shops and stores,—and its extent and advancement, greatly surprised me. A great part of it might have belonged to some of the more substantial and prosperous cities and towns of England. In general character, it struck me as being most like Birmingham, with some of the larger London streets intermixed. There were park-like suburbs around, uniting it with rising townships of wide extent. These surrounding towns have still houses of boards, or of zinc, and, in some few instances, of canvas. The Government offices and public buildings of Melbourne surpass anything in England to be found out of London; and the Houses of Legislature, with the Treasury, &c., when finished, will, in their sumptuous style and decorations, rival the Senate Chambers and buildings in Paris.

*Sun., Dec.* 16.—Preached morning and evening at Wesley Church, Lonsdale Street,—a large gothic structure, with tower, spire, transepts, and chancel, all on a good scale, and in good keeping. The congregations were immense, and the excitement I experienced while preaching to so many whom I had known in England was greater than I can easily describe.

*Mon., Dec.* 17.—Wrote letters, and received visits from friends.

*Tues., Dec.* 18.—Left Melbourne at eight o'clock in the morning for Ballarat, Mr. Draper kindly accompanying me. Travelled to Geelong by railway, over wide-spread pasture and arable lands, and arrived there by eleven; having had a stoppage on the way, through the failure of a bridge over a creek. We now got into a huge, swing coach, with fifteen or sixteen persons inside, and with nearly as many outside. It was a long, boat-like conveyance, on leathern springs, of American construction, and driven by a dashing American coachman. We had all kinds of persons with us as fellow passengers: Chinamen, in their blouse-like dresses, and with their long tails curled up behind their heads; long loose-limbed colonists, with stiff, grizzly beards; gentlemen gold-seekers; and rough, enterprising labourers, with their wives and children. The road was good in some places, but rugged and jolting in others. The land on both sides was mostly fenced in, except where we drove through the bush and scrub, and had to drive over plank and "corduroy" roads at full speed. In loose and swampy parts they saw trees in two, from the top to the roots, and then place the flat-side of the half trees upon the ground, and the coach rattles and jolts over the round upper half of the trees. Roads thus formed are called "corduroy," from their striped resemblance to that material.

There are inns at every stage; and on the road we often met bullock-drays, going slowly and heavily down to the capital, laden with bales of wool for transit to England. At intervals, by the way, were to be seen settlers' huts and clearings, with trunks and charred stumps of trees, and with the gradually-acquired stock feeding on the field and forest-like pastures around. Here and there would be seen a larger dwelling, of more substantial material, with larger herds of cattle, and with park-like grounds in its neighbourhood. It was surprising to see, as we went along, what wide, spacious plains opened to us on either hand, which in their primitive condition were entirely free from bush and scrub, and had not more trees upon them than would be desired for ornament, or for the shelter of cattle. It seemed as if the settler had nothing to do, in such parts, but to plough up the turf, and turn out his flocks and herds; for no primeval forests were there to be rooted out before cultivation began. In other parts, gentle slopes and shady glens were seen, and over them long ranges of hills, wooded to the summits, giving breadth and variety to the landscape. Some of the trees were large and grand in their forms; but they were nearly all gum trees, which shed their bark instead of their leaves, and thus present, in stem and branches, a stripped and naked appearance. There was, also, the lack of rivers and streams. Otherwise, if there had been greater variety of foliage, and the winding of flowing water, the scenes in our way would not unfrequently have been equal to the best parts of Yorkshire.

About five o'clock in the evening we found ourselves at the point of descent from an elevation into a valley where a street of two miles, or more, wound its serpentine length between stores and houses of various materials, but chiefly of wood; and with the ground on either hand, in the valley, and up the sides of the hill, all in heaps and hollows, covered with machinery and temporary dwellings; while in various directions, amidst the disembowelled yellow-white earth, were running, in gullies and channels, streams of muddy water. This was BALLARAT, and its gold-diggings. Our American Jehu had dashed along at a quick rate previously, but now he hurried forward his "eight-in-hand" at their utmost speed, and galloped furiously down the hill into the town. We drove with wonder through the strange street, with its variously formed structures and stores—some of boards, some of zinc, others of brick and stone;

and so oddly and grotesquely fashioned and coloured, that they seemed more like the temporary show erections of a pleasure-fair than the buildings of a central thoroughfare in a township of forty thousand inhabitants. We gazed curiously upon the "signs" and names of the possessors from different nations, gaudily painted on the fronts of the motley erections, as we passed along, and saw sleek-faced Chinamen and bearded Europeans mingled together upon the pavement at the sides. At length we emerged from the more hastily constructed portion of the town, and ascended the upper part, with its substantial buildings of good, ornamental styles of architecture. On the arrival of the coach at the hotel, we were cordially welcomed by Wesleyan friends, and I preached in their larger chapel in the evening.

*Wed., Dec.* 19.—Mr. Draper and myself, with the Rev. John G. Millard, superintendent minister of the Ballarat Circuit, and Mr. Oddie, circuit steward, drove in a spider-wheeled phaeton to the agricultural lands of the neighbourhood; and after passing through spacious grounds, reserved for botanical gardens and other ornamental purposes, we saw large fields of many acres standing thick with corn. We went some ten miles out, and found extensive plains of rich arable and pasture land, with rising villages and hamlets, and roads being laid out and beaten down for traffic. A series of well-moulded hills of rich clothing bounded the prospect; and swampy, outspreading lakes varied the scene pleasantly. After visiting one of our ministers at a country station, baptizing an infant child of English emigrants, and seeing large farmsteads of prosperous colonists, we returned to Ballarat, to look more closely at the gold-digging region.

We now took to our feet, and passed "Golden Point," so named from its extraordinary amount of precious produce. The earth was honey-combed; the valley gaped with holes, and was filled with gullies and drains of water, in every direction. Squatters, merchants, soldiers, sailors, farmers, shopkeepers, miners, shepherds, artisans, college-graduates, and freed convicts, were all herded together in search of the yellow prize. It seemed a huge human ant-hill; and sound and excitement of labour were everywhere heard and seen. We passed from part to part, hearing from our attendant, who had been at Ballarat from its commencement, strange stories of the scenes and deeds of that place when gold was first discovered in it, and when parties went in every direction "prospecting," as the term is currently applied in Australia to restless searchers in auriferous regions for hid treasure. His recital of struggles for certain localities by multitudes arriving from week to week; of privations and sufferings endured by diggers, and their alternate states of destitution and enrichment, extravagance and profligacy; his pictures of their quarrels with licensing officers, and among themselves; of their epidemics and deaths; their treacheries, thefts, and murders, filled us with shuddering wonder, and drew from us loud exclamations as we went along. But we were scarcely noticed by the diggers, whatever might be our looks or words of amazement; for they were too earnest in their work to give any heed to us. In one place we had pointed out to us the spot where the largest nugget of gold ever discovered in the world was found by a party of four men, at a depth of one hundred and eighty feet from the surface. It weighed one hundred and thirty-four pounds, and is described as being of the size and form of a ham; and was named, "the welcome nugget." We were shown the strata of the earth; and how the richest deposits are in veins of blue clay, and are found mostly in rounded or water-worn lumps of various sizes, varying from a quarter of an ounce to two ounces in weight. Not unfrequently the gold is incorporated with round pebbles of quartz, the original matrix of the precious metal; less frequently in irregular smooth pieces of from four to seven ounces' weight. The greater quantity, however, is washed from the clays in the form of minute rounded or flattened grains. Upwards of one hundred millions sterling of gold has been produced by Victoria since the discovery of its treasure in 1851, and Ballarat has contributed more than one-fourth of that amount. The gold from here, too, is of the finest quality. It averages twenty-four carats, and is worth eighty-three shillings per ounce, being considerably more valuable than our composite gold sovereigns. The diggings and washings at Ballarat, at the time we visited it, had slackened in their production of gold; and the greater part of that obtained was not, as formerly, from the gullies, but from a considerable depth, and from quartz crushed by machinery. Many whom we saw at work were rewashing the heaps of excavated soil so hastily searched by early diggers; and they found it worth their time to expend labour on the old material. They were thickly clotted and bemired with their labour in the muddy pits, ravines, and water-courses, and some of them had the look, as well as the garb, of desperadoes. It was pitiable to see their wives and little children in the miserable huts erected for shelter amidst these muddy heaps and holes, and in which they had their homes by day and night.

We afterwards went to what is called "the Chinese Camp," where some three thousand Chinamen were located together, on an eminence near to their side of the gold-diggings. Their dwellings were, as might be expected, of the light boarded kind, with small rooms and cupboard-like shops in front. There were, in the midst of their frail, crowded structures, a joss-house for their gods, and a large theatre for their sports. As they knew our guide by his efforts to benefit them religiously, they allowed us to look at their abodes, shops, cooking-rooms, and gaming-houses, and even courteously invited us to partake with them of cakes, tea, and fruit. Their numerous gaming-houses were crowded with eager-looking actors, at the counters or boards. In their dwellings and shops were suspended idol-shrines and lanterns. We saw scarcely any women among them. Their wives are left behind in China, as hostages, we were told, for the return of the men to their own country; but others say that they are afraid to trust their wives among the colonists. A few of them, who, I suppose, have made up their minds to settle permanently in Australia, have taken Irishwomen for wives. But the reports of domestic morals among the Chinese are awful; and from what I heard and saw, I do not wonder at the prejudice existing in the minds of Anglo-Saxon colonists against them. It was melancholy to reflect that three thousand of such sensual and depraved beings had been gathered at the gold fields of Ballarat to mingle and compete with Europeans; and that more than forty thousand of them are dispersed over the colony of Victoria! As we left this saddening sight, the short twilight passed away; the din of labour ceased; and in one direction we could hear a few bars of the sweet German hymn; in another snatches of a roaring song by boisterous sailors; in another the harsh sounds of quarrel, or the echoes of laughter. With space and distance the discordant sounds blended into a general hum; and when the last sound died away, as we re-entered the Methodist parsonage of Upper Ballarat, we recounted the old saw of England, that "One half of the world does not know how the other half lives."

*Thurs., Dec.* 20.—Left early in the morning by coach for Geelong, where we were expected at a public meeting in the evening. Arrived there a little after noon. Geelong is the second town of importance in the colony of Victoria, and is situated on the western side of Port Phillip, on a picturesque and sheltered slope of the bay, at a distance of forty-one miles from Melbourne by the railway. It has a population of twenty-five thousand, and has some good streets, shops, warehouses, and public buildings. In its central and principal thoroughfares, and in the character of its buildings, it is not unlike the clean, healthy town of Huddersfield, in the West Riding of Yorkshire; and it is as well situated, by fall of ground, for drainage. The outskirts of the town are, as might be expected, more scattered and irregular in their dwellings. The river Barwon runs about a mile behind it, flowing towards its outlet in Lake Connewarre, through which it discharges itself into the sea. The scenery contiguous to the river is beautifully picturesque, and the Barrabool hills around, being remarkably fertile, are occupied by productive farms and vineyards. We had a large, enthusiastic meeting in the evening, were kindly greeted by ministers of various denominations, and found many among the audience whom we had known in England. We were hospitably entertained by our superintendent minister, at Geelong,—Rev. Joseph Dare. At his pleasant manse by the chapel, I was re-joined by Mrs. Jobson, whom I had left to follow me to Geelong when I went from Melbourne to Ballarat.

*Frid., Dec.* 21.—Detained at Geelong by the indisposition of my wife till the afternoon, when we returned by railway to Melbourne.

*Sat., Dec.* 22.—Spent the day in writing letters, and in receiving visitors.

*Sun., Dec.* 23.—Preached at Brunswick Chapel, Melbourne, in the morning, and in our grey granite gothic chapel, with its square tower, at St. Kilda, in the evening. The heat was great, and the excitement as much as could be borne.

*Mon. Dec.* 24.—Wrote letters, and exchanged visits with friends from England. Day exceedingly hot, but night cool. Musquitoes troublesome.

*Tues., Dec.* 25.—A strange Christmas-day, being intolerably hot; and no prospect of gathering around the fire with relatives for Christmas-cheer:—Christmas being the Australian midsummer. In the morning we went to the Botanic Gardens, which are stored with plants, animals, and birds, native to the colony; and then drove past the Government-house, and amidst the forest clearings of the roads and fields of the neighbourhood, finding it difficult, in some parts, to make our way in the carriage, through ruts and swamps. Beyond the Government domain, towards the east, the sweep of scenery was large and impressive. Unbroken dark forests crowned the hill; and in the distance was the long range of the "Blue Mountains." As we drove from part to part we heard everywhere on the gum trees the cricket-like insects,—usually called locusts by the colonists,—hissing their reed-like, monotonous noise; but no song-bird, either large or small, gladdened us with its music. In the evening I preached at Prahran, in a large iron chapel, on the Christian believer's love to the unseen Saviour, and to a full congregation gathered from the houses of wood, brick, zinc, and iron of that populous suburb of the capital.

*Wed. and Thurs. Dec. 26 and 27.*—Went over various parts of Melbourne, acquainting myself more fully with its plan, arrangements, public institutions, &c., and had pleasant converse with our ministers of the city:— the Rev. Messrs. Waugh, Binks, Hill, Wells, and others.

*Frid., Dec. 28.*—Left Melbourne by the "Black Swan" steamer, at half-past ten in the forenoon, for Tasmania.

---

MELBOURNE, for the period of its existence, is, undoubtedly, the most wonderful city in the world. It is the growth of a single generation: indeed, mostly of the last ten or twelve years. Earlier it was only a long straggling village, or embryo town, with stumps of felled forest-trees in its streets. Now it is a large city, extending two and a half miles in length, one and a half in breadth. On all the land sides,—amidst park-like scenery,—it is surrounded with thickly-populated and richly-ornamental suburbs. It has at present 120,000 inhabitants, and its numbers are constantly increasing. The streets are wide, well paved, and well laid out; and you see in them stores, shops, and houses of good architectural styles: some resemble what are seen at the west-end of London; but for the most part they resemble those of a good second-class city, or enterprising English town. The city is already rich in public buildings, and these are continually on the increase. Some of them, for Government and Legislative uses, are even sumptuous in their character and decorations. A dark-grey granite is obtained from the hills on which the city is built, which would seem to be all but imperishable in its consolidated hardness; and this, with freestone dressings, supplies good materials for massive public works. Many of the shops and warehouses are of grey-white grit stone, clean and ornamental, as in the best streets of Manchester and Liverpool. The broad footways at the sides of the streets are thronged with busy, enterprising men of all nations, but chiefly of the Anglo-Saxon race, and from the old country; while the macadamized roads between are filled with waggons, carts, bullock-drays, and various vehicles of merchandise. Some of the drivers of these carriages, as well as other passengers on foot and horseback, show by their garb of high-leathern boots and "cabbage-tree" hats, as also by their sun-burnt, unshaven faces, that they are from the interior of the colony, where men have to rough it. But, mingled thickly with these, are gentlemanly-looking merchants and tradesmen, portly and flourishing as in Hull or Bristol; while ladies of gay dress and equipages move to and fro, at certain hours, for promenade, and for purchases. Indeed, throughout the city there is a "well-to-do" air with the inhabitants. Rags and beggary are almost unknown. No tattered urchin tips his cap at the crossing, and, with scraggy besom in hand, besieges you for halfpence. All but rakes and profligates are well-dressed; for all who *will* work *may* work, and that at wages which will feed and clothe them. The most helpless are, perhaps, "fast" young men who go there as clerks, accountants, and "editors," and not to work out of doors. These, really, glut the market. But all who are willing to earn their bread by the sweat of their brow may do so in Melbourne. Money is not now so plentiful as it was; and wages are not so high; but a common labourer in the field, or breaking stones upon the road, has from seven shillings to ten shillings per day; while a mechanic, or an artisan, will have from fifteen shillings to twenty shillings. Rents are not so costly as they were, having fallen, on the average, one-half within the last six years. My host paid at one time as much as £4,000 a year rent for his house and store, and these were not at all of more than ordinary pretensions. Servants' wages are still high: a good female servant has as much as from thirty to forty, and even to fifty pounds a year. These circumstances give the inhabitants a free independent bearing; and it is impossible to go through the streets of Melbourne without perceiving that it is an energetic and flourishing city. It has, lengthwise, nine spacious thoroughfares, or principal streets, which are crossed by streets equally broad and imposing; and these are intersected at right angles by numerous narrower streets, running parallel to the larger streets, and branching out into the outskirts of the city in all directions. Three railways issue from its busy centre, upon which have been expended not less than eight millions sterling. The city is daily washed and kept clean by an abundant flow of water brought from a distance, and of such fall and force that in case of fire the part in danger may be immediately deluged. The public buildings are scattered about in various parts, but are chiefly on elevated sites; and to stand in the heart of this young metropolis, and reflect that on this spot, a few years ago, where now 120,000 persons have their homes, where merchants and tradesmen exchange millions sterling, where learning has its university and appended colleges, where the press issues its daily and weekly newspapers by thousands and tens of thousands; and where there are orphans' homes, hospitals for the sick, and asylums for the insane;—To stand here and reflect, that but a very few years ago all this was an uncultivated wild, where untutored savages and poisonous reptiles had their dwelling,—is creative of no common emotion.

In this crowded metropolis RELIGION is not overlooked or forgotten. As in the "United States," and as in Canada, there is a general reverence shown to it and to its ministers. The Sabbath too is outwardly observed. Nearly all Christian communities have their young and flourishing churches here. Equality of Christian churches is distinctly recognised. At present £50,000 are annually distributed among them, according to the respective numbers returned; but this is not likely to be continued long. Year by year the grant is a subject of angry contention. More than once it has been condemned by a large majority of the Representative Members, and has only been retained by a majority of two or three in the Legislative Council. State assistance to Education is also given to the annual amount of £125,000. This sum is distributed among two classes of Schools,—"Denominational" and

"National,"—the former being four times as many as the latter. The first Gospel sermon preached in this section of the island-continent was by Joseph Orton, a Wesleyan missionary, who had accompanied the enterprising Batman from Tasmania across Bass' Straits to Port Phillip. It was preached in April, 1836, beneath the shadow of the forest trees on the crest of Batman's Hill. The service was attended by the colonist and his household, and by a goodly number of the aborigines, who, attracted by the novel scenes and sounds, crowded near to learn what was meant. The text was, "Except a man be born again, he cannot see the kingdom of God;" and the sermon has been described by one who heard it as being most powerful and impressive; so that all—including the poor ignorant aborigines—were awed and bowed under it. This was the first Methodist seed sown on the virgin soil of this region of Australia, and it has issued already in an abundant harvest. Within the colony of Victoria we have at present 44 ministers, 249 chapels and preaching-places, 43,627 persons forming our congregations, 335 local preachers, 147 day-school teachers, 5,646 day scholars, 1,722 sabbath-school teachers, 13,631 sabbath scholars, 5,909 full and accredited church members, with 522 on trial for membership. The Wesleyans in the colony also supply £2,500 per year for Missions to the islands of the Pacific. Melbourne has its proportionate share in these Methodist efforts and distinctions. The best and most imposing ecclesiastical structures of Melbourne belong to Methodism; and in character and size are like the large gothic chapels recently built by the Wesleyans in London and Liverpool. One of them, a large imposing building in Lonsdale Street, is of grey granite with freestone dressings: it has a tower and spire, and transepts, and is in appearance the cathedral of the city. This, and some other chapels of Melbourne, were mainly built out of £40,000, realized by the sale of a small piece of land formerly occupied by the Methodist Missionary Society in Collins Street,—a street which has become the principal artery for trade and merchandise in the capital.

My first sermon in Australia was preached in this Lonsdale Street Church, which was densely crowded. And never shall I forget that wedged mass of living beings, nor the sight of them, when, after the reading of the Liturgy from the desk by the Rev. James Waugh, the resident superintendent, I went up the spiral staircase of the beautiful cedar pulpit, and, in giving out the verse,—

> "God of my life, through all my days,
> My grateful powers shall sound Thy praise;
> My song shall wake with opening light,
> And cheer the dark and silent night,"—

looked forth upon that sea of upturned, eager faces, browned with the Australian sun, nearly all of persons in middle life;—many of the men with stiff furze-like beards and long hair, and some of the women worn and subdued by the heat; and the vast assembly sprinkled all over with countenances familiar to me from preaching to congregations in different parts of our parent country; so that on a careful computation, afterwards made, it was reckoned that I knew one-third of the whole, either in their own faces, or in their family-likenesses. The effect of a voice familiar to so many of them, and calling up at a moment, as by a single link, a host of home associations, was indescribably exciting. In all directions eyes gushed full with tears; faces flushed and quivered with emotion; and a sigh of deep feeling heaved and swayed the mighty mass, until it waved before and around the preacher like the swelling billows of a sea. With imposed restraint upon a soul moved to its utmost depths at the sight, I preached from the 103rd Psalm, on the grateful remembrance of Divine mercies, and found that the spirit and tone of my audience were in full accordance with the theme. In the evening of the Sabbath the large building was still more densely crowded; and our subject of meditation was the Lamb in the midst of the throne. The collections proved the strength of gratitude and love influencing the congregations; and it may be humbly hoped that the services of that day in Lonsdale Street Church were not in vain.

At BALLARAT, also, Methodism is energetic and prosperous. I preached to some twelve hundred persons in the larger of our gothic chapels there; and found it had been mostly copied from one of my own published designs. Here were many old Cornish friends, with their serious and devout faces; and who as miners, at Ballarat, and other places in the colony, have had encouraging employment in search for gold-ore. Some poor prodigals in the far country that night said, "I will arise and go to my Father;" and at the close of the service the ministers and circuit-officers presented to me, on behalf of the assembly, an Address of congratulation and welcome, expressive, also, of their love and loyalty to British Methodism. I was glad to find that Wesleyans there are not only striving to keep themselves from the evil that is in the world, but also labouring to carry on the cause and work of God in the town and in the region around. There are two Wesleyan Chapels in the townships of Ballarat, containing together accommodation for some two thousand worshippers. In the Circuit there are twelve day-schools: the one at Ballarat is large and flourishing, and is conducted by a teacher from our Training-Institution at Westminster. And there are twenty-four societies and congregations in the Circuit regularly visited by the ministers and local preachers. Of the latter there are as many as forty-three, whose names appear on the Circuit-Plan; and of these, three-fourths, and more, are from Cornwall. I found also some zealous friends from Islington, to whom I had ministered in past years; and who, living in the forest and the bush, hold religious services weekly in their own dwellings for themselves and neighbours. I had not the opportunity of inquiring particularly into the state of other Christian churches at Ballarat. They are not so large or prosperous as the Wesleyans; but they have several places of worship; and, according to their means, are serving their generation by the will of God; and, generally, there is good fraternal feeling existing among different religious denominations. It was, however, melancholy to learn, that a native Chinese missionary, who had been extensively serviceable to his own people, and who had been voluntarily supported by the benevolent of all churches, had just been dismissed from his place and work, by clerical intolerance, for attendance at Wesleyan worship, and his place among the idolatrous and degraded Chinese left unsupplied. I was not able to visit other towns in the gold-field region of Victoria, though importuned by the ministers and people of our flourishing churches there to do so. But I was assured that in general features, both civilly and religiously, Ballarat might be viewed as a fair specimen of principal places in the auriferous district.

In GEELONG there are several good ecclesiastical structures; and our own gothic church there, with its enlargement by transepts, is not inferior to any building in the town. Our superintendent minister (Rev. Joseph Dare) is an intelligent, large-hearted, eloquent man; and by his talents and catholicity of spirit deserves the favour he has both with his own people and those of other Christian communities. He has the largest connexion of churches under his care of any Methodist Circuit in the colony, and, with his colleagues, labours in the surrounding parts, to carry forward the cause of Christ at a rate equal to the advance of emigration and settlement. In his Circuit there are as many as thirty chapels and preaching-places; and, in addition to the resident ministers, there are thirty local preachers. The meeting which was held at Geelong in the evening of our visit, was one of Methodist welcome to myself and Mrs. Jobson. It took place in a large spacious building,—the Mechanics' Hall,—and was numerously attended both by Methodists and by ministers and members of other religious bodies. I met there, among other ministers known to me, a son of the late Rev. W. Scales, of Leeds. He has a Nonconformist Church in the town. I also saw several who had been members of my congregations in England. The Rev. D. J. Draper, our able and energetic chairman of the District, presided. An Address was presented, expressive of the views and feelings of the Methodists of that part towards myself and those whom I had gone to represent, which was supported by speeches from several ministers and lay-gentlemen; in reply to which I spoke at length on the state of Methodism in the old country, and on the duties of Wesleyans in all parts of the world. It was a good meeting, and glowed with Christian feeling.

The secular prospects of this youthful colony of VICTORIA are truly promising. It is little more than ten years since it was separated from New South Wales for self-government; and yet it is now foremost in commerce among the Australian colonies, and scarcely surpassed by any other colony of the British empire. In extent of territory it is nearly equal to the United Kingdom, and is exceedingly rich both in gold and cultivable land. It has a population of 550,000, chiefly from the old country; being more than sevenfold the number of its inhabitants in 1851, when first separated as a distinct colony. It has forty incorporated towns; is traversed by railways and macadamized roads; and has electric telegraph-wires extending, not only to the adjoining colonies of New South Wales and South Australia, but also across Bass' Straits to Tasmania. And with its salubrious climate; its large yearly exports of gold, wool, tallow, hides, &c.; and its large annual imports of British goods and manufactures, it may be viewed in relation to Great Britain as worthy of the honoured name it bears. Many exciting stories are told of its sudden fluctuations, of the glut of its markets with unsaleable goods, and the ruinous consequences thereby upon firms and individuals. And many a prophetic warning of coming ruin may be heard from squatters and large landholders, whose miles of acres are being distributed among "new chums," as they arrive. But the colony advances steadily from year to year, and still proves attractive to industrious settlers from all parts of the world. In my travels into the interior, I found persons from the factory life of Lancashire and Yorkshire, gathering up their produce, and raising their cattle on their own freeholds, purchased at twenty shillings per acre, with the prospect of good provision for their rising families, as well as a speedy competency for themselves during the remainder of their lives. In its social and political character it appears to a hasty European visitor unsettled and unsafe. The unguarded speeches of "Representatives," and the frequent changes of the "Ministry," are strange and startling; but it must be remembered that the young and enterprising colony is adjusting itself to self-government only recently acquired. A free, independent bearing appears here among all classes, as may be expected among a people who have all emigrated to improve their condition, and in a country where no hereditary forms of rank exist. The tendency is, undoubtedly, to democratic equality, civilly, as well as religiously. Five years ago a principle tantamount to manhood suffrage was introduced into the colony, and, as we have seen, preponderance of state-aid to religion only lingers a while as a relic of the past. In such circumstances, antecedents give no privileged *status* to individuals or churches; and for a time, at least, nobility and establishments are alike impossible. The Imports of the colony amounted, in 1859, to £15,622,891, and were in the following proportions:

—Produce, or Manufacture of the United Kingdom, £10,263,468; of British Possessions, £3,242,325; of other foreign places, £2,117,098. The Exports of the same year amounted to £13,857,859; of which £9,122,137 represented gold, and £1,756,950 wool. Nearly all the exports were shipped direct to Great Britain; amounting to 634,113 tonnage, and freighting 2,026 vessels.

## CHAPTER V.

TASMANIA—River Tamar—Launceston—Stories of the Old Convicts—Last Night of the Year 1860—Coach Journey from Launceston on New Year's Day, 1861—Beautiful Scenery—Reaping on New Year's Day—Arrival at Horton-College—Sunday-School Children and New Year's Festival—Coach Journey renewed—Tales of Sportsmen—New Face of Nature, Trees, Birds, and Insects—Arrival at Hobart-Town—Notes on Tasmania—Return to Launceston—Re-passage of Bass' Straits, to Melbourne.

---

*Frid., Dec.* 28.—I took but a single passage in the packet for Tasmania, and left Mrs. Jobson behind at St. Kilda. We had some interesting company on board. A judge shared my sleeping-cabin. Another passenger was an influential member of the House of Legislation from Melbourne. He was going, like several others, a voyage of change and health to Tasmania. There were, also, several gentlemen of the legal profession, and a clergyman from Cornwall, now in charge of the College at Adelaide. With these I had free and friendly conversations, and from them learned much that was instructive concerning the colonies. Our passage over Bass' Straits was tossing and turbulent: some would describe it as stormy; but by this time I had become fully at home on the sea, and could rest like a storm-bird upon the swelling wave.

*Sat., Dec.* 29.—At early morning Tasmania,—or as

it was formerly called, "Van Diemen's Land,"—was in sight. By half-past twelve we approached the mouth of the River Tamar. The scene before us was far more pleasing than the approach to Australia. It was varied with patches of cheering bright green and lawn-like turf. After we entered the winding river, the shore on either side was exceedingly beautiful. In some parts, it was broken into romantic forms of shelving and protruding rocks, covered with luxuriant shrubbery, which wrapped its roots in fantastic figures around the stony protuberances; and, in other parts, it was clothed with forest trees down to the water's edge, except where it was cleared for dwellings. Here and there the river opened with fine broad bays, hemmed round with gracefully moulded hills thickly covered with wood; and beyond these lofty purple-headed table mountains appeared in the distance, bearing the names of "Ben Nevis," and "Ben Lomond." The river combines the scenery of the "Dart" in the West of England, and of the "Hudson" in America; and in several parts has as bold and richly-clad elevations by its side, reflecting themselves in its glassy surface, as are seen at the sides of the Hudson in the passage from Albany to New York. As we advanced, numbers of long-necked black birds were seen diving into the water, and remaining some time before they again made their appearance. At stated points there were dark barrel buoys resting on pile-driven stands. On these, other aquatic birds of great length and peculiar form were perched, and would stand, I was told, for hours without moving. The course of the river's channel is only to be traced by the aid of these buoys,—there not being sufficient water, except in the very channel, for a vessel of any size. We reached Launceston at half-past four in the afternoon, having sailed up the Tamar forty miles. I was met and welcomed to Tasmania by Messrs. Sherwin and Crookes, members of the House of Legislation, and by the Rev. T. B. Harris, son of the Rev. Thomas Harris, of our home connexion. Mr. Sherwin drove me to his pleasantly situated villa, where the surrounding gardens were full of English flowers and fruits, and where I received every attention and comfort that a stranger in a far-off land could desire.

*Sun., Dec.* 30.—Preached twice in the Wesleyan chapel of Launceston to large and attentive congregations, and made collections on behalf of Foreign Missions. Was impressed with the outward observance of the Sabbath in the town, and with the order which was seen in the streets, considering what had been the character of many of the inhabitants in earlier times.

*Mon., Dec.* 31.—Walked over the town of Launceston with my kind host, to observe its principal features; and after dinner at Mr. Crookes', in company with himself and other friends, went in a boat to see a most romantic and picturesque gorge at the north-west corner of the town, where the South Esk river flows into the Tamar. It is as if volcanic force had riven asunder some huge mountain rock, and left a deep channel to flow between. The rocks on either side stand on large broken masses, with trees and verdure scattered over them, and towering in bold, upright forms overhead. Leaping from our boat, we clambered over rocks and through brushwood to another gorge above, and came to the edge of a vast deep basin, into which there rolled, over scattered rocks, a large volume of water from other gorges above. The rocks and wooded hills at the side of the basin were reflected in the clear mirror of the lake; and their shadows, contrasted with the bright sky above, formed a grand picture. This region, I was told, is fearfully prolific in poisonous snakes and reptiles, common to the colony.

On returning to the town we passed the "Bastile" of the old convicts, and had recalled to us many a story of former days, when the banished ones were marched in fetters to church, and there publicly exposed to the observation of all. Both men and women had their hair cropped close. The men would play at cards in the gallery during the service; and the women wore iron-collars with sharp prongs, or spikes, to prevent them from reclining their heads for indulgence in sleep. Such treatment, as may be supposed, did not produce love or reverence for Sabbath-worship; and in too many instances the clergyman officiating contented himself by formally "doing duty." At that time there were as many as fifty thousand persons of the convict class in Tasmania. This number has been considerably reduced by the rush for gold to other colonies; and this island is no longer a penal settlement. Also many persons of most respectable character and life have voluntarily chosen this colony for their abode. Still, however, not a few remain in it who were themselves convicts, or who are immediate descendants of "transports;" and the mixture and intermarriages with them are such that a visitor has to be careful, in some companies where he may appear, not to make too close inquiry concerning the reasons of removal from the old country. Not a few of the worst of the "old hands" have drunk themselves to death, yet a sufficient number of them remain to constitute a formidable class. They are able in Launceston, to the annoyance of my worthy friends, Messrs. Sherwin and Crookes, and of many other free settlers, to elect to the Legislature, from among themselves, a representative who, under the influence of intoxicating liquor, has disgraced himself in the House of Assembly. This class action tends to perpetuate the memory of the past concerning the character and position of parties, as well as to give great offence to the free settlers. After all, however, it must be admitted that the general order in society, and the outward reverence for religion, are surprising.

LAUNCESTON is a town containing about ten thousand inhabitants, and is situated within a sort of horse-shoe circle of hills at the junction of the North and South Esk rivers, which, by their confluence, form the Tamar. Its streets and shops are in the more level part below, and extend downwards to the wharf at the edge of the water. The sloping elevations around the town are sprinkled over with the dwellings of the genteeler class, and are tastefully adorned with gardens and vineyards. There are three Episcopal churches in Launceston, two Presbyterian, one Baptist, and one Primitive Methodist chapel, together with our own large Wesleyan chapel, which holds from eight hundred to one thousand persons, and which has a minister's house and good Day and Sunday school-rooms adjoining. We have also a second chapel and school, on the rising ground near to Mr. Sherwin's. The Roman Catholics have a large chapel in the town; and both priests and people are zealous to make proselytes to their faith. There have recently been erected some good government buildings, in the Tudor style of architecture, a

Mechanics' Institution, and a public suite of rooms. There is a fine open square in the middle of the town, with ecclesiastical structures at the sides, and with a Paris bronze fountain in the middle. On the whole, Launceston is a pleasant and picturesque town, and it is truly English in its character.

On the last night of the year 1860, we held a public meeting in our larger chapel, having the mayor of the town in the chair. Ministers of different denominations attended, and in their addresses, as well as by their presence, manifested a truly catholic spirit. The passion for Missions is not so strong in this part of the world as in Methodism at home, not having had so many years for nurture; yet we had a really good meeting; and the collections made on this evening and on the previous Sabbath, produced one hundred and fifty pounds. I did not know so many persons, proportionately, in the congregations here, as I had known in the congregations of Melbourne; yet there were some to whom I had ministered the word of life in Manchester, Leeds, and London, whom it was interesting to meet, from my knowledge of their family relationships. The Watch-night service was to commence in the chapel almost immediately after the missionary meeting; but having to leave by coach the next morning early, I did not attend that service.

*Tues., New Year's Day*, 1861.—At five o'clock in the morning left Launceston for Hobart-Town, by a four-horse coach, which daily runs in fourteen hours from the principal town in the north of the island to the capital city, or principal town in the south. The road is very good, having been made by convict labour, and having had no amount of necessary work spared from it. The coach was well horsed, and reminded one, as it bowled over the macadamized surface, of the best days of the "Age," "Highflyer," and "Red-Rover," along the famed North Road of England. The resemblance would have been complete, only there lacked the guard's cheery horn. The country is mountainous, and yet pleasant in its general aspect. Two chains of mountains run through it longitudinally, called the eastern and western tiers, and the great road passes through a cultivated valley between. The best arable land is in the northern part of the island, and the landscape, though mostly indigo-green, yet exhibits more variety of tint than Australia, and is far more English in its appearance. English flowers and fruits thrive here in full perfection; sweet-brier hedges perfume the way for the traveller; and the climate is salubrious and pleasant. Familiar names from the old country are given to the principal mountains, some of which rise from four to six thousand feet above the level of the sea. Towns and villages, with their cottages, houses, shops, gardens, and places of public worship, all look as if they were English. It has been observed that the Englishman reproduces his home wherever he goes; and this may be fully seen in Tasmania. It appears in the small, slab-built hut, smothered with geraniums and honeysuckles; in the dairy farm house, with its trailing vines, climbing plants, surrounding flower-garden, and orchard of apple and pear trees; and in the solid stone mansion, flanked by oaks from the old country, with its smooth green lawn in front, its tastefully formed flower and strawberry beds at the sides, its surrounding domain of paddocks and pastures, divided by hedges of hawthorn and sweet-brier, and with its clustered hay-stacks, corn-ricks, barns, wool-sheds, and outhouses. Almost every house we passed had its garden; and in the very smallest garden would be seen the simple flowers of our childhood, such as primroses, pansies, cowslips, and daisies; while the sweet little violet shed its perfume under hedges of ever-flowering geraniums, that were, in some instances, ten feet high. In many of the gardens were seen the English beehive. As we rode through the country, we saw the golden corn waving in the breeze over fields of many acres, or bending to the sickle of the reaper. This seemed strange. It was more like an English New Year's Day to see signs of holiday and feasting in the towns and villages as we passed through them. And where we stopped to change horses, it was pleasant on alighting to receive from the portly innkeeper in his doorway the old English greeting of, " A happy New Year to you, Sir!"

Some of the trees and the birds in Tasmania render the scene un-English, if you let your eyes dwell upon them; for here, as in Australia, the gum-trees are indigenous, and, though evergreen in their foliage, shed their ash-grey bark entirely from boles and branches; and flocks of green and gold parrots and parroquets flash to and fro in the sun, with their brilliant colours, while swarming crickets, or "locusts" on the leaves, chirp unceasingly their summer song. We passed through Perth, Cleveland, Campbell Town, and Ross, in which towns we saw Methodism had its chapels; and, in the greater number of towns, I was met and cordially greeted by Methodist ministers resident in the several neighbourhoods. About a mile beyond Ross we reached Horton College, where I alighted to look over our educational establishment there. It is a neat brick building of Tudor style, with stone windows and dressings, near to the road, backed by round-moulded hills, and surrounded by arable and pasture lands. It was built at a cost of from four to five thousand pounds, the money being chiefly provided by Captain Horton, a retired merchant sea-officer from Lincolnshire, who lives on his garden and farm opposite. It is a high class collegiate school, accommodating at present some sixty students; and recently obtained, on Government examination of education in the colony, the most satisfactory commendation. The Rev. William A. Quick is its president; Mr. Fiddian, who so signally distinguished himself in literary examinations and prizes in England, is its head-master; and under him there are other efficient teachers. Only one wing of the building has yet been erected; when the other wing shall be added, the college will accommodate one hundred students. The villa of Captain Horton is most pleasantly situated among surrounding garden-grounds; and I spent a cheerful evening in company with himself, his wife, the ministers of the neighbourhood, and several intelligent and social friends, who resided in that part of the colony. It was delightful to see the school-children sporting themselves in the surrounding fields, on this their New-Year's festival, and to hear their merry voices ringing out among the hills the music of their Sunday school ditties and songs, as they went home at sunset, in Captain Horton's farm-waggons, to Ross and other adjacent places. This, too, was English-like; it reminded one of happy Sabbath school festivities in dear old Yorkshire and Lincolnshire.

*Wed., Jan. 2.*—Went forward by coach to Hobart-Town. The scenery on the second day pleasingly resembled that which I had passed over on the first; but in some parts,—such as from the descent of "Constitution Hill,"—it was increasingly impressive in boldness and grandeur. We drove through more towns and villages bearing English names; but in one region of our drive there were hamlets which, from their nomenclature, one would suppose had been first peopled by Crusaders, being called Jericho, and Jerusalem, with the river "Jordan" to water them. In our course, the forests on the mountain-ranges at the sides thickened and darkened; and we were joined on the coach by some Kangaroo-hunters, and their large Scotch-deer-hound-like dogs. I listened earnestly to the relation of their sports, and to the wonderful accounts they gave of the daring conflicts they and their dogs had braved with their bounding game. They had been on the high table-land, where there are large lakes,—one of them, they said, as much as ninety miles in circumference, and more than three thousand feet above the level of the sea. These lakes form the heads of several rivers; and are surrounded by extensive plains and forests. Some of the male kangaroos, called "boomers," were described as being four or five feet high, and as having sprung, by the power of their tails and long hinder legs, as much as a dozen yards at a bound. When brought to bay by the dogs, they had fought desperately; and had placed their backs against the trees, so that they could not be seized from behind. This enabled them, both by mouth and limbs, to deal savagely with their antagonists. Our hunting companions could also tell of opossum-shooting by moonlight, and of the peculiar habits of the "wombat," or native badger. They also proclaimed themselves well acquainted with the haunts of the Tasmanian eagle, which is fearfully destructive to lambs;—they had seen the emu, or Australian ostrich, running wild; and talked of shooting-sport with black swans, pelicans, cormorants, and penguins, as well as with hawks and vultures.

Some of the trees we passed were of gigantic growth, with trunks as much as five or six feet in diameter, and wild flowers and heaths of great luxuriance and beauty were, in parts, spread over the ground,—while orchids and elegantly interwoven creepers gracefully festooned the extending branches. Moths were seen almost equal in size to small birds. The wren, the king-fisher, and diamond-birds of brilliant plumage, appeared at intervals. Some of the feathered songsters were musical, yet they were not equal to the singing-birds of Europe; and, on the whole, the voice of the cheerful magpie, which, instead of the noisy chattering it makes in England, here often seems to mock the flute, was the most pleasing to my ears. Our road lay through increasingly neat towns and hamlets as we advanced. We crossed a lake-like branch of the Derwent river, at Bridgewater, on a sort of tramway, made by convict labour; and after passing through New Town, with its orphan-schools on the right, and its shops, houses, and places of worship on the left, we descended, among suburban villas and cottages, into the main street of Hobart-Town, arriving at the coach office by about seven in the evening. I found there a group of Methodist friends waiting to welcome me. One of the sons of the late Rev. John Waterhouse, the first general superintendent of our Australasian Missions, drove me to his pleasant residence at Sandy Bay, from which I could survey at leisure, and with advantage, both the harbour and the town. Here I found the widow of Mr. Waterhouse, residing with her son; and spent the evening with a company of friends, in answering inquiries concerning Methodism and its supporters in England.

*Thurs., Frid., Sat., Jan. 3, 4, and 5.*—Went about Hobart-Town, viewing it from different points; visiting its museum of Tasmanian animals, birds, and productions of various kinds; and also made excursions to the more picturesque parts around. During these days I had also very pleasant intercourse with our ministers and with Wesleyan friends,—finding here also several Methodists whom I had known at home. Some of the surrounding scenery is fine and romantic, particularly on the drive round Brown's Hill, and from Kangaroo Island. The Government domain, too, is large and imposing, as viewed from the water at the south; and the Botanical Gardens and Queen's Park adjoining, are extensive and pleasant. On the Friday evening I preached to a good and respectable congregation at Brien's Bridge, about five miles north of the city, from John xiv. 1-3;—dwelling upon the attractions of our Father's house, in which there are many mansions. Tender thoughts of home were present with all of us; and the service was one of much feeling. It was at this place that the Rev. Joseph Orton, our missionary, preached his first sermon in Tasmania.

*Sun., Jan. 6.*—Preached twice at Hobart-Town; and, being the first Sunday in the year, renewed the "Covenant," according to Wesleyan custom. The attendance in the morning and evening was large, and in the afternoon, at the renewing of the Covenant, the lower part of the chapel was well filled. I did not know so many in the congregation, or in the church, as I knew among our people in Victoria: still I knew several of them; and this day is for ever solemnized by the fact that in it Mr. Dunn, a wealthy banker in the city, and one of our church-members, heard his last sermon; for he was almost immediately afterwards removed by death to the eternal world.

*Mon., Jan. 7.*—At five in the morning returned by coach to Launceston, to be in readiness to cross Bass' Straits the next day for Melbourne.

Hobart-Town is situated on sloping hills, by the side of the broad Derwent water, just where it opens to an immense sea-harbour, and at about forty miles' distance from the southern boundary of the colony. The city contains nearly twenty thousand inhabitants. It has good, well-paved streets, lined with large shops and stores, and is adorned with public buildings of respectable character: among them are numerous churches and chapels of the several denominations. The heart of the city—where business is carried on—is on the lower ground near the river; and cottages, villas, and terraces and gardens cover the sides and crests of seven hills, which bound Hobart-Town. The large harbour is exceedingly safe and commodious, and has many good warehouses at its head. The entrance from the sea southwards is between outlying islands, and by bold rocks and cliffs, with olive green hills of pleasant mould. Hobart-Town, from the harbour near to Kangaroo Point, with its shipping, hills, and buildings, varied by shrubberies and gardens, and backed by Mount Wellington,—which, with its grand basaltic columns, rises four thousand two hundred feet high, and casts its dark, solemn shadow over much of the scene from its roots down to the water's edge,—forms a picture of sombre magnificence,—especially as seen reflected and doubled in the glassy face of "Sullivan's Cove" in front. It has its markets, newspapers, cab-stands, &c., much after the pattern of English towns of similar size; and, in all respects, gives unmistakeable proof that it belongs to Great Britain.

———

TASMANIA is a valuable and attractive colony. In its extreme length it is two hundred and fifty miles, and in extreme breadth two hundred miles; but in configuration it is very irregular. Its general form is that of a heart, with the point turned toward the south; and from the chain of rocky islands running from its north-east angle, over the one hundred and twenty miles of Bass' Straits to Victoria, some express no doubt of its having been, at a former period, a part of the mainland of Australia. Indeed, it is said, that Ben Lomond is the culminating point of the Australian Alps. The contents of Tasmania are reckoned to be about twenty-four thousand square miles, or some fifteen millions of acres, making it appear that it is nearly as large as Ireland. There belong to it as many as twenty-three small outlying islands, some of which are mounted with light-houses, and others are noted for mineral treasures and precious stones. Its surface is very uneven, and displays almost every variety of scenery. The lofty mountain, the verdant valley, the wild, bold, rocky shore, extensive sheep-lands and cattle-plains, waving cornfields, dark unbroken forests, and highly cultivated gardens and pleasure grounds, are all to be found in it. The general character of the island is mountainous, with many lovely valleys between the numerous elevations, rendered abundantly fruitful by rivers and streams, which descend from the high lands, and water large tracts of country in their course to the sea. In the western range of mountains are large subterranean caves, said by those who have seen them to be, with their meeting stalactites and stalagmites, and crystal pillars supporting roofs of immense height, exceedingly grand and sublime. Common English flowers, fruits, and vegetables, flourish in the island; the plants and trees of almost all quarters of the globe thrive in it; and scientific men have pronounced its climate to be, at different periods of he year, equal to the climates of France, Switzerland, Italy, and the best parts of the Mediterranean. On the whole, perhaps, it may be pronounced the most healthy climate in the world,—being never too hot nor too cold. It has abundance of good soil and valuable timber yet unappropriated, and awaiting the enterprise of man. Much of its soil is remarkable in fertility; and after years of production, without the aid of manure, still yields large crops. Some of its trees are of gigantic size, measuring from two to three hundred feet in height, and being of corresponding girth. The pine and the gum tree attain immense growth; while the myrtle is not like our small fragrant shrub, but is a large, spreading tree, from fifty to two hundred feet high, in the hollow trunk of which several persons may shelter at the same time. Coal is found in most parts of the colony, and is sold in the market for from thirty shillings to two pounds per ton. Gold has been discovered in several localities, though not in such quantities as to repay the emigrant digger. Other mineral treasures are known to exist in the island; but no earnest attempt has yet been made to develope them. Its corn ranks among the best in the world, as declared at the Great Exhibition of 1851; and its wool commands a high place in the home market. Although, till 1853, it was a penal colony, the convict class hardly form a fourth of its ninety thousand inhabitants; many of the "old hands" having rushed to the diggings across the Straits, when gold was discovered in New South Wales and in Victoria; and the state of society is such that it is no uncommon thing for persons, even in lonely parts, to leave their doors unlocked when they retire to bed. Many harrowing tales are told of robberies and murders by bushrangers and outlaws; but they are all of past periods, and not of the present. The black aborigines, once so perilous, and who used to come into the towns by fifty together, have dwindled down to some dozen old people, and are protected and supported, in one place, by Government. From its commencement, the colony has been resorted to by settlers of unquestionable respectability. Their gabled cottages and imposing mansions, in the midst of lovely gardens and park-like scenery, have an English aspect which cannot fail to delight the sons and daughters of Great Britain. Churches, chapels, and schools are spread over its fourteen counties, and its two hundred towns and villages. The Church of England numbers, by its comprehensive mode of reckoning all not claimed by other denominations, about one half of the population; and on this account receives large Government aid. The Roman Catholics number some seventeen thousand in Tasmania, and have a seat for their chief prelate in the Legislative Council of the Government. Presbyterians, Independents, Baptists, and most of the Christian denominations in the old country, have their churches and ministers here. Methodism has its network of Circuits spread over the island, and has its chapels, preaching-places, and schools, in every place of importance. The first Methodist sermon preached in Tasmania was by the Rev. Benjamin Carvosso, in 1820, when detained at Hobart-Town on his way to New South Wales he stood upon the steps of the Court House, with Mrs. Broadbent at his side, and warned the sinful people to flee from the wrath to come. Our first regularly appointed missionary here was the Rev. William Horton, a relative of Captain Horton, the generous patron of the college near Ross. Now, we have in Tasmania 69 chapels and preaching-places, supplied by 11 ministers and 46 local-preachers; and we number 2,000 fully accredited church members, 2,000 Sabbath and day scholars, and 6,400 regular attendants on Wesleyan services. In addition to the support of its several agents and institutions for itself, Methodism in Tasmania supplies £1,000 a year for the spread of Missions to the heathen in the islands beyond.

Since 1856 the government of the colony has, for the most part, been committed to itself; and though some strange things may, at times, have been said and attempted in the Legislative Council and House of Assembly, yet there can be no doubt of the general and hearty loyalty of Tasmania to England. It gave proof of this recently in its noble subscription to the "Patriotic Fund" for the aid of the Widows and Orphans of the Crimean War, of a sum equal to 35s. 8d. for every householder, or of 6s. 3d. for every soul in the colony: a subscription unparalleled, in its proportion, within the British dominions.

In my way back to Melbourne I gathered additional information on the resources and prospects of Tasmania from a plain, common-sense man, formerly of Brigg, in Lincolnshire, my own native county. In a comparatively short time, he had, by labour and farming in the northern part of the island, obtained a competency for himself and his family. Good, cultivable land can be had there for twenty shillings per acre in the more eligible parts, and for ten shillings where less so. Sheep-farming in the best counties, and on clean runs, is a profitable investment for capital, and returns as much, in some instances, as twenty-five per cent. Cattle, to the number of nearly 100,000, are depastured in the island, and sell for £12, and up to £16, a head. There are in the colony more than 20,000 horses, some of which are of good breed, and fetch large prices. The northern part of the island is more productive of corn than the southern, and may be called "the granary of Tasmania." Large exports are made from it by shipping, at its nearer port of Launceston; and now that the convict system is abolished, and the bad prestige of its arrivals taken away from Hobart-Town, it is not improbable that the northern port will be more prosperous than the southern. The greater nearness of Launceston to Australia will be likely to favour its growth and prosperity. Immense quantities of fruits and vegetables are sent from Tasmania to Victoria; and of the total exports from the colony in the year 1858, amounting to considerably more than one million, Launceston made nearly one hundred thousand pounds above half the total sum. Wages for masons, carpenters, plumbers, &c., range from 7s. to 14s. per day. Shepherds, farm-labourers, and servants, range from £25 to £50 a year, with rations or living. Beef and mutton range from 4d. to 8d. per pound; bread is 9d. the four-pound loaf; and tea 2s., or 2s. 6d., per pound. Wearing apparel and house-rent are both more expensive than in our own country.

---

*Tues., Jan.* 8.—Left Launceston by the "Shepherd King" steamer, at ten in the forenoon. We had a goodly number of respectable passengers on board. Our cargo of fruit and vegetables, for Victoria, was also heavy. The weather was fine, and it was pleasant crossing Bass' Straits to-day.

*Wed., Jan.* 9.—Arrived at Melbourne by three in the afternoon; and spent the remainder of the day in packing up and preparing for departure.

# CHAPTER VI.

VOYAGE from Melbourne to Sydney—Port Jackson—Reception at Sydney—Opening of the Australasian Conference—Paramatta—Return to Sydney—University—Bible Society Meeting—Beautiful Suburbs and Neighbourhood of Sydney—The last Native—Again to Paramatta—Richmond—Bullock-Drays and Loads of Wool—Splendid View of Sydney and its Harbour—Botany Bay—House of Legislation—Notes on Sydney and New South Wales—The Australasian Conference and Methodism on the other side of the Globe.

*Thurs., Jan.* 10.—ABOUT ten in the morning left Sandridge pier, Melbourne, with my wife and several of the ministers from Victoria, Tasmania, and South Australia, for Sydney,—where the Australasian Conference of Wesleyan ministers was to open on the 17th of the month. The sea-breeze was refreshing after the heat on land, which had been almost suffocating, from the hot wind blowing over the northern interior, that had recently prevailed.

*Frid. and Sat., Jan.* 11 *and* 12.—We had some tossings at sea, so that many passengers were confined to their berths much of the time. Mrs. Jobson and I escaped sea-sickness, as usual; but, our cabins being crowded and close, we experienced considerable discomfort; and I had little or no sleep during the whole of our passage from Melbourne to Sydney. Through the roughness of the weather, we had to bear out further to sea than we should have done if it had been smoother: so that in the whole of our course of from five to six hundred miles we saw but little of the coast, and where we saw it the interior of the country was not discernible.

*Sun., Jan.* 13.—Arrived at the "heads" of Port Jackson by four o'clock in the morning, under drizzling rain. We wound our serpentine way amidst the hills and the islands of the harbour, and reached the quay at Sydney in another hour; but remained on board till seven, when a friend of my youth, the Rev. John Eggleston, President of the Australasian Conference, a talented and successful preacher, and Secretary for our Missions in this region, came, together with the Hon. Alexander M'Arthur, son-in-law of the Rev. William B. Boyce, to welcome us ashore; and Mr. M'Arthur drove us up in his carriage to his mansion at Glebe Point. I was sorely weary, for want of sleep; and most of my ministerial companions were unable, from the effects of the voyage, to fulfil their appointments for the day. Knowing, however, that I was expected by the people, I preached at Bourke Street in the morning, and again in the evening at York Street Chapel, and in both instances to large and exciting congregations.

*Mon., Jan.* 14.—Visited, by special invitation, the mansion of Mr. Mort, a gentleman of great taste, who has erected a splendid gothic house at a distance of about two miles from Sydney, on a beautiful hill, overlooking the wide water which runs from the "heads" to the harbour of the city. The house is stored with a superb collection of pictures by the best masters, brought here from England. I was agreeably surprised to find a mansion of such taste, and so rich a collection of pictures, at such a distance from the old country, and in this new southern world. The real refinement of the company, who, at Mr. Mort's invitation, had come to view the pictures, was also a surprise to me in this quarter of the globe. The dress, equipages, and bearing of the guests, seemed to me equal to what are found in connexion with *élite* gatherings in London; while the views and opening prospects from the surrounding balconies and grounds were almost as fine as the Lake of Lucerne, without, of course, the panorama of snow-crested Alps beyond. In the evening I attended a large meeting in York Street Chapel, to receive public congratulations from ministers and friends on my arrival amongst them. I found there many whom I had known in England; and nothing could be more respectful and hearty than the welcome they gave me. Many a burst of both British and Methodist loyalty broke forth in the meeting; and much feeling was evinced at the remembrance of scenes at home.

*Tues. and Wed., Jan.* 15 *and* 16.—Most of the time devoted to letter-writing for England, and to social intercourse with friends; and the remainder of it spent in the "Stationing-Committee" of the Conference, among representatives from the several colonies and islands of the Pacific, who, at this preparatory meeting, sketch out a draft of ministerial appointments for the Circuits, as nearly as possible according to the recommendations of the annual District-committee meetings, to be afterwards modified, or confirmed, by the Conference.

*Thurs., Jan.* 17.—The Conference opened, and continued proceedings until Saturday, February 2nd; during which seventeen days I attended regularly its sessions, preaching and holding public religious services in the different chapels of the city and neighbourhood on Sundays and week-evenings. At nearly all these services, there were those present who had been in my congregations at home; and some were the sons and daughters of parents I had known intimately. Reminiscences of early days and associations were affecting beyond expression; and many whom I had not known before thronged around me at the doors of the vestibule, with inquiries concerning the "fatherland," as if I had been acquainted with all persons in it. The chapels were usually wedged full inside; and, in some instances, crowded round outside far into the street, or grounds adjoining; so that in this, the Australian midsummer, the heat was oppressive almost to suffocation. Yet the effects of excessive perspiration and of confined atmosphere, upon the preacher, were not what they would have been in England. There is a reinvigorating power in the air of Australia not known here; and with almost daily services, both protracted and earnest, I experienced nothing of the "clergyman's sore throat," nor had scarcely the full ring of my voice at any time impaired. The tunes sung were English; and they were sounded forth with a strength and fulness of voice found only in old Yorkshire. And here, in this elder colony, were a due proportion of aged persons; so that the general aspect of the assemblies was still more British than in the younger colony of Victoria, where but few in the congregations are advanced in years. Indeed, the order, tone, and appearance, at the public services, were so truly English, that one might have imagined they were held in the heart of Yorkshire, Lincolnshire, or Lancashire, rather than fifteen thousand miles distant from our shores.

*Sat., Feb. 2.*—At six o'clock in the evening went by rail to Paramatta, which is about fourteen miles west of Sydney, and which is one of the oldest settlements in the colony. The clearings and dwellings in the way did not present much novelty of feature, except that here and there would be seen standing upright in the fields, and around temporary abodes, charred stumps of trees. Mrs. Jobson and I were hospitably entertained at Mr. Byrnes', who with his friendly wife and family spared no pains to make us feel at home in the strange land. We found here the heat more humid, and the musquitoes more troublesome, than in Sydney; but such kind attentions were rendered us, that we could scarcely think of more personal comfort than that which here fell to our lot.

*Sun., Feb. 3.*—Preached at eleven in the Wesleyan chapel of Paramatta to a full congregation; but was so oppressed with moist heat, that I was scarcely able to proceed with the service. In the afternoon a storm came down on the town, and a deluge of water tore up the streets into gullies, rendering them almost impassable. Preached again in the evening, the heat having somewhat abated; and afterwards, with Rev. John A. Manton, our able superintendent minister at Paramatta, and Rev. D. J. Draper, from Victoria, administered the sacrament of the Lord's Supper to church-members.

*Mon. Feb. 4.*—After breakfast, was driven by Mr. Oakes in his carriage through and around the town, alighting at points of interest on our way, and visiting orange orchards belonging to our friend, who drove us.

Paramatta lies in a hollow, screened by the rising grounds about it from the cooling breezes of the sea; and it is this, its low and sheltered situation, which accounts for the steaming heat that at times rises from it. Otherwise, the town, which has in it some four thousand five hundred inhabitants, and mostly old settlers, is good and pleasant; so much so, that it is quite a place of resort for change and recreation by the residents at Sydney. Paramatta has some excellent buildings, both private and public; and its main streets have in them good shops and stores; but its intervening gardens and grounds are spacious and numerous, so that a rural character is largely preserved for the town. Many an English oak, planted by early settlers, may be seen in Paramatta, though the tree will not be so large and robust as if it grew in the old country. Oranges and vines are found here growing in abundance. Several large structures remain to show that, formerly, when Paramatta was the seat of Government, and a convict settlement, it was a place of importance. Among these are the Government House, with its surrounding domain, now deserted; penitentiaries and prisons for refractory criminals also remain, but they are left to fall into decay. The drives around the town are pleasing and picturesque; the rising lands on every side are carefully cultivated, and tastefully laid out in orchards, and for agriculture. Amidst the more central buildings of the town, rises, with imposing effect, the double-towered church originally built by the lady of Governor Macquarie, for the first and good clergyman of the Church of England in the colony, the Rev. S. Marsden, who so fraternally co-operated with Methodist missionaries for the establishment of Christianity, both in this colony and in New Zealand. The old church, with its leaden spires, is not unlike Southwell minster in its general aspect. And the massive red brick parsonage of the devoted and laborious clergyman is on the side of the hill west of the church. There is an air of general prosperity pervading the place, and the residents are celebrated for their generous hospitality. Most denominations of Christians have their churches and places of worship at Paramatta. It was an early station with the Methodists. We have two chapels in it, which are soon, it is hoped, to be superseded by larger and more spacious structures. Most of our ministers of public name in Australia have resided here at one time or other. It was here that the devoted and laborious Walter Lawry terminated his missionary life. I saw the broad-eaved cottage in which he died, and also the cemetery on the side of the hill opposite, in which his remains are interred. In his old age scandal was busy against him with her many tongues; but his name is in this part as ointment poured forth.

At eleven in the forenoon, Mrs. Jobson and I left Paramatta in the steamer for Sydney, accompanied on our way as far as Ryde by Mrs. Byrnes and her daughter. On driving to the steamer we passed some factories in the valley, at the side of the water, which, from a mile distant, runs as little more than a broad stream through the town. Soon after we started, the river opened out to considerable width. It resembled the upper part of the Thames, between London and Richmond; only at intervals it was skirted by branches of adjoining forests, and more scooped out into graceful coves and bays. At Ryde we saw large orchards of oranges and lemons, and visited our minister, the Rev.

R. Amos, resident there. Afterwards, we took another steamer for Sydney; but before we reached the city a heavy thunder storm fell upon us, and shrouded river, rocks, and trees in dark, solemn grandeur. The weather cleared sufficiently to show us Cockatoo Island, a strongly fortified place of banishment for refractory criminals. Here we crossed the harbour to the landing pier of the capital; and there found our friend Mr. M'Arthur waiting for us with his carriage, to convey us to the Glebe.

*Tues., Wed., Thurs., and Frid., Feb.* 5–8.—Devoted to letter-writing, visitation of friends, and of public institutions. One evening was pleasantly spent at the University, where Dr. Woolley, the Principal, gave us and our friends of the Glebe handsome entertainment, amidst his clerical professors and associates. The buildings of the University are large, richly ornamented in the decorated style of gothic architecture, and are highly creditable to the architect and to the city. The stately hall is nearly equal to the best halls of our colleges at Oxford and Cambridge, and is rich in effect by its Westminster Hall-like open roof, supported by corbel-angels, and by historic windows of good coloured glass. It has a spacious, well-stored library, a choice museum of Egyptian, Greek, and Roman antiquities, enriched and arranged by Sir Charles Nicholson, and excellent lecture and class rooms. Some £75,000 of public money have been spent upon it; but the central tower over the principal entrance has yet to be erected, as well as some necessary appendages; and £25,000, it is reckoned, will be required to complete it. There is no religious test in the University. Adjoining grounds have been granted by the Government to different

Christian denominations, upon which to erect colleges for the instruction and training of youth in their respective tenets. But little has yet been done in this direction; and some fear the results upon youth of the most influential families of the colony thus left unguarded, by college and religious training, against latitudinarian principles.

*Sat. and Sun., Feb. 9 and 10.*—Obliged to remain indoors and in bed, by severe illness, arising from over-labour and exhaustion; so could not go to Maitland for religious services there, as intended.

*Mon., Feb. 11.*—Somewhat better. Attended and spoke at a large and spirited meeting of the Bible Society. Our friend, the Hon. George Allen, president of the society, was in the chair; and I was glad to be able to show and express the catholicity of British Christianity. At this meeting, however, it was apparent, that Protestants are under more restraint in speaking of Popery than in the old country.

*Tues. and Wed., Feb. 12 and 13.*—Wrote letters, transacted official business with the President of the Conference in the day time; and in the evenings, by the considerate and generous arrangements of my host and his neighbours, the Allens, met, in social parties, different classes of citizens and colonists, from the deputy Governor downwards.

*Thurs., Feb. 14.*—Was driven to the "heads" of Port Jackson by Hyde Park, Surrey Hills, and Paddington, passing the soldiers' barracks, and several large houses on spacious grounds, possessed by old convicts, or their immediate descendants. Then, by a road over sandy hills and mounds, we drove through a pretty suburb, tastefully named "Waverley." Having reached the "heads," we stood on the shelving edge of the stony cliff beyond the lighthouse, and looked from its dizzy height over the wide water. Before us lay the entrance to the harbour, with the red floating light within, and hills covered with wood beyond; while on our right stretched the blue expanse of the Pacific Ocean. I sketched this view from the overhanging crag of the cliff. We returned by another road nearer the harbour, skirting its bays and coves. It was a charming ride. The drive over hill and dale, and round projections and inlets, diversified the views sweetly. Villas girded with trees stud the sloping hills, and the harbour is dotted in different parts with lovely islands. Beyond these is Sydney, with its towers and spires; and the far background is formed by a long line of blue mountains rising against the sky.

We passed on the road the last remnant of the aborigines who inhabited this part of the Australian continent. He was named "Ricketty Dick," from his having had a paralytic stroke that disabled his limbs. He sat by the roadside, scantily covered by his dark, tattered blanket, with his hands open in front, soliciting alms. He moved, to take up the bit of silver which was thrown to him, with difficulty; and then crawled into his dog-kennel-like hut among the trees, behind. Food is usually supplied to him from the houses of the gentry near; for, however cruel might be the conduct of the first European settlers to the poor natives, wherever any of the aborigines now remain, they are universally treated with consideration and kindness, so far as their own dispositions and habits will allow.

On our way back we passed through Darlinghurst

and Wooloomooloo, genteel and healthy suburbs of Sydney. The ground over which we passed in this drive, and which was so generally studded with stately and tasteful houses, was all covered with scrub but five years ago.

*Frid., Feb.* 15.—Went with Mr. M'Arthur, at half-past six in the morning, in a light conveyance to Paramatta, where we breakfasted at Williams's excellent family hotel, and then drove to Windsor along a well-made road, seeing good land and farmsteads on the way; several of them being possessed, or let, by the old convicts. By half-past one we reached Windsor, a village-like town by the Hawkesbury River, consisting of two long streets of shops and cottages, with gardens at the sides. It contains a large Wesleyan chapel, and a massive Episcopalian church of brick, with a plain, spacious Roman Catholic chapel. Driving over swampy ground, through the intervening woods, for four or five miles, we reached Richmond, another town like a large village, with streets laid out at right angles, and none of them paved. It is a pleasant, rural place. The high hills over the Hawkesbury River are covered with dense forest, and are richly picturesque, both in forms and clothing. Beyond these is the long range of the "blue mountains" with their sugar-loaf points. We intended to have gone further on, for a more extensive view, and to have ascended the green hills; but a storm of lightning and rain set in; so we were glad to take refuge for the night in a rural inn, where we had very comfortable accommodation.

*Sat., Feb.* 16.—Left Richmond at half-past seven in the morning, for return to Sydney by another and a less cultivated route. For twenty miles, or more, the road, after the heavy fall of rain the night before, was very trying to our horse; for we had to pass over swamps, amidst stumps of trees, and through thickly entangled bush and scrub. Our way lay for some time through the forest. We passed some trees of gigantic size and growth, and heard the odd medley of cackling, bray, and chuckle notes from the " Laughing Jackass." The land where cleared was good, and in parts opened to us extensive farmsteads, with numerous cattle, and large flocks of sheep. We overtook several heavily-laden bullock drays with their wool packs, on their way to Sydney. Some of them were dragging their ponderous loads slowly along through the deep ruts of mud roads, and others were resting by road-side inns, and sheltering weary teamsmen stretched out at full length under them for sleep. In some instances, these loads of wool were dragged by eight or ten oxen. The rough, bony, sun-browned men by their side have whips, short in the stock, but with long cow-hide lashes, which, after whirling round their heads, they throw with amazing skill to the extremity of their team of bullocks, so as to hit with fearful certainty any lagging animal on the ear, nostril, or other tender part selected. We rested some time at one of these way-side inns, and saw, while there, much of rough colonial life. We saw the bushman, tall, spare, active, and wiry, canter up the road, and come leaping with loose rein over fences till he reached the inn door, where, with face, hands, and throat burnt to a ruddy bronze, he quenched his thirst. We saw the stocksman, with gaunt frame, long limbs, and weather-worn, seated upon his bony, long-limbed steed, on which he has his home, driving his cattle before him to the stockyard, aided by skilful dogs. And we saw traveller after traveller enter for refreshment and for rest. We could not pass further into the interior, as we had intended; for the recent rain had broken down the roads at several parts so as to make them impassable. We, therefore, returned to Sydney, reaching Mr. M'Arthur's mansion in the evening.

*Sun., Feb.* 17.—Preached again at Newtown, a suburb of Sydney, in the forenoon. The chapel is new and large, and is a good specimen of decorated gothic, mostly taken, in its general design, from our "model chapel" at Stockport, only much increased in dimensions. Preached in the Hon. George Allen's neat Grecian chapel on his own estate at the Glebe, in the evening.

*Mon., Feb.* 18.—Crossed the harbour of the "North Shore" in company with a valued friend and able minister from England, the Rev. William Hessel, to view from the highest elevation on that side of the water the landscape of the far interior. It was a wondrous sweep of brown green scrub and forest, with here and there a glint of water in it; and was bounded in the distance by a long blue mountain range. Turning our backs upon this vision of the wilderness, and descending a little, we had, perhaps, the grandest panorama of the capital that can be obtained from any point of view. Down from our feet extended a mass of the dense green foliage which so commonly meets the eye in Australia. Seats and villas of the gentry were scattered among it; and on the right hand a pretty large collection of houses of the working classes, forming what may be termed a hamlet. Then the wide blue waters of the harbour stretched away on either hand, with small steamers plying across it to their several points, and with ships of merchandise lying at anchor before Sydney. The land on the other side of the water was composed of a countless number of beautiful and swelling rounded hills, here and there extending their bases into the harbour, so as to make it look like a fringe of indentations. The summits of the terraced hills before us were crowned by the houses, spiral churches, and other public buildings of the city, with the signal flag-staff in front, the government house on the left, and the University in the distance on the right; the whole forming a panorama of almost unsurpassed beauty. It was from our stand-point on the rocks of the north shore that I sketched the view which forms the frontispiece of this volume. It has been copied as nearly as possible in colours, that my readers may gain some idea of the hues of an Australian landscape; but this process of art gives a very inadequate representation of the scene.

*Tues., Wed., Thurs., and Frid., Feb.* 19, 20, 21, *and* 22.—Spent in the examination of Sydney and its neighbourhood, in writing letters, transacting public business, and in preaching in the several chapels of the city in the evenings.

*Sat., Feb.* 23.—Passed a pleasant day with a large pic-nic party, who accompanied us to the "heads" and the "middle harbour," in a steamer generously obtained for us and our friends of the Glebe and of the University, by George Wigram Allen, Esq., who ranks high in the legal profession. This gentleman is the eldest son of Hon. George Allen, and son-in-law of Rev. William B. Boyce. The "middle harbour" is even more romantic than Port Jackson, and in bold rocky scenery covered with trees and shrubbery, surrounding deep crystal water, is equal to the finest scenes at the Scotch lakes.

*Sun., Feb.* 24.—Preached in the morning in the large Congregational Church, Pitt Street, belonging to Rev. W. Cuthbertson, B.A., a talented Independent minister: a collection of nearly one hundred pounds was made on behalf of that church. In the evening preached a farewell sermon at Sydney, in York Street Wesleyan Chapel, to an immense crowd. The heat was intense, but did not seem to interfere with the fervour of the service.

*Mon., Feb.* 25.—Passed a pleasant morning at the residence of Mr. Fairfax, the energetic proprietor of the "Sydney Morning Herald." The house has a picturesque perch on the shoulder of one of the highest hills at the side of Port Jackson; and is Elizabethan in its style, with high, pointed, wooden gables. It commands, from its terraces and grounds, most extensive views of the harbour, city, and inland country. Mr. Fairfax is from Warwickshire, and by intelligent perseverance has made his position one of the most elevated and influential. His newspaper is the "Times" of Sydney and New South Wales; and out of the fortune amassed by it he has recently expended £30,000 upon handsome freestone offices for the printing and publishing of his daily journal. The "Herald" is said to have a circulation of from seven to eight thousand daily, and to be worth to its proprietor £10,000 a year. It was surprising to see how soon the white sandy soil of his grounds and gardens had become covered with verdure, fruits, and flowers. In the evening met Dean Cowper, with several of the principal clergymen and Nonconformist ministers of the city, and some distinguished official and professional gentlemen, at the Hon. George Allen's, Toxteth Park. Mr. Allen had generously assembled these interesting guests, in order to make us acquainted with colonial society. It was a cheerful evening, profitably spent, and closed with religious worship, in which Churchmen, Dissenters, and Methodists fraternally and audibly united.

*Tues. and Wed., Feb. 26 and 27.*—Ill through exhaustion, and not able to leave my bedroom.

*Thurs., Feb. 28.*—Went with my host and Mrs. Jobson to view the world-known "Botany Bay." On quitting the suburbs we crossed "Lachlan Swamp," where the water filters itself through the sandy soil, and is afterwards collected for the use of the city, and conveyed thither in pipes. This vast sponge-hollow is a region of snakes and reptiles, some of which are large and deadly.

BOTANY BAY, undeservedly but indelibly branded as the high place of exiled felony, (for it never was occupied more than a few weeks as a convict settlement,) is a large round indenture of some miles into the land, with a narrow opening to the sea, a few miles south of the "heads" of Port Jackson. There is a great variety of shrubbery and trees around it, but no remarkable profusion of flowers; yet it was the splendour of its new floral show, as well as I remember the account, which caused Dr. Solander, the companion of Captain Cook, to give it the name of "Botany Bay." By the side of it is an hotel, with beautiful grounds, and a curious and valuable menagerie of Australian beasts and birds; while within the house are preserved the stuffed forms of numerous snakes and reptiles. I spent some time in minutely examining these, and in observing their respective peculiarities. This place is much resorted to by the citizens of Sydney in their family and pic-nic parties; and we were gratified to learn from a board at the entrance of the grounds, that the keeper of the hotel, who is a Wesleyan, closes it against all visitors on Sundays. Lovely as is the scenery skirting the bay, and comparatively near to the capital as it is, yet it has not been chosen for suburban residences. Perhaps the dishonoured designation attached to it has prevented this; for it would not be the most pleasant association with the name of a gentleman resident there, to have his letters directed from England to him at " Botany Bay."

In the afternoon of Thursday I went to Balmain, another suburb of the city, across the water, to call upon friends, and to select a cabin for our return to England in the " Jeddo," which was in an arm of the harbour behind. I had previously been at Balmain, opening a tasteful gothic chapel, designed by Mr. Mansfield, jun., who was also the architect of the excellent new chapel at Newtown, in which I preached. We were kindly entertained at the pleasant villa of Rev. R. Mansfield, (father of the architect just named,) who some time since retired from ministerial service among us, but who yet occasionally preaches in our chapels of the city and neighbourhood, and is highly esteemed. We also found, in a rural cottage by the water, the daughter of a family with whom we were intimate in Manchester, and who, with her husband and children, resides here. Our steamship promised well by her appearance; and on returning to the shore we saw the " John Wesley," our tight and buoyant missionary ship from the isles of the Pacific, waiting for Rev. James Calvert and his associates, who were expected to be at Sydney in a few days, from England. On our return from Balmain to the Glebe by water, we fell into the hands of a sharper, who charged seven shillings for rowing us across. In the evening we visited the Exhibition of the "Society of Arts," in Pitt Street, and found in it many instructive specimens of the produce of New South Wales. The varieties of wood, and the samples of gold from the colony, were especially interesting. Mingled with these were numerous works of art. Those in marble and different metals were excellent; but the colonial paintings were very inferior to English. On the whole, however, the exhibition was good, and even surprising, in so distant a part of the world.

*Frid., March* 1.—Was driven by the Hon. George Allen to the House of Legislation, and went with him through both the upper and lower chambers; hearing the debates, and observing, once more, the order and character of the proceedings. Large and handsome buildings are about to be erected by the Government on a new and beautiful site, commanding a view of Port Jackson. The plans approved are upon an estimated cost of more than half a million sterling. In the evening I had a farewell meeting in York Street Chapel with the Wesleyan Societies of Sydney, and addressed them on personal piety, family religion, and the duties they had to perform for God and for Methodism in the land of their adoption.

*Sat., Mar.* 2.—At two in the afternoon, after packing up during the morning, Mrs. Jobson and I left the hospitable abode of my good and princely host, the

Hon. Alexander M'Arthur, bidding a tender farewell to him, his charming wife, and lovely children, as well as to a large number of ministers and friends, who crowded the pier to witness our departure, in the "City of Sydney" steamer. We left Sydney for Melbourne at three in the afternoon, grateful for the affectionate kindness shown to us during our protracted stay in the capital; and saddened by the thought that, probably, we should see but very few of our friends *again* on earth.

I spent full seven weeks in Sydney and its neighbourhood, having, as noted in my journal, friendly intercourse with all classes of persons, and free access to all sources of information. It is a wonderful city for situation. The harbour is large and fine, and in capacity, safety, and romantic grandeur, equal to any harbour of the world. It is entered seven miles distant from the capital, by as striking a portal as the coast could possibly supply. The opening from the ocean is two miles wide, between majestic headlands, three hundred and fifty feet high. The passage is then serpentine, through what may be called a series of lakes of pure blue water, indented with picturesque bays, and coves, bordered and surrounded with richly wooded, rocky hills, that are dotted and crested with mansions, villas, and cottages, of every variety of form and style. All this part of the water is called "Port Jackson." The foliage on the rocks, hills, and cliffs around, though not as leaden and monotonous as in wholly uncultivated parts, yet is somewhat dull to English eyes; and lacks the warmer greens, golden yellows, and the rich browns, of our European landscape. It is heavy in colouring. As you proceed, the passage narrows, and numerous lovely islets dot the channel, clothed luxuriantly with trees and verdure. Turning round one island, covered with fort and batteries, that command the entrance at its straitest point, you enter the harbour, which is two or three miles wide, completely landlocked, with good anchorage, and securely sheltered from storms. Here are seen extensive docks, wharves, ship yards, and landing piers, thronged by vessels of various tonnage, while, rising terrace-like above these on hill over hill, and far away on the left and the right, are the buildings of this metropolitan city of the parent colony.

Not much of the character of Sydney can be seen until you land, and climb your way to the main streets; but, then, all is so thoroughly English, that the visitor might well suppose he had been by some mysterious power borne over the fifteen thousand intervening miles, and suddenly put down into some familiar part of the British metropolis. George Street, and Pitt Street,— the two long parallel streets running up through the city from near the landing,—are more than two miles long, eighty feet wide, and are enclosed on either hand with handsome warehouses, shops, and stores, equal to anything seen in Liverpool and Bristol. The streets are well macadamized, the pavements at the sides are broad and well kerbed, and the lofty edifices are mostly of clean freestone, taken from the rocky bed of the sites on which they rest. The crowds, the stir, and the gay equipages, would almost lead you to suppose you were in Piccadilly, or Regent Street, of our own metropolis; while the various public cries of "Fish, ho!" "Old clo'!" the shouts of omnibus conductors for "Paddington," "Surrey Hills," &c., and the hail from the driver on his perched-up seat behind his "Hansom,"

P

with stretched-out whip, of "Cab, Sir?" all remind you of dear old London. The only reminders in the streets that you are on foreign ground, are that here and there you see, amidst slender vehicles and gay equipages, on the middle carriage-way, a bullock-waggon, dragging its heavy load down towards the quay; and that, on the pathways at the sides, you meet rough, sunburnt men from the interior, clad in loose clothing, bound around the waist with broad buckled straps, and wearing muddy leathern boots, which reach far up their thighs.

The public buildings of the capital are numerous, and may be favourably compared with those of our second-class cities and towns, if not, in all instances, with those of first rank among us. Some of the more recent structures are as imposing, and as consistent in style, as the public buildings of our principal seaport and manufacturing towns, and have almost a marble purity in their material. The parks, grounds, and gardens of the suburbs, are large, spacious, and well laid out. The Government domain, with its winding walks amidst rocks and trees by the sea side, is romantic and beautiful; the Botanical Gardens, with their grand Norfolk pines, containing almost every variety of tropical plants and flowers, and in which, as you saunter along, you may hear the military band playing some familiar air, and ending with "God save the Queen," are delightfully situated around a cove of pure water, where numerous pleasure-boats, of various forms and colours, ply to and fro; and "Hyde Park," though within the city, and poor in trees and verdure, as well as limited in its extent, when compared to our own great western outlet, is, nevertheless, a healthy lung or breathing-place for the citizens, and is surrounded with terraces, mansions, and ecclesiastical structures of striking character.

Sydney, in itself and immediate suburbs, contains, according to the last census, 92,642 inhabitants. Its climate is hot in summer, but dry and salubrious; yet, at times, terrific storms of thunder and lightning, rain and dust, sweep over the city, and plough up its roads into deep ruts and trenches. There are also storms of heated dust, which pass over the city, and move like a compact wall across it, darkening the sun, reddening the sky, withering the trees, and making the scorched earth crack under them, as if it were a globe of brittle pottery. These hot dust storms are terrific in their aspect to strangers. One would suppose that the seals of the Apocalypse were being broken, that the day had come which shall "burn as an oven," and that the elements were about to be dissolved with fervent heat. These visitations are called "brickfielders" by the colonists; I suppose because of the brick-dust swept onwards by them in their course from the brick-fields adjoining, and from their brick-red glare. They bear along with them pulverized, sandy dust, which penetrates every crevice and key-hole of the most sheltered abodes. At these times, the thermometer rises to one hundred, and more, in the shade, and all things are still and breathless. The "brickfielders" are usually followed, before the day closes, with "southbusters," as they are named, from their coming from the sea at the south; and then the mercury will suddenly sink down forty or fifty degrees, until fires and great coats seem desirable. One of these "brickfielders" passed over Sydney while we were there: when it seemed, as we looked from our balcony at the Glebe towards the city, as if the Last Seal were opened, and the destroying angel had received his commission to go forth. It was a scene fit for the tragic pencil of Martin. We were told that sometimes these Australian siroccos last for two or three days, and that then the effects are fearful. Birds drop dead from the trees, insects die, dogs and cattle put out their tongues with burning dryness, and trees and plants shrivel up like bunches of scorched sticks and straws. Scarcely a blade of grass, or a leaf upon a tree, is left; and human beings fall down dead in the streets. In the interior, bush-fires kindle and burn with fearful fury. Some old colonists affirm that these storms are moderating, as internal cultivation advances. It is to be hoped that it will prove to be so.

The evenings at Sydney were, at times, singularly beautiful. The moon was so bright and large that you could see to read by it. The stars, too, were brighter and larger than ours in appearance, and seemed to drop like pendent lamps of glittering crystal from the deep blue dome above; while the flooded light of moon and stars upon the bays and coves of the surrounding harbour, made them shine like polished mirrors. The change of heat and cold from day to night was sometimes sudden; and, doubtless, the sudden changes in the atmosphere have their effects upon the complexion and constitution of the weaker sex; for, though blooming earlier, yet they fade sooner than under our cooler and more equal sky.

Society in Sydney is in the highest ranks nearly as refined and accomplished as in England. A border line is observed between the descendants of convicts and the families of free-settlers, as far as practicable; though in trade and merchandise, where wealth is possessed, society is, of course, as open and free in one case as in the other; and where special merit has appeared in any one of the proscribed class, the Governor, or some other high official, has led the way in public recognition. I attended the Governor's levée, on the departure from New South Wales of Sir William Denison; and the dress, order, etiquette, and show, could scarcely have been excelled at a royal drawing-room in England. The military and naval commanders, government officers, bishops, professors of the University, clergy, and ministers of different denominations, attended in their respective costumes and dresses, and presented a brilliant scene; while the soldiers, volunteers, and lines of carriages on the government domain, and the regatta boats on the harbour around, were stately and imposing. But there is a lower class of character and life in Sydney as well as a higher. There are "slums" and dens of infamy and crime, where the dregs of human corruption seethe, ferment, and break out in terrible violence. There are more than five hundred public-houses in Sydney and its immediate neighbourhood, and some of them are as dark and cellar-like as any that can be found in our own "Wapping," or that could have been found in St. Giles', while others are as gay and garish as our own street-corner gin-palaces. Drunkenness and gambling are of gigantic strength in Sydney, as at Melbourne, and destroy their victims with fearful rapidity. The "great social evil," too, is apparent in the streets, both day and night; and that though woman's household service here has large remuneration. Thirty, and thirty-five, pounds a-year is a common wage for servant-maids; and then there are holidays required, and various conditions imposed, which are provokingly embarrassing to mistresses of households. Indeed, throughout colonial society there is a freedom of speech and manner surpassing what exists in the old country. Labourers and servants of all classes speak and act with greater independence; boys in the streets shout their ridicule upon "new chums," as newly-arrived persons are called; and little children, though not so precocious and assuming as in the United States of America, nevertheless, are ready to assert their "rights." Money is more plentiful; and though expenses may be greater, so as to reduce materially real profit, yet the handling of heaps of gold and silver gives conscious importance.

It is not, however, by the cesspools alone that the character of a city is to be judged, or by its servants, and boys and girls, though these are features not to be overlooked or left out of the account. There are dregs of society everywhere, and always will be while human nature remains fallen and depraved; and in hot, exhausting climates, these may be looked for. The sun suckles serpents and vipers while it colours flowers and ripens fruit. But in general character,—in its bulk and strength of middle-class, as well as in its higher and lower ranks,—the Society of Sydney is equal to the society of our chief cities and seaports in England. The main drawbacks to my own personal comfort in Sydney, where I was so generously welcomed and hospitably entertained, were, the oppressive heat which for hours in mid-day unbraced the loins of the mind, and prevented pedestrian exercise in the open air; and the pungent bites of musquitoes, which in the evening, whether in public, social, or private life, come buzzing against your cheek with a peculiar *whir*, fixing their blood-suckers in the flesh, and then, after drawing their full potion, flying off with a flutter of triumph, leaving a blotch behind, which, until ripened to a yellow head, is far more irritating than a healing blister. At night, too, unless securely veiled by musquito curtains, these little insect fiends have great pleasure in tormenting you, by darting their truculent proboscis into your flesh, and drawing your blood. And they have evidently a high relish for the round fat part of the hand, from the wrist bone to the little finger. If this part be exposed from under the coverlid for five minutes, it will be sown all over by them with bumps and blisters, not to be forgotten till the next night, if so soon. They, too, like the boys in the streets, have wanton pleasure in vexing "new chums." These, however, are but small drawbacks, comparatively speaking, to the general excellence and advantages of Sydney, as a place for visit, or residence. There is an air of settled comfort and dignity in it, such as we have in our cities at home, and such as is not found, to an equal extent, in the cities of the younger colonies. The "volunteer" spirit is alive in it, as it is also in other parts of Australia. There is now in the colonies a force of more than ten thousand volunteers; and when I was in the capital of New South Wales, the volunteers were efficiently performing military duty for the Government in the place of regular regiments shipped to New Zealand to quell the rebellion among the natives. The game of cricket, and other English sports, may be daily witnessed in the suburbs of Sydney. On the whole, it is a large, prosperous, and charming city; and, though on the other side of the globe, and in the "ends of the earth," has been described as being more English than England itself.

An opinion might be expressed on the character and

proceedings of the Legislative Chambers of Sydney; and a question asked, If self-government had not been given prematurely to the colonies of Australia? In the Lower House of the elected representatives of the people, there are demagogues and talkers, who evidently speak for out-door effect, and who say strange things at times, as well as in a strange manner. On one night of my attendance there, I heard an earnest discussion on the proposed abolition of capital punishments for the colony, and which, with a gallery filled with "old hands," brought out all the extravagancies imaginable in relation to such a subject; yet with all the clap-trap employed for popular hearing, there was strength and principle enough in the House to resist and overturn the measure; and there was an evident respect to England in her firm retention of this law of "death for death," and "blood for blood." And some delicate and manly things were well said, and generally acquiesced in, on the sacredness of woman's purity to be preserved from ruffian violation by dread of punishment, which were truly creditable to the assembly. It is still an experiment to be tested by time whether universal suffrage, as practically given, is not premature; but with all the spouting by political adventurers on colonial independence and self-sufficiency, loyalty to British government cannot be doubted; and some short time since, when a prominent member of the House, of the class referred to, proposed colonial independence, a resolution of indignation was immediately moved, seconded, and would have been carried,—if the proposition had not been almost immediately withdrawn,—declaring that the proposal was contrary to the views and feelings of the colony, that the paper on which it was written should be torn in pieces by a menial, and a sweeper of the House sent for to remove it with its accompanying dust from the floor. The members of the Upper Chamber are now, by nomination from the ministry, in office for life; and in their position and stake in the country, as well as by their intelligence and independence, are a seasonable check upon the legislation of the colony. My host, the Hon. Alexander M'Arthur, is now a member of the Upper House; and the Hon. George Allen has long been such, as well as chairman of its committees.

The COLONY, of which Sydney is the capital, is large and prosperous. It was as large as England, France, and Germany; but in 1859, it had as much as ten times the area of Great Britain separated from it for the new colony of Queensland, which, if supplied with adequate and cheap labour, may become what it has been proclaimed, a future cotton-field for England. In some parts, New South Wales is lovely and picturesque, deserving the name, given to it by Captain Cook, from its resemblance, in his view, to our ancient home principality. On the sea-side it is garrisoned by high towering rocks, which rise from three to six thousand feet above the level of the water. Within, its arable and pasture-land is extensive and good. It produced in gold, last year, £1,718,194. It has mines of various metals, and of coals, which are rich in produce. It has orange-groves and vineyards, and fruits and flowers of every variety of climate. Grapes of the finest quality are produced in the colony, not only for the table, but also for the manufacture of excellent wine. It is intersected in all directions with excellent roads, some of which are "metalled" with hard basalt from its own "blue mountains." The royal mail proceeds from Sydney to all towns in the interior, and letters are delivered with punctuality and dispatch. Postage-stamps are here used for letters as in Britain. Stage-coaches run to inland towns, and steamers ply along the coast between different seaports. Telegraph wires communicate with most places within the colony itself, as well as with the colonies adjoining. Alpacas and llamas have been recently introduced into New South Wales, and in both fat and fleece are equal to the flocks of South America. It has large exports of hides, leather, wool, timber, oil, and other merchandise; and, by the construction of railways, it is opening ready ways to different towns of the interior, not reachable by rivers, and to which there had been but indifferent means of access. It is superior to Victoria in the length of navigable rivers; but is still Australian in its deficiencies in this respect, and calls for increased attention to inland irrigation, and to the treasuring up of the waters which abundantly fall upon it. New South Wales supplies full employment to all who seek it. Mechanics and artisans obtain twelve shillings and fifteen shillings per day; labourers, seven shillings and nine shillings: destitute poor, there need be none, except of the sick and blind; and for these there are suitable institutions provided by the public.

There is less fluctuation in New South Wales than in Victoria, owing to its being an older and longer established colony; but, at times, circumstances occur to disturb and depress its prosperity. The "squatting interests," or large land-holding for sheep and cattle-runs, are at present disturbed by ministerial measures. It is too much to expect that miles upon miles of land shall be permanently in the hands of one man, at a small annual rental, when many are waiting to purchase his "hold" in divided portions, at a price which will materially increase the government-revenue, and bring the soil into cultivation; though in all such measures vested interests ought not to be overlooked. Some of the "squatters" have made enormous wealth. One, whom I met in company as Sydney, had netted as his profits in the last year, from a joint hold of land, £15,000; and others have much larger holds than he and his partners. The "Land-Bill" just passed has broken in upon the repose of some of these; and in several instances which I heard of, both in Victoria and New South Wales, "squatters" were removing to Queensland, where tempting offers of longer security are made on fourteen years' leases of extensive sections of land. But there is room enough yet in the oldest colony for cattle and sheep-breeding on a large and profitable scale; and as such it will still be resorted to by energetic and wealthy emigrants. Some of the unexpecting sons of England's nobility are of this class; and among them are not unfrequently found graduates of English universities, who, in their solitary homes by the forests and the plains, have the best and newest books of British literature for indoor reading, and who *con* their well-worn copies of Homer, Horace, and Virgil, in the open woods and fields. There is also a little uneasiness at present in the gold-regions, through the prejudice of Anglo-Saxons against Chinamen, who, having come over for a season from their own country to the colonies, herd together, and save as much in their living as they can, that they may carry away with them as large an amount of wealth as possible. This is not the most favourable service for the colonies; and the habits of the Chinesemen without wives, or families, are offensive to Britons, while the knowledge of the prejudice of races in the United States of America strengthens the objection to have them in the same neighbourhood. But it is unworthy of Anglo-Saxons and of Englishmen, to disregard the laws of their own government, as they have recently done at Lambing Flat, and to install Judge Lynch for terrifying and expelling the Chinese. Such questions as these may be expected to disturb, at intervals, a rising colony, without interfering with its growing advancement and prosperity.

RELIGION in this colony, and in its capital, is reverenced, as it is throughout Australia. Ecclesiastical structures are numerous. Most Christian denominations in the old country have their off-shoot churches here, with their respective ministers. The Church of England has its various ranks of clergy; but the bishop was sadly chagrined, when I was in Sydney, to find by a legal decision against him in the highest colonial court, that he had not the power of an English diocesan over his clergy, and could be excluded by an objecting clergyman from a church in which it had been published the bishop would hold a service for ordination. Nor is there a disposition in the colony to increase the status, or enlarge the power, of the dignitaries of the English Church. It is not viewed, or intended, to be there "the Establishment." There, as in Victoria and Tasmania, a growing effort is made, year after year, to abolish State-aid to religion, which, no doubt, will succeed before long. The knowledge that Roman Catholicism is greatly aided and sustained by Government grants, also, weighs with many Protestants. Roman Catholicism exhibits large numbers in Australia by emigrations and removals from Ireland. It is there seen in mitred pomp and state at public assemblies and ceremonies, beyond what usually appears in our home-country. At the levée for the Governor-General, which I attended, the episcopal dignitaries of the Romish Church came in stately carriages, having episcopal armorial bearings upon them, and attended by livery-servants. Protestants see this, and, knowing how much Popery is there strengthened and supported by Government aid, claimed by it on the census number of adherents, they are willing to make the sacrifice of their own Government grants, and thus leave the false system to stand, or fall, by its own resources. This willingness spreads rapidly through all the Australian colonies, and has already expressed itself in several of them by a majority of votes accordingly. Probably, in a few years, it will prevail in all Legislative Assemblies there, both in the Upper and Lower Houses; and, as it has already done in South Australia, will abolish Government aid to religion altogether. The Day-schools of New South Wales are of three kinds,—Denominational, National, and Private. Together, these number 739, having in them 32,840 scholars. The Sunday-schools of the colony number 313, with 16,590 scholars. The total grant for ecclesiastical purposes made by the Government in the year 1859 was £42,967. Of this, the Church of England had £22,292; Roman Catholics, £12,683; the Presbyterians, £4,698; and the Wesleyans, £3,109. The entire population for New South Wales is returned at

336,572, exclusive of 23,450 separated with Queensland. The total quantity of land granted, leased, and sold, in the colony, to 15,715 occupants, is 27,663,365 acres. The exports for 1859 amounted to £5,800,926, and the imports to £6,772,049.

METHODISM holds a good and prominent position in Sydney and in New South Wales; though in Government returns it does not appear to such advantage as churches which number both moral and immoral, unclaimed by others. It was commenced at Sydney, in 1812, by Mr. Thomas Bowden, the worthy father of Mrs. Allen, of Toxteth Park, who in that year formed a Methodist class in the city. The first Wesleyan missionary sent to New South Wales was the Rev. Samuel Leigh, who arrived at Sydney in August, 1814. The first Wesleyan chapel was the one in Princess Street; built and given to the Connexion by Mr. James Scott; and which still remains in use, with a minister's residence adjoining. This chapel was opened by the Rev. Walter Lawry, in 1819, our second missionary to New South Wales, and the brave pioneer of Methodist labourers in the islands of the South Seas. Now, in Sydney and its suburbs, we have some eighteen chapels and preaching-places, which are mostly well attended, and some of them are of excellent architecture. It has, also, its Methodist Book Room, and its Methodist Journal, which bears the name of "The Christian Advocate and Wesleyan Record." In the colony, Methodism has 35 circuits and stations, 276 chapels and preaching-places, 42 ministers, 178 local or lay preachers, 256 class-leaders, 7,456 Sunday-scholars, taught by 877 teachers, 23,751 attendants on its ministry, 3,820 fully accredited church-members; and, besides supporting these agencies and institutions, it supplies £3,000 a year for foreign Missionary work among the natives in New Zealand, and in the islands of the Pacific.

As already stated, our Annual Conference of Wesleyan ministers, in Australia, was held in Sydney. It opened, as I have said, on the 17th of January, and continued seventeen days. It was held in the York Street Chapel; and was attended by most of our ministers of New South Wales, by ministers from the colonies of Victoria, South Australia, and Tasmania, and by missionaries from New Zealand and the islands of the Pacific,—some sixty ministers in all. It was a good Conference. It was orderly and dignified in its proceedings, and considerate and satisfactory in its measures. The ministers on the floor of the chapel were, in large proportion, young, as we regard ministers in Methodism; but they were intelligent, gentlemanly, and earnestly attentive to business. In front of them, and also on the platform, were older ministers, who had been the pioneer-labourers in Australia, and who had their position and cares by years and experience, as they would have in the British Conference. An elder among them was Nathaniel Turner, our first missionary to New Zealand, who there as also in the Pacific Islands, hazarded his life for the name of the Lord Jesus Christ. We had, also, on the platform the Ex-presidents, Manton, Butters, Draper, and Eggleston: all noticeable and impressive men in their persons and countenances, as well as by their missionary labours in earlier and harder times. The Rev. Stephen Rabone, formerly a successful missionary in the South Sea Islands, was the appointed president;

the Rev. Thomas Buddle, from New Zealand, was elected secretary; and scattered up and down in the Conference were missionaries and ministers of familiar name, such as Watkins, the appointed president for next year's assembly at Adelaide; Buller, from New Zealand; Watsford and Adams, from the islands;—the latter, brother to Professor Adams, of Cambridge, who discovered the planet Neptune;—with Ironside, Bickford, Ward, Chapman, Hurst, Harris, Waugh, Binks, Hessel, Waterhouse, Oram, Rigg, Cope, and others, known and loved by many in our part of the world. Though few attendants, compared with the four or five hundred ministers at an English Conference, it was, nevertheless, an affecting and impressive scene. It was only seven years ago that the Rev. Robert Young, my honoured predecessor, the first deputation to Australia, and the Rev. William B. Boyce, our active and devoted general-superintendent, and first president there, who had laboured so efficiently for this object, formed the Affiliated Conference of Australia, and established Methodism there for independent government and support; and now the ministers who could leave their circuits to attend a Conference were, on the platform and scattered over the lower part of a large chapel, a goodly company. They all received me with the heartiest affection, and gave me as cordial a greeting as could possibly be given to a brother by a body of ministers. They evinced strong emotion at the mention of the fathers of the British Conference, and of the love of all their brethren to them. They received the official Address from the British Conference, delivered to them, with marked courtesy and respect; and they heard an accompanying extempore address with attention and signs of fraternal gladness. Throughout the entire proceedings they showed the truest veneration and love both for the parent Conference and the Methodists of England. We discussed together, freely, and at considerable length, vital and delicate questions on the relative position and powers of the parent and the affiliated Conference; and in all not an ungenerous sentiment, or ungentlemanly word, was spoken. We argued fully the pressure of the large Mission-work upon the colonies, and which amidst financial difficulties bore heavily upon their home-funds and personal comforts, when as fine a flame of missionary zeal burst forth as ever kindled in a missionary meeting at home.

The Reports brought by the chairman of the districts were very encouraging, and showed that in the southern region of the world Methodism is a mighty power, which is steadily and rapidly progressing. Our intelligent and faithful missionaries from New-Zealand told us of the triumphs of the Gospel in their respective fields of labour among a population of nearly 80,000 colonists and settlers, and more than 56,000 native New-Zealanders. They made known to us that we had 63 chapels and preaching-places in the two Districts of Auckland and Wellington, for English worshippers, with 4,787 attendants at public worship, 737 church members, and 1,375 Sunday-school scholars; while in the native department we have 140 chapels and preaching-places, 154 native local-preachers, 110 native class-leaders, 3,791 scholars, 180 native Sunday-school teachers, 6,247 native attendants at public worship, and 1,546 native church members. They spake with sadness of the war then raging in New-Zealand; describing it as being far from the rude, brutal rebellion which some supposed; and said that by misrepresentations of the designs of the British Government upon their lands, a sort of William Tell feeling of patriotism had been roused among them that would not be easily allayed. They told us how Christian natives who had been misled into the conflict, took with them native preachers, and held daily worship in their respective tribes; but rejoiced to assure us, that most Methodist converts, and nearly all our various agents among the natives, had been loyal to the government and throne of Britain. In the interval of Conference-sittings, the Rev. Thomas Buddle gave me some free translations of poetical compositions by native New-Zealanders,—one of which I here subjoin. It was chanted by a blind native at the gathering of his tribe for a *korero,* or native assembly for discussion on war with the Government.

> "The wind blows keenly,
> Its blast has sorely pierced me.
> The stars are hidden from me;
> And I tremble like the birds
> That flutter, when dark clouds
> Fly across their path.
> Who has created this night of sorrow
> That now o'erspreads the land?
> Who is he, that conceived
> This thought of war?
> Why does he not return
> By the same plebeian path
> That brought him here,
> Nor dare to tread on sacred ground?
> From the councils of the great ones
> Hast thou come
> To break our long repose?
> Whither wouldst thou lead us?
> End now thy strife
> And leave us pure,

> That we may rest in peace.
> Who is the evil spirit
> That prompts to war?
> Bid him keep at distance,
> Lest maddened by his wiles
> We fall into the snare of Rongo,
> The man who came to fetch us.
> Withdraw thy stretched-out hand,
> Return it to thy bosom undefiled—
> Pollute it not."

The missionaries from the Friendly and Fiji Islands gladdened our hearts with their reports. They stated that in groups of islands where a few years ago there was not a Christian, and where cannibalism prevailed in its most fearful forms, there is scarcely a heathen now to be found. Their returns for the two Districts named, showed that in them Methodism has 629 chapels and preaching-places, 262 native ministers and catechists, nearly 2,000 native school teachers, 34,431 day and Sunday scholars, 18,554 native church members, and 81,410 native attendants on Methodist worship. A letter was read from King George, our local preacher at Tonga, asking counsel on a law of divorce which he found it difficult to uphold; and several most interesting topics on Missions were brought before the Conference. It was with gladness the tidings were received at one of our sessions, that the Rev. James Calvert, the friend and companion of the late Rev. John Hunt in Fiji, and a band of ministerial associates from England, had already embarked for the South-Sea Islands, and might be expected there in March or April. Medical assistance is much needed for the missionaries sent to the Friendly and Fiji Islands, and for their wives; and if such could be supplied, it was stated, missionary labour and life would be prolonged.

From what I learned of the Rev. Joseph Waterhouse, the chairman of the Fiji District, his disinterested, self-denying, and efficient services, mark him as a worthy son of our first general-superintendent of those Missions.

The GENERAL SUMMARY of returns made at the Australasian Conference of Wesleyan Methodism which I attended at Sydney, for Australia, Tasmania, New-Zealand, the Fiji and Friendly Islands, is as follows:— 955 chapels, 628 other preaching-places, 175 ministers, 775 day schools, 41,565 day scholars, 1,292 Sunday-schools, 62,794 Sunday scholars, 33,964 church members, and 181,468 attendants on Wesleyan worship. The total amount expended in the year on the Missions in New-Zealand and the Islands was, £16,535; of which £5,005 were supplied from our Missionary Society in England, and the remainder from the colonies and from the Mission-stations themselves. Towards this the Islands contributed £3,000 in net proceeds from oil.

One reflection forces itself upon the mind on reviewing the statistics of our Missions in this part of the world, and that is,—what triumphant encouragement we receive for persevering effort, when we sum up the amount of success vouchsafed by God in proportion to the means which the church has hitherto employed for evangelizing the heathen! This encouragement is given under every variety of human condition and circumstances, where the church has been earnest and persevering in missionary efforts. In Ceylon, for instance,—which I visited on my way, and which may be viewed as a field for experiment in our Eastern Mission, and as the stepping-stone to India,—there the religion of Jesus Christ has proved successful in the midst of Buddhism, Hinduism, and devil-worship. The history of our Missions there is briefly this. In 1814, Dr. Coke, the honoured founder of Methodist Missions, and who for his apostolic labours must be ranked among us next to Wesley, after having crossed the Atlantic eighteen times to plant and organize Missions in the West Indies and America,—and after having endured much persecution for his evangelistic efforts among the oppressed negroes, and for his open denunciations of slavery,—sailed from England with a band of six youthful missionaries for the East. But while crossing the Indian Ocean, he was suddenly removed from the scenes and services of this mortal life to his eternal reward. He was found dead, one morning, on his cabin floor, having died when alone in the night; so that the missionaries who accompanied him, and who had relied upon him as a father, after having with tears committed his body to the deep, had to land at Ceylon without a human guide and friend. In their orphanhood, they betook themselves to their work among the natives, distributing themselves by lot over the island. Since then faithful men have been sent in succession by our Missionary Society, and the result is what I have recorded in an earlier chapter. A net-work of organized churches is spread over the most populous parts of Ceylon. These are under the efficient instruction and training of native teachers and ministers; and though the influence of corrupt and idolatrous systems is still powerful in the island, yet the leaven of Christianity is in the midst of the native mass, and in due time will, undoubtedly, leaven the whole lump. Here are the first fruits of our Missions in India and the East.

The encouragement vouchsafed to the Christian Church has been still greater in Australia. Within some thirty years Christian missions were commenced there; and amidst the most unfriendly circumstances imaginable. They were commenced among convicts, and among colonists and settlers, many of whom were worse than the convicts committed to their custody. Yet the preachers of the Gospel, sent from time to time, persevered in their evangelistic efforts, and followed the population in its progress; and the result has been such as I have already hastily described. The Australian colonies are Christian throughout; and though exhibiting, in some respects, revolting forms of wickedness, yet the profession of Christianity is universal, and flourishing churches are everywhere found in them.

But the most encouraging example is seen in the Islands of the Pacific. There, within little more than thirty years, the principal groups of isles were peopled by barbarous savages and ferocious cannibals; and now, almost universally, their inhabitants are professing Christians. There, where the Church has shown itself to be earnest in the supply of missionaries, converts have increased and multiplied, until, in the island groups I have named, heathenism has no more place. There cannibalism is so loathed and abhorred, that it is not allowed to be mentioned among the people. There are hundreds of chapels, and hundreds of school-houses, of native workmanship, in which many thousands assemble from week to week, and day to day. There the Sabbath is kept holy to the Lord. There marriage is established, and polygamy abolished. There an infantine literature is growing rapidly; and there thousands a year are provided by the native churches for the spread of the Gospel into regions beyond. Could any proofs be more demonstrative, that if the Christian churches of England will send forth their messengers in adequate numbers, either to the more refined millions of the East, to European colonists and settlers in distant parts, or to the barbarous savages of the very darkest regions, success will be realized in *proportion* to the agency employed? Only let the churches of Christ send an adequate number of missionaries to India, China, the multitude of the isles, and to the interior of Africa, and these heathen regions shall assuredly be evangelized: these realms of sin become the kingdom of our God, and of His Christ!

# CHAPTER VII.

DEPARTURE from Sydney—Return to Melbourne—House of Legislation—Meetings with Friends and Ministers—Opening of New Church at Collingwood—Passage to South Australia—Extreme Heat on Arrival—Visit to Kapunda in a Mining Region—Sabbath Services—Welcome at Willunga—Vineyards on the Hills—Plains and City of Adelaide—Farewell Breakfast—Notes on South Australia—Western Australia—General Views of the Island-Continent—The Aborigines.

---

*Sat., March 2.*—PLEASANT passage down the harbour, in which, gleaming, still and green, at not more than an arm's depth from the surface, the ravenous shark might be seen. On reaching the "heads," and passing into the ocean, we found the weather rough, and the water tossing. Before evening we steamed by the mouth of "Botany Bay;" within which, on the north side, we could see the monument raised for M. le Receveur, the French naturalist in Captain Cook's expedition; and in the boisterous state of the wind and water we could readily perceive how that first chosen harbour was an insufficient shelter for ships, against the roll of the ocean, and was likely to be abandoned for the deeper and safer inlet of "Port Jackson." Soon we bore further out to sea, and, before it was dark, lost sight of land.

*Sun., March 3.*—Sea still rough; and so many passengers confined to their berths, or prostrate on deck, that we could not hold religious services on board.

*Mon., March* 4.—Sea smoother. By noon, saw Wilson's Promontory, with its white lighthouse on a rocky height. We passed between it and the picturesque, stony, off-lying islands. Towards evening it again became rough and stormy; but we rode finely into the harbour of Port Phillip, by eleven at night.

*Tues., March* 5.—By six in the morning we were at Sandridge pier, where the Rev. D. J. Draper met us, and from thence conveyed us to his house at St. Kilda, as our home during our stay at Melbourne. Went to the Parliament Houses, to gain a little better understanding of the character and proceedings of legislative assemblies for Victoria. The Upper Chamber is a superb and sumptuous room, as highly decorated, and almost as richly picked out in gold upon its mouldings and ornaments, as any state-room in Paris; and the Council seemed composed of orderly and gentlemanly members. The Lower Chamber is a substantial and stately room; but not so elaborate in its finish as the Upper. It was crowded at this time to hear explanations from a sharebroker, who had retired from the ministry through judgment against him, on a legal trial, for his part in certain business transactions. He explained at length, but feeling was strong against him, and it was afterwards spoken out by members in the opposition. The general aspect of this assembly was inferior to our House of Commons; but it was superior to that of the Congress at Washington, and fully equal to the Lower House in Canada. The style of speaking which I heard was orderly and creditable.

*Wed., March* 6.—Went over the Methodist Book-

Room, and the extensive premises adjoining. Drove round the Wesleyans' Emigrant Home, which, at the rush to Victoria, was a welcome asylum to many; and visited the Free Library of Melbourne. This library is on an extensive scale, and is in a building of good style. It is open gratuitously to all classes, and for both sexes; and while much frequented in the evenings by the working-classes, as well as by the higher classes in the day-time, it has never yet been seriously abused. The people view it as their own, and are voluntarily and unanimously its guardians. Already this library possesses an extensive collection of historic works, and its books of all classes are well arranged.

*Thurs., March* 7.—Reception-meeting given to me in Lonsdale church. Previously, there was a social tea-meeting in the large rooms on the premises, which were thronged in all parts; while the yards and grounds were covered over with gigs, carts, and waggons, belonging to friends who had come from a distance. At the reception-meeting in the large church, the Rev. D. J. Draper occupied the chair; and delivered a manly and thoroughly English speech. An Address was presented to me, supported by speeches from our own and other ministers, by the Hon. A. Fraser, and by J. T. Sumner, Esq., J.P., son of the late Rev. John Sumner, in the home Connexion, and a leading merchant of the city. I spoke, in reply, on the state of religion and Methodism in England, and on what they, whom I represented, desired the Wesleyans of Australia to be.

*Frid., March* 8.—Met the Methodist ministers of Melbourne, and their wives, at Lonsdale Street parsonage, and spent with them some very pleasant hours.

Several of them I had known in the old country; and the Rev. James S. Waugh, our host, I had been agreeably associated with on visits to Ireland. He is editor of the "Wesleyan Chronicle" at Melbourne; and, as a remembrancer of our meeting in Australia, gave me a precious relic of early Methodism, in the Hebrew Bible, daily used by the Rev. Thomas Walsh, whose extraordinary proficiency in the original language of the Old Testament has been recorded by Wesley; where he states, that this early Methodist minister knew every Hebrew root by heart, and could tell how often any given Hebrew word occurred in the Old Testament, and in what place.

*Sat., March* 9.—In the morning occupied with preparations for departure; and in the afternoon visited Mr. Webb, sen., of Brighton, in whose spacious gardens we plucked grapes, figs, mulberries, almonds, and various fruits in abundance. . The scene from the sea-shore, in front of his house, was exceedingly pleasing; and in its long, flat sea-beach, with fishermen, and here and there a lounger from the city, would have suited well the pencil of Collins.

*Sun., March* 10.—Opened a large new gothic Methodist church at Collingwood, by preaching in it, morning and evening. The church, passages, yards, and street adjoining, were thronged; and proofs of God's healing mercy to sinners were given. The heat of the day was great, and my clothes hung close and heavy upon me through profuse perspiration. This being my last day in Melbourne, I felt stimulated in preaching, by the consideration that my ministry in that city was about to close for ever; and that, in all probability, I should never again, on earth, see the ministers and people who had welcomed me so ardently. Affecting home reminiscences, by the sight of familiar faces, strengthened this feeling; so that, as ofttimes before, I lay awake through the night from intensity of excitement and emotion.

*Mon., March* 11.—Left Melbourne at nine in the morning, by the "Aldinga," for Adelaide. Ministers and friends accompanied us to the pier; gave us tokens of remembrance; and, lingering till our departure, beckoned to us their affectionate farewells. We had a good vessel, and made our way quickly from Hobson's Bay. As we passed into the open sea, we met a large emigrant ship from England, with five hundred persons, or more, on board. They crowded over all parts of the deck and rigging, eager to catch the first sight of their new home. It was an impressive sight, especially with the consideration of how various and anxious were the thoughts of these emigrants, who had braved the mighty deep, and were now about to set their feet on a strange land.

*Tues., March* 12.—Fine day at sea. Coast line on the right, low and flat. In the evening passed Kangaroo-Island, with its lighthouse, and with bush-fires burning upon it.

*Wed., March* 13.—Rose at six, and found that we had advanced far up St. Vincent's Gulf, and were fast approaching Port-Adelaide. Arrived there soon after seven, and felt the heat very oppressive. It required some exertion to get my luggage safely landed; and though some working men from England, who had known me in Manchester, gave all the assistance they could, yet, by the time I reached the railway-station, I was nearly prostrate with fatigue in the consuming heat. The thermometer was 107 in the shade, and 154 in the sun. Friends from Adelaide, led by the Rev. William Butters, (formerly known to me at Hibaldstow, in Lincolnshire,) soon arrived by the train to welcome us, and to accompany us on the seven miles' line to the city. We passed over a flat country almost as parched as Egypt, stopping at three or four stations, for small towns and villages in our way, and reached Adelaide by nine. We were driven through the city to Mr. Butters' house, called the "parsonage;" but I was so faint with heat, that I was hardly able to breathe. We languished through the day, scarcely speaking to our kind host, or to the friends who called to welcome us to South Australia. In the evening we drove out; but there was little air to feel even in an open phaeton. By bedtime, however, a breeze sprung up from the sea, and there was a cooler night than any of us had expected.

*Thurs., March* 14.—Walked through Adelaide, and viewed it from different points. In the afternoon, we went by train to Kapunda, fifty-two miles,—passing by Gawler-Town,—and I preached in the evening to a large congregation in a good gothic chapel. Kapunda is a town produced by settlers in a mining region, which surrounds it, and is not unlike some of the smaller towns in Cornwall. In my congregation I found several Cornish and some Lincolnshire friends. A productive copper mine is the chief attraction of this place,—the land around not being very good.

*Frid., March* 15.—Rose early, and looked at Kapunda and the mining district around. After breakfast left by train to return to Adelaide, having with me the Rev. W. Butters and Ald. Colton. Our train rushed round some sharp turns, but went safely. The country through which we passed was low and stony. Here and there was seen the bed of a river, or a stream, but dried up, and trees were growing in the dry channel. "Water-holes" appeared at intervals, but they seemed to have little water in them. It was thus with Gawler River, which we crossed midway on our return. Bush-fires were raging both on the mountains on our left, and on the fields towards the coast on our right. The land over which we passed seemed scorched to hard sterility; yet some of it, we are told, was so fertile, that sixteen years in succession it had borne corn, and that without being replenished in vigour by manure of any kind. On our way we saw flour-mills at Gawler town and other places, showing that we were in a grain-producing region.

*Sat., March* 16.—Engaged with preparations for the Sabbath, and in writing letters for England.

*Sun., March* 17.—Preached in Pierie Street chapel in the morning to a large and attentive congregation,— the yard and grounds of the neighbourhood being covered with the vehicles of persons from the country. In the evening preached in a handsome and crowded spacious new gothic chapel at North Adelaide, with turrets in front, open roof within, and with flying-buttresses at the side. Slept at the Rev. Jabez Waterhouse's, who is our resident minister at North Adelaide, and in all respects worthy of the name he bears.

*Mon., March* 18.—Wrote letters in the morning, and in the evening attended an enthusiastic reception-meeting in the chapel at North Adelaide. The Rev. W. Butters, chairman of the district, and deservedly honoured in Australia for his talents and services, occupied the chair. This meeting was preceded by a social tea, where there were several I had known in England; as there were, also, at the Sunday services.

*Tues., March* 19.—Went to Mr. Padman's villa, situate in a picturesque suburb two miles from the city, and at the foot of a long range of mountains, where we finished our letters for the next mail; and then enjoyed the pleasant garden and companionship of our friends. Mr. Padman is the son of the late Rev. Thomas Padman, in the ministry at home; and is a prosperous merchant of the city of Adelaide. At night we saw bush-fires raging on both sides.

*Wed., March* 20.—Went from Adelaide to Willunga, (which is thirty miles from the capital, in the opposite direction to Kapunda,) accompanied by the Rev. Messrs. Butters and Waterhouse, and their wives. We had a pleasant drive near the sea-coast; and saw large tracts of good land in our way, and hills well moulded. We passed by several of our country chapels, which were neat gothicized buildings in brick. Abundance of trees were seen in the valley on our left as we approached Willunga, and on a range of hills running out at our right into the sea. Within a mile of the place of our destination, some forty friends on horseback met us, and then turning round preceded us on the road. Opposite our large gothic chapel at Willunga, a high triumphal arch, richly decorated, with evergreens and flags, and with the word "WELCOME" upon it, spanned the road. On reaching it the horsemen drew up and joined the crowd in a shout of the old English "Hurrah!" which made the plains and the hills behind echo and re-echo. After responding to this unexpected salutation, we drove on to Rev. Robert C. Flockart's, formerly known to me as a hearer at Spitalfields Chapel, London, and who is an energetic, successful minister here. I repaired to the chapel, replied to the Address there presented to me; and after a social tea-meeting, which filled the building, preached to the multitude. Here, also, as in other places, were many hearers whom I had known in England.

*Thurs., March* 21.—At half-past nine, left Willunga, accompanied by our friends. On the triumphal arch, the word "FAREWELL" was inscribed in large letters. At the end of thirteen miles, in returning, we rested our horses at a way-side hotel, where some "snapper-fish" was served up to us: this fish is one of good taste and flavour. We reached Adelaide in the afternoon, having lingered somewhat on the road, to view the surrounding country. In the evening, we went up to North Adelaide, and spent the night at Mr. Kain's, a wine-merchant from Guernsey. This gentleman had married the daughter of the Rev. T. W. Smith, minister with us at home. Here we met several intelligent friends; one of them a relative of the Hardys, a well-known respectable Wesleyan family, of Barrow, in North Lincolnshire. How strange it seemed to find, on the opposite side of the globe, wherever we went, so many whose faces and names were familiar to us!

*Frid., March* 22.—Went to the Hon. G. M. Waterhouse's, at Irecombe, to spend the day with the son of our first general superintendent in this part of the world. He is an intelligent and influential gentleman, who has, perhaps, as much power in the colony as any one that can be named, and is chief secretary. He lives twelve miles from Adelaide, on a part of the mountain range, behind the city. To ascend with less difficulty, and to see the country, we went sixteen miles round, upon roads which had been cut by hard labour through the rocks and at the sides of the hills. On our way, before we left the plains, we saw some excellent land. It was well cultivated; and at intervals there were deep water-holes in dried beds and channels, in which water is stored for dry seasons, and to which thirsty cattle rush, sometimes to drowning and death. At Irecombe, Mr. Waterhouse has on his estate, professedly of retirement, vines and other fruit trees, which yield him a large income. We walked with him round his pleasant vineyard, and into his orchards, seeing, as we passed along, birds of gay plumage feeding rapaciously upon the fruit. We heard, too, the sweet note of the magpie, which here, as in Tasmania, is musical. Most of the day was spent in conversation on the colony of South Australia; our host being familiar with all its concerns and interests.

*Sat., March 23.*—Left Irecombe, and returned to Adelaide, by a more precipitous, but more direct road. On descending the hills, we had before us a view of the vast plains of Adelaide, which I can liken to nothing seen elsewhere. On our left were large, well-rounded hills, covered with blue and purple green vegetation. Before us, and far away to our right, extended a vast level plain, looking at this torrid time of the year like the dried soil of a desert: yet it is a locality of extreme fruitfulness, and produces some of the best grain of the world, as the awards of the National Exhibition of 1851 show. The city of Adelaide was in the middle of this plain, but slightly on our left. From the city, onwards, there was the bed of the river "Torrens," nearly empty, but the shallow water winding curiously in its deep channel. Then there were the two curving sheets of glassy water,—St. Vincent's and Spencer's Gulfs,—stretching their lake-like forms from the land to the sea; and beyond all, skirting the entire panorama, was the great Southern Ocean, bounded by the blue horizon; while in our immediate foreground were richly coloured hills, broken by deep rugged cuttings, down which we were driving. On our descent, I sketched this scene, being one of such richly varied features. The afternoon and evening were pleasantly spent with friends at Mr. Colton's, where we slept.

*Sun., March* 24.—Preached in the morning again at North Adelaide, and in the evening again at Pierie Street. In the evening his Excellency the Governor, Sir Richard Graves M'Donnell, attended, with several of his Executive and Legislative Council; but it was difficult to find room for them. It was a day of deep, concentrated emotion, which, combined with the intense heat of the season, seemed to drain the energies of body and soul.

*Mon., March* 25.—Attended a Farewell Breakfast given to us in " White's Room," as the large public hall of the city is called; and met there some four hundred and fifty persons, who paid five shillings each for tickets of admission. The Treasurer of the colony, (formerly a worshipper at City Road, London,) the Hon. G. M. Waterhouse, Mr. Foster, of the " South Australian Register," and several members of both Houses of Legislation, were among the company; and there were in it some who had been friends of my youth, in Lincolnshire and elsewhere. A Farewell Address was presented to me, and I spoke in reply on Christianity and Methodism, and what Australia might be and do, if faithful to Christ. Afterwards we went to the Botanical Gardens,—which might be called Zoological, as well,—and observed, with unspeakable interest, the novel forms of Australian and Tasmanian mammalia and birds. The kangaroo in all its varieties (*Macropus giganteus, M. nemoralis, M. fruticus,* &c.) was here; and I had proof, in their wonderful leaps, of the powerful spring there is in their hind-legs and tails. The marsupial animals, as is well known, are abundant in this far southern world. Among them are some very destructive species, which we saw in these gardens, —such as the pouched wolf, (*Thylacinus cynocephalus,*) which the settlers call the " zebra wolf," sometimes the "tiger," and at other times the " hyæna." It is a very powerful animal, of the size of a large dog, with short, stumpy legs; its colour is a brownish yellow, with black bands transversely along the back. This creature is found in Tasmania only, and destroys sheep, kangaroos of the smaller species, and, in fact, almost any living creature which comes within its reach. It is becoming scarce. A more revolting creature is the *Dasyurus ursinus*—also a carnivorous marsupial. Colonists, in Tasmania, where only it exists, at first found it very abundant, and called it the " devil," from the havoc it made among their sheep and poultry. This animal is not larger than a bull-terrier, but it has most powerful jaws. It is covered with shaggy black hair, with white bands, or patches, on the chest and shoulders. The wombat (*Phascolomys fossor*) is another Tasmanian marsupial, and is often called the " badger " by settlers. It was the most comfortable-looking creature we saw, being so exceedingly fat and plump. Its rabbit-like head, also, rendered it a good-humoured looking animal; and we were told it is sometimes kept tame. The flesh is also said to be good eating. It burrows in the ground, lives on roots and plants, appears at night only, and is found at times to be a yard long. The birds, in this interesting collection, were rich in variety, and some of them splendid in plumage. The beautiful little "ground" and "grass" parroquets were seen in full perfection.

*Tues., March* 26.—Left Adelaide for the Port of Glenelg, where we were to take the steam-ship for King George's Sound,—the point of our embarkment for England in the "Jeddo." The distance from Adelaide to Port Glenelg is six miles. We were driven there in a coach and four, and were accompanied by friends, in their private carriages, who followed us in procession the whole way down to the pier, where they watched our departure in the "Balclutha," and beckoned us "farewell," as long as we were in sight. We left the port at two: the weather was favourable; and soon we were out of sight from the shore, reflecting, as we paced the deck, that our mission to Australia was finished!

---

From the foregoing notes of Travel in South Australia, it will have appeared that the colony has in it no bold mountain-scenery to strike the visitor, but is pleasantly diversified with hilly ridges, which enclose an extensive alluvial plain of great fruitfulness. In scarcely any part are there trees growing so thickly together as to assume the forest character, though the ground is by no means devoid of timber. There are three principal mountain ranges, bearing the names of Mount Lofty,

Mount Barker, and Mount Wakefield. These are all well wooded, and the gently undulating grounds and pleasant valleys which intervene between them and the level plain have trees upon them. Nor, with the exception of the lower course of the Murray, is there in the colony any inland water deserving the name of lake or river; though, as in the other Australian colonies, there is by rain a fall of fresh water upon it almost equal to the fall in England. The great Lake Torrens, of horse-shoe form, and which makes so large a figure upon the map, is merely a tract of soft, muddy ground; and the river Torrens, shown in some earlier prints of Adelaide as bearing on its bosom ships of war, is not unfrequently so dry a channel that it may be crossed without wetting the feet. Still the colony is prosperous and attractive. It contains an area of 300,000 square miles; exceeding in its contents all Germany; and, with its two large gulfs, has a coast-line of nearly 1,500 miles. The climate is exceedingly hot in summer, as noted on the day we arrived; but then, the evenings, generally, are cool and refreshing; and the other parts of the year are described as perpetual spring. The plains on our arrival were dry and parched; but on a slight shower of rain the verdure began to bud, and almost in a day seemed to tinge the soil with tender green: a sufficient indication of what other seasons would produce in clothing for the land. And that South Australia is a prosperous colony may be seen from the statistical returns of its steady increase in all departments of commerce and revenue. It has not the discoveries of gold to attract eager multitudes from distant parts, as in Victoria and New South Wales; but other precious minerals crop through its surface, and yield large returns. It has fifteen mines of copper, lead,

s

iron, and tin, now at work, which, during the last ten years, have produced in exports upwards of three millions sterling; and, besides these, large sections of ground, in different parts, have been leased to companies and individuals by the Government, and these leaseholds are known to contain valuable deposits of the various metallic ores. The copper ore commonly yields twenty per cent. of metal, and requires but little labour to obtain it, or take it away. The famous "Burra Burra" Mine, about ninety miles north of Adelaide, usually yields twenty-five per cent.; and the ore found there at times has yielded as much as seventy; so that its shares, originally purchased at five pounds, are now worth one hundred and fifty pounds. The discoverers and early shareholders of this mine realized large fortunes from it. One proprietor who purchased one hundred original shares at five pounds each, found himself within three years afterwards in the annual receipt of £11,000. The iron ore, in some parts, is so rich that it may be wrought at the forge as soon as taken from the earth. The deposit of soil by the sea, in what are called the plains of Adelaide, is particularly fitted for the growth of corn. It has no trees upon it to be cleared away, and can be worked without renewal, as already noted, for sixteen or eighteen years. South Australia has now as many as seventy-three flour-mills, and the number is continually increasing. The land is well distributed, being sold chiefly in allotments of eighty acres, at twenty shillings per acre. And it is plain, by the yearly increase of cultivation of vines, that this colony will eventually become a principal wine-growing colony. Several proprietors already get thousands of gallons a year, and dispose of them at six shillings per gallon, nett. The grapes are of the very finest quality, and grow luxuriantly. So that, all things taken into account, while it is not so pretentious and stirring a colony as Victoria, or even New South Wales, yet South Australia is prosperous and attractive. It is, like the other Australian colonies, subject to hot dust-winds from the north, which drape both town and country in a denser and darker livery than a London fog; but these clouds of penetrating impalpable red powder never continue long, being soon swept away by the southern breeze. Bush-fires, too, such as we saw burning on the hills, are common in summer. During the very hot weather the dry grass and scrub ignite from any accident, and flame away for miles, like the grass on the American prairies. The scene at night is threatening to a merely European eye; but the settlers learn to take little notice of it, unless it come dangerously near to them. The elective principle has here been introduced for the colony. It has two Chambers;—one the House of Assembly, composed of thirty-six members, and the other the Legislative Council, composed of eighteen members. The executive is vested in the Governor, whose council consists of the heads of departments, having ministerial responsibility. The House of Assembly is elected for three years. The vote is by ballot, and there is no property qualification for the franchise. The population of the colony, by the last census, is 127,000; the total imports for a year, £1,639,591; and the total exports, £1,783,716. The total quantity of land sold to the end of 1860 was 2,033,761 acres, for which £2,606,605 had been paid by the purchasers, being at the average rate of some twenty-six shillings per acre.

ADELAIDE, the capital, is a large city, well laid out with wide macadamized streets, that intersect each other at right angles; and these are well relieved by open squares, and by the surrounding domain of nearly half a mile's breadth, for the recreation of the people, called the "Park Lands." The metropolis consists of two portions, named North and South Adelaide, which are united by a massive iron bridge that spans the river Torrens, and cost for its erection £22,000. The shops, stores, and Government buildings, are down in South Adelaide; and private residences mainly cover the higher ground of North Adelaide. Many miles of street have been laid out in the two portions of the city. The inhabitants are more staid and settled in their bearing than in the capitals of the sister colonies; and trade seems to be carried on in a more safe and steady manner. In and about the city there are good public buildings; and near it there are populous suburbs, clustered pleasingly together, under such familiar names as Kensington, Norwood, and Stepney. Adelaide, lying in the centre of a vast plain, having a radius of several miles in each direction, with park-like suburbs on every side, and richly clothed hills at the back, is a well situated and pleasant capital.

RELIGION, both in it, and through the colony, is wholly sustained by the voluntary efforts of the several denominations. No Government money is here given to any section of the Church; but every community of professing Christians is left to itself. The Episcopal Church is feeble, comparatively. The bishop, in his gabled residence at North Adelaide, is supported by a beneficent endowment from Miss Coutts; but most of the clergy have to eke out their scanty livings by teaching, or by cultivating vineyards. Roman Catholics, too, though said to number seventeen thousand in the colony, having no State aid, are feeble and low. Congregationalists, Baptists, and the Free Church of Scotland, as well as the German Lutherans, have their churches in the capital and in the colony. There are some three hundred Jews in South Australia, who have their synagogue in Adelaide. Methodism is strong and prosperous here. By the Government returns, it numbers nearly twice as many attendants at its worship as are found in connexion with any other Christian body. It was the first religious community organized and established in the colony. It was introduced by two excellent men, Messrs. East and Boots, who had worked together at Kingscote, on Kangaroo Island; and who, in remembrance of Wesleyan services at home, had there worshipped God together in their carpenter's shop, with as many as could be induced to join them. Immediately upon the formation of the settlement, and before any house could be erected upon the surveyed allotment of Adelaide, a class-meeting was held by Mr. Abbott, in a rude hut on the bank of the river Torrens. This was the first place of Methodist worship in the city. The next was in the kitchen of the English wooden house of Edward Stephens, Esq., son of the late Rev. John Stephens, known and venerated in British Methodism. In this kitchen, Methodism was first organized in 1837, for Adelaide and South Australia. The foundation-stone of a chapel in Hindley Street was soon afterwards laid by Mrs. Edward Stephens, daughter of the late Mr. Baron, of Hull. The appointment of local-preachers followed, and, true to the missionary character of Methodism, the services of one of them were wholly given to the Aborigines. Before the end of the year 1838, the Rev. William Longbottom, a Wesleyan missionary, proceeding from Tasmania to Swan River, was, with his family, wrecked on the coast of South Australia, when he took the charge and oversight of the church thus providentially prepared for him by the previous and voluntary association of the Methodists there. Since then Methodism has continued to advance; and now, in the colony, there are 138 chapels and preaching-places, 15 ministers, 182 local-preachers, 216 class-leaders, 5,952 Sunday-scholars, 3,129 church-members, and more than 20,000 regular attendants at its public services. The total cost of its church-property has been £68,000. It has expended upon ecclesiastical buildings during the last year upwards of £4,000; and beyond supporting its ministry and its numerous agencies and institutions within the colony, it supplies, annually, more than £1,000 for Missions to the heathen in regions beyond Australia.

*Wed., March* 27.—The weather cool, and the sea rough. Steamer rolled much; and a fine horse on board, valued at three hundred pounds, died with fright. The owner was with us, and bore his loss bravely. He was an intelligent, well-informed, extensive land-holder in Western Australia; and the information he gave me concerning that colony agreed with the previous communications received from other intelligent informants who had long known it.

WESTERN AUSTRALIA is the poorest and least prosperous of all the Australian colonies, and seems to be almost struggling for existence. Although it is full thirty years since it was founded; is eight times as large as the United Kingdom; and boasts a coast-line of 4,000 miles; yet, through mismanagement, and a series of disasters, it has progressed but little; and its resources are only slenderly known, compared with those of the other Australian colonies. For want of sufficient free labourers it was made, at its own request, a penal settlement in 1850; and some whom I conversed with in Victoria are of opinion that this was what seriously checked the immigration of a better class. Others, however, like my experienced friend on board, who had lived there, contend that, if it had not shared the convict system, the colony would not have been so far advanced as it is; and are urgent that a larger number of prisoners and ticket-of-leave men should be sent from the parent-country to Western Australia. From what I saw of the working of the convict system at Albany on my way out, and from what I heard from ministers and friends who had resided in the colony, I should say, that the latter opinion is correct. And, as far as I could learn, for the "banished ones" sent there, the situation and circumstances of Western Australia are most appropriate. There is no running away, except to starvation and death; and in the arrangements made for remuneration and freedom, there is powerful motive for industry and reformation. There are in the contents of this colony strong inducements to emigrants. The general aspect of the scenery is said to resemble what is found on the eastern side of Australia, only the mountains and rivers are upon a less extensive scale. The climate is described as the most healthy known,—the number of deaths reported being surprisingly few in proportion.

There is, I am told, rich loam in "Herefordshire,"—vaguely known as "the country over the hills,"—which, sooner or later, must be thickly studded with farmsteads, and which in itself would not only produce corn enough for the consumption of all in Western Australia, but also yield a large surplus. Some express a hope that the rumoured discovery of additional metallic treasure will attract more enterprising persons towards it, and make it less and less dependent upon convict labour. At the end of 1859 there were eight copper and four lead mines being worked in the colony. The "Wheal Fortune" copper mine yields, on the average, twenty-eight per cent. of metal: and the "Geraldine" lead mine eighty-four. Horses, which are bred in great numbers, and cattle, with hard, durable timber, are, at present, among its most valuable commodities. The total exports of 1859 show an increase of £93,037, against £78,648 in 1858. From the Government returns for the end of 1859, it appears that there was then in Western Australia a population of nearly fifteen thousand; the increase in five years not having been more than four thousand. About four-fifths of these are Protestants; but I am informed that the Roman Catholics, from colonial land in their possession, support high-class school establishments, to which Protestants send their youth, perhaps, too confidently, for education. The Wesleyans, who in numbers rank next to the Church of England, have two English missionaries: they are stationed at Perth and York, and itinerate in the surrounding country, preaching in some eleven places of worship; but from communications received from them, it is plain they have been little encouraged in their isolated fields of labour.

*Thurs. and Frid., March* 28 *and* 29.—Sea calmer, and weather warmer.

*Sat., March* 30.—Saw land by three, P.M., and anchored in King George's Sound at eight.

*Sun., March* 31.—The "Jeddo" arrived by half-past seven in the morning. We went on board; saw our cabin, which had been reserved for us from Sydney; and then were rowed ashore, where we heard a good sermon in the small Episcopal Church at Albany on the Resurrection of Christ,—it being Easter Sunday. After the service, we again saw many natives here with their skin-dresses and spears. By half-past two we went on board the "Jeddo," and about an hour afterwards set sail, taking our last farewell of Australian land.

---

OUR views on this vast Island Continent had greatly enlarged since we touched at King George's Sound in December, 1860, on our way out. We had measured it by travel to and fro in lengths of 500, 600, and 1,300 miles in our several stages. We had entered its bays and harbours; had tossed up and down in its straits and gulfs; and we had rushed along on its railways, or jolted over its plank and "corduroy" roads in the interior. And though we knew when we came the length and breadth of the colony, as being 2,400 by 1,700 miles, with a coast-line engirdling it round of 8,000 miles;—though we had been told it was nearly equal in superficial contents to all Europe; that it would hold all its nations; and that if lifted up bodily to be put down against the United Kingdom, it would make a land-passage either to the East on the one hand, or from Ireland to America on the other,—yet it was not until we had travelled about and upon it, and had personally observed it for successive hundreds of miles, that we could appreciate its extent. How ancient, or how modern, may have been its origin, we could not learn, with all inquiries concerning its geological formation and structure. The signs of volcanic agency present themselves in almost all parts; and on the east, especially, the ever-toiling mason insect has built up massive and far-extending reefs of coral, that serve as a vast breakwater against the surge and roll of the Pacific Ocean. Its mountain-system is peculiar. Instead of running lengthwise with the continent, as in the countries of the old world,—where every range, however tortuous, agrees in general with the length of the country in which it lies,—the mountains of Australia stretch transversely from north to south; while the Australian continent is longest from west to east. Indeed, if viewed in relation to the scientific theories based upon investigation of the earth's crust on the northern side of the globe, this "great South Land" is full of anomalies and contradictions. And so it is with its animal and vegetable productions. It has *black* swans, *white* eagles, quadrupeds with birds' bills, cherries growing with stones outside, and trees which shed their bark instead of their leaves. It is not strictly correct to speak of Australia as "Our Antipodes;" for a straight line passing through the earth's centre from us to the opposite side of the globe would emerge at "Antipodes Island," S.W. of New Zealand, and not through Australian territory; but the time of our winter is the Australian summer; and while the coldest winds here are from the north, the coolest there are from the south. What the interior of Australia is cannot yet be told. Exploring expeditions, with troops of horses and camels, have gone forth to search their way across from south to north; but up to this time there is a vast blank of knowledge around the inner regions. Whether there be an inland stony desert, from whence the hot winds come charged with their heated dust, or a vast central lake, which produces violent inundations that overwhelm large tracts of country, and swell the rivers with mighty torrents, is not yet known. And hitherto almost each succeeding explorer has contradicted, by personal observation, the conjectures of his predecessor. Stuart's Diary, in his recent expedition, would lead us to conclude that the interior of Australia is, in rich grass land, mountain-ranges, and metallic ores, fully equal to the outward boundaries.* For full and positive knowledge, however, of the character and contents of the central interior we must wait awhile. But the large extent, the great importance, and the priceless value, of this island-continent on the other side of the globe, to England, and to the world, demand consideration and acknowledgment. Here is territory at the ends of the earth, holding in its bosom mineral treasures the most precious, overspread with lands rich and fruitful, and extending through every variety of climate: territory nearly as large as Europe, girdled round with a noble coast-line, full of fine bays and safe harbours;

* Since the above was written, the testimony of Stuart on the character of the interior of Australia has been confirmed by the Report of the only surviving member of one of the exploring parties referred to in preceding lines. But, alas! Burke, the enterprising leader of the party, and nearly twenty of his brave attendants, now sleep in the silent wilderness, where they fell through exhaustion.

situated midway between America and Africa, and at the extremity of Asia, with "the multitude of the isles" scattered over its seas; fast filling with an energetic Anglo-Saxon race allied to Britain by birth, political constitution, and commerce; and who are there reproducing English homes, English farmsteads, and—beyond any other British dependency—importing, for the increased multitudes, English manufactures.* To Great Britain, such an ally is beyond all calculable value and importance in its situation and worth. Nor is it less important in its moral and religious relations. It is a *Christian* land, in the midst of dark, idolatrous, and heathen regions. It has already its Bible Societies and Missionary institutions, and is sending forth its agents to surrounding nations and tribes; though, sixty years ago, it was itself but a desert and a wilderness, peopled by a few savages. It has in it the inalienable love of British freedom and rights of conscience. It has established in all its colonies the mighty engine of a free press. It is the determined foe of despotism and persecution. And in the great battle of Armageddon, which is as likely to be fought on the other side of the globe where Satan has had his seat so long, as it is on this side, it shall be, if faithful, and "valiant for the truth," among the strongest and most honourable of the agencies employed by Christ in the universal coming of His kingdom.

Several questions have come more or less under consideration in the colonies, which will, doubtless, engage

* The last returns give for Australia, Tasmania, and New Zealand, nearly one million and a quarter of colonists and settlers: two thirds males, and one third females,—the discrepancy in the relative numbers of the sexes being mainly in the newer colonies. The total imports for these are £26,742,686, and the entire exports £23,163,080.

further attention before they shall be decided; such as the reduction of the price of waste lands, so as to encourage their occupation by settlers, and to bring them more speedily under cultivation,—protective duties on colonial produce, so as to secure for it preference over foreign importations,—the payment of members of the legislature,—the reconstitution of the Upper House or Legislative Council,—the entire abolition of State aid to Religion,—the substitution of one Education Board for the present conflicting systems of "National" and "Denominational,"— and the establishment of a Federal Government for the union and benefit of the whole group of Australian colonies. These and other questions are more or less discussed in all the colonies, and will be likely to supply in them topics of popular excitement for years to come. The last-named question—that of Federal Government—is not so ardently entertained as it was some time ago. In 1857 the question was mooted by the youthful colony of Victoria, and was favourably responded to by the sister colonies, as well as encouraged by the Imperial Government at home. But since then, the colonies have been fully occupied with their own self-government; and, probably, as time advances, and each colony shall have decided constitutional questions for itself, there will be less and less disposition to surrender to a general and comparatively irresponsible Government power possessed and felt by the colonies separately. And it is a significant fact, that in the recent appointment of a successor to Governor Denison for the parent colony, Sir John Young's official title is that of "Governor-in chief of New South Wales," instead of "Governor-general," as on previous similar appointments.

One enigma presents itself to the reflecting mind in relation to Australia, which a visitor and traveller there like myself cannot escape the consideration of,—that is the fate of the poor ABORIGINES. A visitor sees remnants of their different tribes in every colony, and one learns everywhere that they are fast fading away both in strength and numbers.* They are the lowest and most degraded of the human family; have persistently withstood all attempts to civilize and Christianize them, and in another generation, probably, will have entirely ceased to exist in the hitherto occupied portions of Australia. Poor, wretched beings! inferior in figure and feature to untutored Africans. Dark earth-brown in colour; with sloe-black savage eyes widely set against their high cheek-bones and under protruding bushy black eye-brows; with distended nostrils, wide mouth, broad, pouting lips, matted, long, black hair, shrunken frame, long thin arms, short outspread feet, spindle-legs, bedaubed and greased from head to foot, and without decency and shame. Such were the natives I saw in the different colonies, in their forlorn groups of men and women,—with their sickly children, and lean, hungry dogs; and though in climbing trees, hurling the boomerang, or throwing the spear, they exhibit in their attitudes and movements vigour and grace which would ally them with the great Papuan race, so widely spread over the vast south-eastern hemisphere, and show them to be the descendants of an enterprising and skilful people,—yet as soon as they resume their ordinary forms and modes of life and countenance, they exhibit a feeble, dejected, and

* It is estimated that in all the Australian colonies there may remain of them some 200,000.

dispirited look which tells of wretchedness and destruction. It is reported that in the north, where they have been less disturbed by Europeans, the aborigines are a bold, athletic, and valiant people. It may be so. I suppose from concurrent testimonies on this question it is so. But I can only write of what I saw; and those which I beheld are among the most feeble and abject of the human family; and had upon their very frames and looks the signs of dejection and death.

Laudable and praiseworthy efforts to rescue the dark natives from their impending fate have been made in all the colonies by the Government, as well as by voluntary associations and benevolent individuals; but with almost universal failure. Whatever might be the dishonourable conduct of early colonists, who, for safety or amusement, hunted and shot down this "black game" in the woods and forests, no ill-treatment of the aborigines is allowed now, with impunity. On the other hand, paternal tenderness and compassion towards them has in recent times been carried almost to excess. No expense, or labour, has been spared on their behalf; yet they refuse continued association with the civilizing race, and waste away in their own wretchedness. Numberless instances are quoted of education and employment of the aborigines by European colonists; but, almost in every case, the native child or servant, taught and clothed, has gone back to the wild tribe to which he or she belonged, and sunk back into barbarism. In some few instances conversions to God have been known among them; and our Wesleyan Methodists, who, like most other Christian communities in the land, organized special Missions for them, have had, in more than one case, religious teachers raised up among the natives; but sooner or later the seed died in the ground, and brought forth no fruit. A short time before I was at Adelaide, the Legislative Council for South Australia had, in concern for the wasting aborigines, appointed a special committee to inquire into their state, and into the best means to be employed for their rescue and improvement. The Hon. G. M. Waterhouse was on that committee, and reported to me its proceedings and results, as well as presented to me official documents concerning it. That committee examined the most competent witnesses to be obtained, both Europeans and natives, and found that the rapid decrease of the aborigines was attributable to infanticide, the women, or "gins," being unwilling to bear the burden of more than one or two children; to certain rites performed upon young men of some tribes, impairing their physical powers; to the introduction among them, by Europeans, of more aggravating sensual disease than existed previously; to excess in the use of intoxicating liquors; to promiscuous intercourse of the sexes among the youth of the natives as well as with Europeans, by which the births among the aborigines were seriously reduced; and to the great disproportion of males and females in the several tribes. In addition to these causes of diminution in numbers, it was also explicitly elicited, that the adoption by the natives of semi-civilized habits, such as sleeping in thin tattered blankets, instead of thick and warm opossum rugs, was inducing pulmonary disease, which had become extensively destructive and wasting to their lives. The evidence supplied gave other fearful glimpses into their state of ignorance and degradation. Cannibalism was more than hinted at. There seemed to be no knowledge, or idea, of a supreme Being among them, except that of a dark spirit who came forth at night prowling abroad to inflict disease and death. Deeds of treachery, murder, and blood, were referred to, as well as sensual rioting among old and young the most revolting. And the testimonies borne by benevolent labourers for the sinking race, on their own failures and disappointments, were the most disheartening. The doom of this people creates in us afflictive thoughts on the fearful consequences of sin to nations; but the filling of the vast island-continent with a better and prosperous race silvers the edge of the black cloud which hangs over the mind while we think of the Australian aborigines. In God's counsels concerning nations and tribes we must humbly and reverently acquiesce: "the Judge of all the earth shall do right!"

# Part Third.

## RETURN HOME.

# RETURN HOME.

## CHAPTER VIII.

VOYAGE back from Australia to Ceylon—Visits to other Buddhist Temples—Interior and Fort revisited—Farewell to Ceylon—Voyage to Bombay—Caves of Elephanta—Ramble through Bombay—The Parsees—Voyage from Bombay to Aden—Voyage up the Red Sea—Scene of the Israelites' Passage—Arrival at Suez—At Cairo—Loss of Luggage—Arrival at Alexandria—Luggage not found—Departure for the Holy-Land.

*Mon., April 1, to Frid., 12.*—VOYAGE over the Indian Ocean, from King George's Sound to Ceylon. At the beginning the weather was rough, but our ship sped quickly along. As we advanced, we had the advantage of the trade-winds, and made twelve and thirteen knots an hour. The weather became increasingly warmer as we approached the tropics, and towards the end of our voyage we were within the "doldrums," or contending trade-winds; so we had doldrum weather, showery and squallish, with moist, "muggy" heat. The thermometer ranged, during our voyage, from 70° to 90°. Sir John D—— and his lady, friends of our hosts at the Glebe, Sydney, were on board. Sir John had been acting for the Chief-Justice in New South Wales, and from some years' residence in the colony, as well as from his associations with courts and officials, increased my information concerning Australian life and society.

Captain B——, also, a retiring police magistrate, was with us, and several " squatters;" so that there was no difficulty in obtaining any particulars desired in my inquiry concerning the colonies. Our fellow-passengers joined us devoutly in the religious services of the Sabbath, and were pleasant and intelligent companions. Captain Soames was a good commander of the ship, and the crew were orderly and well-behaved. We reached the harbour of Point de Galle by six on Friday evening; but as no pilot came to us before sunset, we were not able to enter; so the ship beat about on the outside of the reefs through the night.

*Sat., April* 13.—In the harbour by seven in the morning. Breakfasted on board, but went on shore in the forenoon, and drove up to Rev. John Scott's. The captain reported to us, that his passage from Sydney to Galle was the quickest ever made.

*Sun., April* 14.—Preached in the forenoon in the Presbyterian Church, and in the evening in the Wesleyan Chapel to large congregations; the majority of our passengers in the " Jeddo" being present.

*Mon., April* 15.—Drove into the Fort; and in the evening to Bonavista, where we visited the clergyman, and went to Mrs. Gibson's native school, of which he has the oversight. About thirty native girls are boarded and educated here, and about thirty more attend daily. After sketching the harbour from this point, returned to the Fort, and held a prayer-meeting, at which I addressed a goodly number of persons.

*Tues., April* 16.—Went to a celebrated Buddhist temple on a hill in the neighbourhood of Galle. In the house adjoining there were some half-dozen priests. I talked at length with the chief-priest, an intelligent and learned man, who made earnest inquiries concerning England and Australia. He led me through his establishment, showed me his collection of pictures and books; and in the visitors' book, which he kept, were the names of Bunsen, Pritchard, and other celebrities. In his study he had the Scriptures, and some Christian tracts, in Singhalese; and he fain would have had the use of our Singhalese press at Colombo for the printing of some work on Buddhism which he had prepared. It was explained to him how that could not be allowed with a Christian missionary's press; and when asked why he and his people, if they believed in their system of religion, did not send missionaries to propagate it in England, he shook his head, and said, the English were too firm and resolute to afford any hope of success; they were not like the people of the East. At a slight hint, he put on his best saffron robes and sandals; took his large fan and white handkerchief in his hand; and stood in his verandah to be sketched. He was a venerable man, of good form and features; but the younger priests who stood around, and eagerly looked on, were not so well favoured. They had a dirty, monkish look, though ablutions and bodily cleanliness are strictly enjoined upon them by Buddhism. The temple adjoining was a hexagon in form, and of moderate size. It was covered with Italian tiles, and had a verandah all round, with hanging lamps. On opening the door, a large yellow figure of Buddha was seen sitting within a glass-case, and having a table for flower-offerings in front. There were several smaller figures, also within the case; and all over the temple walls, within, were painted yellow-robed figures of Buddha. The priests seemed to set little store by the flower-offerings; for they swept them from the table most unceremoniously, to make space for the sketch-book. The court in which the temple stood was, in its enclosure and objects, similar to that at Belligam, described on a former page; and between it and the dwelling of the priests, was a canopied reading-stand, whence the priest rehearsed the doctrines of his sect from Buddhist books. The whole establishment was surrounded by lofty cocoa-nut trees, and a profusion of foliage. On returning to the Fort I went with Mr. Scott into the civil courts, and was courteously invited by Mr. G—— to sit with him upon the bench, and observe the trials. They were conducted through an interpreter; the hall was crowded with natives; and the legal practitioners were both natives and burghers.

*Wed., April* 17.—Went some miles up the Gindari river, and saw some fine open scenery, with rice paddies at the sides, and natives ploughing with oxen. Buffaloes were enjoying themselves in the water, as before. The river was of strong volume in several parts, and whirling eddies appeared at its turns; but our frail bark of native manufacture, sheltered in the middle for us with palm-leaves, was skilfully managed by the Singhalese boatmen, and we went smoothly and rapidly along. Some pleasant villages lay over the fields, both on our right and left; and it was interesting to observe the natives, in their bright and picturesque costumes, going to or from market, on paths across the cheerful green fields. In our river-voyage we purchased oranges, plucked for us from the trees: these fine fruit were indescribably refreshing in the heat of the day. On our return, we breakfasted on curries, kindly prepared for us by Christian natives in a bungalow, or rest-house, by the water.

*Thurs., April* 18.—In the forenoon had conversations with native ministers and catechists. In the latter part of the day engaged with packing. During the interval of our visits to Ceylon, our clothes, books, and papers, left there until we should return, had been affected by the moist heat of the atmosphere. Our clothes were found damp and clammy, our books faded in the binding, and our manuscripts and writing-paper mouldy and stained. Missionaries, with their books and papers, suffer no little annoyance and loss from this cause.

*Frid., April* 19.—Went down to the Fort, and found that the "Nemesis," for Suez, had already one hundred and fifty first-class passengers, with fifty children, from India, on board, and was also expected at this port to take up passengers from China and Australia, so that she would be fearfully overcrowded, and that down the hot Red Sea passage. We complained of this, after large payment to secure suitable accommodation. An offer was made to us of much better provision, if we would go round by Bombay in one of the Peninsular and Oriental Company's steam-ships, just ready to depart. For health and life, as it seemed to us, we accepted the offer; and at half-past two in the afternoon took our farewell of beautiful Ceylon, and sailed for Bombay in the "Singapore," with about sixty first-class passengers. This steamer was smaller than the one we had quitted, but we had a good cabin assigned to us.

*Sat., April* 20.—Cape Comorin in view at our right. Sea smooth. Very warm weather. Cabin close.

*Sun., April* 21.—We had service on deck, under a double awning, but it was exceedingly hot. During the day the Malabar coast was in sight.

*Mon., April* 22.—The sea was still smooth, and the weather very hot and close. The coast on our right kept in view, with several islands, and the picturesque settlement of Goa,—the Portuguese possession of such bad fame for the doings of the Inquisition.

*Tues., April* 23.—Continuance of fine weather, and the Indian coast, with mountains at a distance, more distinctly in view.

*Wed., April* 24.—Entered Bombay harbour, by four in the morning. Landed immediately after breakfast. Went to the Clarendon Hotel, and had rooms allotted to us; then to the Peninsular and Oriental Company's office, to secure a good cabin in the steamer next going out, being anxious concerning the passage down the Red Sea. We drove through the city; observed that the real Hindoo was larger and stronger in frame than the Singhalese; and that here the crowd of inhabitants was greater than we had seen in Ceylon. I looked into the houses and shops of the natives, went into their markets, and, as far as allowed, approached the courts, tanks, and interiors of Hindu temples. I was not allowed in any case to cross the threshold of these temples; but I stood at the doorways, and saw what there was within; and in some instances the appearance of priests, the daubing upon the idols, and the stalls of the white Brahmin cow, were offensive and disgusting in the extreme. Nor was I allowed to enter what might be called monastic establishments of priests and devotees; but, for two or three annas, I was permitted to advance to the precincts, and observe the lazy recluses stretched at full length upon their mats. Some of the streets of Bombay are large and wide, with shops and stores at the sides projecting in their upper stories, and highly ornamented in wood-carving and colours. In the dark recesses next the streets the natives were seen at work in their several trades and employments, almost naked, as they need to be in the extreme heat of this climate. Parrots and birds of gay-coloured plumage hang commonly at the shop-windows. There are large outspreading suburbs on the land side of the city, studded with luxuriant gardens, mansions, and villas: a spacious park intervenes between the city and the Fort, in which British soldiers and Sepoys parade, and where the *élite* of the inhabitants and residents drive in the afternoon in their splendid equipages, while the military band plays exhilarating tunes. We observed that, next to Europeans, the Parsees appeared to be the chief persons in importance. On returning, we saw in a crowded street a thorough English Jack Tar inflicting, with clenched fists, summary justice upon some natives who had wronged him; and it was surprising to see how that in the midst of hundreds of stout, large men of India, although alone and single-handed, he struck out right and left, as if with his own pair of hands he could master all the native inhabitants of the city. The Hindoos evidently did not understand such John Bull pluck; and fled on the approach of the English sailor, as if they were children!

In the cool of the approaching evening we drove into the outskirts of the city, and along the sea-shore, where spacious mansions, with their tropical gardens, were abundant, and where the more select of British residents and wealthy Parsees were to be seen; and in our drive we went to a famous Hindu tank and temple, as also to the Parsees' lofty tower, where they expose their naked dead to be devoured by vultures and ravenous birds of prey. The suburb in which our hotel was situated is named Byculla, and has in it many large mansions, surrounded by extensive gardens, tastefully laid out, and rich in tropical flowers and fruits. In these the Palmyra, Date, and Betelnut palms, towered in lofty and graceful forms, as they did also in other suburbs adjoining the city. The evening sky was pure and brilliant; but in the night we could hear the dismal howls of numerous jackals.

*Thurs., April* 25.—Rose at half-past five in the morning, and went to the Island of Elephanta, to see the celebrated Caves. We were taken in a bunder-boat by half-a-dozen Hindoo sailors, and a most patriarchal-looking captain. Elephanta is about five miles from the pier of Bombay, in an oblique direction over the harbour; and we had to be carried ashore by natives of the island, because of the shallowness of the water. We then ascended some one hundred and fifty steps, and reached the abode of a pension-sergeant, who had charge of the caves. He went forward with us, about half-way up the mountain, to the front of the principal cave, which was very impressive, and seemed to bring Egypt back before our eyes. It is a huge excavation in the solid mountain rock,—as is well known,—with moulded pillars, and sculptured figures left in stately and bold relief, so as to form a vast solemn temple underground. It is grievous to observe that much of the gigantic sculpture has been wantonly mutilated and broken. The Portuguese have the discredit of this ascribed to them, in their zeal against idolatry; but whether truly or not cannot be learned. And, certainly, a sense of decency might induce mutilation in some parts, where several of the figures have been made to represent the sensual impurities of idolatry. We breakfasted in the cave, and, after sketching the view and plan of it, went to look at the smaller caves on the left side.

The great cave I found to be by measurement one hundred and thirty-three feet long, one hundred and twenty-five feet wide, and seventeen feet high. The roof was supported by twenty-eight pillars and sixteen pilasters, disposed in four rows. Each column stands upon a square pedestal, is fluted, and has a round, richly-moulded capital; but the shaft, instead of being cylindrical, is gradually enlarged towards the middle. Above the tops of the columns a sort of beam-ridge has been left, running transversely, and is, also, well relieved and ornamented. Along the sides of the huge temple are cut out of the rock from forty to fifty colossal figures; some of which have helmets, and others crowns upon their heads. Several of them have four and six arms, holding sceptres, shields, and ensigns of religion and peace. At the south end, facing the main entrance, is an enormous bust, nineteen feet high, with three faces, representing Siva in his triple character of Brahma, Vishnu, and Rama,—the creator, the preserver, and the destroyer. To the right and left of these are sculptured figures illustrative of these powers; and which, for the sake of decency, have been partially broken by axes and hammers. In the cave on the right, and immediately out of the side on the left, are compartments guarded by naked and helmeted figures, in which are altars, with symbols for worship, offensive to modest eyes. The whole design and workmanship shows considerable skill and progress in art. The date of the temple is shrouded in obscurity. Some absurdly ascribe it to Alexander the Great, others to Semiramis;

but it is, undoubtedly, of Hindoo origin; and, though ancient, not so old, perhaps, as the imposing names which some have connected with it would seem to prove. It is not at present used as a temple; but solitary devotees make pilgrimages to it, and offer their prayers and oblations within it. The smaller excavations, on the left side of the mountain, are of the same character, but are to be described as chambers rather than temples; though, from the remnants of altars, and guardian figures upon the doorways, there can be no doubt of their intended use.

We returned at noon to our bunder-boat, and had to be carried to it by the natives through the shoal water. The wind was now strong, so we had to tack about a great deal, and pass Butcher-island, where a mutinous Rajah is confined. On another island which we passed is a very beautiful white mosque. In the afternoon went and sketched, near the railway station, a modern Hindu temple, where there is a college of priests, and large gardens. On returning to our hotel, by a retired walk through the suburbs, we saw palm-trees tapped at the top, and by incisions in the stumps, for "toddy," or intoxicating liquor, which, when distilled, is called "arrack." The daring and the agility of the natives in climbing these lofty, slender trees, surprise Europeans. The musquitoes were tormentors here, but not so numerously as in some places where we had previously been; and during the day we had caught frequent sight of lizards and serpents.

*Frid., April* 26.—Before breakfast visited and sketched another Hindu temple. It was more ancient than the other, and was coloured white, with red lines in its recesses. Several priests were attached to it, and on its stairs, with outstretched hands, performed their morning devotions. After breakfast, drove to the Peninsular and Oriental Company's office, and found a good cabin allotted to us in the "Orissa" steam-ship, which was to leave the next day for Suez. The remainder of the day was spent in company with Mr. K——, the proprietor of the "Bombay Times and Standard," whose friends I had known in Lambeth, and who, from a return list of visitors, had discovered our presence in the city. He showed us the chief places and objects of interest in Bombay, and its extensive suburbs, and explained to us much of East Indian life and society. The Fort we found to be the principal place of merchandise, having in its crowded, narrow streets, bazaars, stores, and other warehouses. The town-hall, museum, and library, are large and creditable institutions on one side of the "Green," as a central open space is designated; and on the other sides are the Mint and Government offices. Huge bales of cotton strewed the piers and quays, ready for shipment to England; and I was informed that about one hundred millions of pounds of cotton were sent annually from that port to Great Britain, and about half the weight to China. It was interesting, on passing the shops, to see the natives working in gold and silver, and at their beautiful inlaid articles. On leaving the Fort we crossed draw-bridges, passed over the esplanade, where soldiers and citizens were promenading, and entered again the main thoroughfare of the city, observing, at the corner on our right, a good depôt of the British and Foreign Bible Society, with adjoining printing-rooms. The streets were thronged with natives, both in dress and undress; and in different parts we alighted to view Hindu temples and Mahomedan mosques, with their deluded devotees. Myriads of pigeons feed around the tanks; and suspended from the branches of trees by their feet, with head downwards, are numerous large bats, or "flying foxes," as they are sometimes called, with their outspread wings dangling loosely in the air, as if they were pieces of wet leather. In the suburbs, on the Byculla side, there are several charitable institutions, having large piles of buildings,—such as hospitals and schools; and there are, in and around the city, ecclesiastical structures belonging to the Church of England, the Presbyterians, and the Free Church of Scotland. We have no missionary here; and there is only one Wesleyan missionary in the entire presidency of Bombay: our missionaries having been sent more to other parts of India.

The most remarkable people in Bombay are the descendants of the ancient Persians, called PARSEES. They were driven here by Mahomedan persecution, and have shown themselves to be an intelligent, energetic, and gratefully loyal race. It is estimated that not more than 150,000 of them are left in all parts, and that 110,000, or more, are in the island of Bombay. They have wrought their way up to a first position in the city, and successfully compete with Europeans in trade and merchandise. Indeed, they are the traders, bankers, brokers, and accountants of the place, and fill the Fort with their stores, warehouses, and offices. Their dress is exceedingly neat and clean. They have a dark chocolate-coloured covering to their heads, which is between a helmet and a turban, in shape; and some of them wear silk trousers and white tunics, and drive in splendid equipages. Many of them reside in stately mansions in the suburbs, surrounded by extensive gardens. They are characterized by truthfulness, sobriety, and loyalty to England; and every year they are becoming more and more Anglicized in their views of education and domestic life. It is not without meaning that they have been denominated the "Saxons of the East." One of them has obtained a world-wide celebrity by his munificent donations in charity and benevolence of £250,000, and more, given to various objects; and by the bestowment of a baronetcy upon him and his descendants from the Queen of England. Sir Jamsetjee Jeejeebhoy, Bart., the prince-merchant of Bombay, who rose to wealth and honour by his own energy and benevolence, has bequeathed a patrician name to his family.

One custom of the Parsees is revolting to Europeans, and that is the treatment of their dead. When life becomes extinct, the body is wrapped in clean clothes, and placed on an oblong piece of polished stone, which is laid on the floor, while the members of the family sit around it and mourn. Then, before sunset, if possible, the body is placed on an iron bier, and is borne by corpse-bearers to the *Dokhma*, or Tower of Silence, erected in some solitary place, and generally upon a mountain. Across iron grating, at the top of this high cylindrical roofless tower, the naked body is laid, where it is immediately preyed upon by bare-headed vultures, ravenous kites, and other carrion-birds, which hover, scream, and contend there for their victims. The bones, stripped of their flesh, fall through the iron grating into a golgotha pit beneath. This is a barbarous practice by a people so clean, intelligent, and refined, as the Parsees.

My host of the Clarendon was a Parsee; and though he had there a large and airy establishment, yet he had his country house for his family, his private carriage, personal attendants, and lived in first style. He was a sensible, well-educated, well-informed man, and was most courteously communicative on all questions proposed to him.

*Sat., April* 27.—Drove to the Fort at eleven A.M.; bought some trifles of inlaid work from the natives. Took boat, and went on board the "Orissa" at three; dined at six; and at half-past eight we steamed out of the magnificent roadstead of Bombay for Aden and Suez.

*Sun., April* 28.—Read the Liturgy, and preached on board, morning and evening. We had music and chanting, and there were good and attentive congregations, out of our two hundred passengers.

*Mon., April* 29, *to Sat., May* 4.—Voyaged on pleasantly in fine weather.—We had religious service each morning in the saloon at half-past nine, well attended; and on the last day the Arabian coast appeared at our right, like Alpine hills overshadowed by long horizontal clouds.

*Sun., May* 5.—Found ourselves at Aden when we awoke in the morning. We had religious service on board morning and evening; but the Sabbath was sadly desecrated by many, who purchased feathers, baskets, and coral, from Jews and Arabs. Left Aden at half-past six: a hot night.

*Mon., May* 6, *to Frid., the* 10th.—Sailed up the Red Sea under a moderate heat and agreeable weather. Sketched the Sinaitic range, and copied in colours the fiery sunset.

*Sat., May* 11.—Sketched Moses' valley, and the part of the shore said by some to be that where the Israelites crossed; but others contend that they went over higher up, beyond Suez, where the channel has been dried, and filled with the sand of the desert. If here, at the first-named point, one can see how the multitude were shut up to crossing the sea, or going back to the swords of their pursuers; and if the removal of the place of crossing to a shallower part be to lessen the difficulty, such an attempt is vain; for the Passage of the Israelites was a *miracle* wrought by the direct interference of the Almighty, to whom a deep or shallow water was the same. We reached Suez before noon, remained there till three, when under advice from steamboat and railway authorities, we left our heavy luggage to be sent after us, and set off by rail to Cairo. We arrived at the old city of enchantment by half-past six in the evening.

*Sun., Mon.* 12.—Our principal portmanteau was not forthcoming at Cairo, as promised; so we had to hasten forward to Alexandria, to see if it were sent forward with the general luggage for England. I went on board the English steamer, about to leave, to search for it; but could neither see nor hear anything of it. We were strongly advised not to sail without it, but, as we valued it, to remain in Egypt until it was sought for and found. So, while inquiries were made, we resolved to visit the Holy Land, finding that in a Russian steamer, leaving Alexandria early the next morning, we could be at Jaffa twenty-four hours afterwards, and at Jerusalem on the day of landing, if we pleased. We had not spared private expenditure before this in seeing anything desirable, that was not strictly within the range of my mission; and ascertaining that for fifty pounds, or so, we could have guide, guard, provision, and travelling, and yet be back at Alexandria for the next Peninsular and Oriental Company's steam-ship to England,—while to remain in Egypt during the interval, would be to remain among objects and scenes already familiar to us,—we engaged our dragoman, and with an American friend, Mr. Hatfield, who had come with us from Bombay, where he had resided as Consul for the United States, went forth to Palestine.

# CHAPTER IX.

DEPARTURE for the Holy Land—Jaffa—Pilgrims returning from the Holy City—Associations of "Joppa"—Journey to Ramleh—Night at the Latin Convent—Scriptural sites in the journey from Ramleh—Watch-houses—First sight of Jerusalem—Church of the Holy Sepulchre—Holy places—View from St. Stephen's Gate—Valley of Jehoshaphat—The Mount of Olives—Zion Gate—The Jews' Quarter—Mount Zion—Ancient and Modern City—Walls and Streets—Bethany—Church of the Ascension—Sepulchre of the Holy Virgin—Other Sepulchres—Tophet—Aceldama—Jews' Wailing Place—Solomon's Bridge—Second visit to the Church of the Holy Sepulchre.

*Mon., May* 12.—LEFT the harbour of Alexandria, in the Russian steamer, at five in the morning. It was a large, good vessel, and had been built at Greenock, in Scotland. The officers were gentlemanly in their demeanour, and exceedingly attentive to us, both at the table and elsewhere. We were nearly all the first-class passengers on board. Strewn over the deck, in the forepart of the ship, were Mahomedans, with their many wives, returning from Mecca; and both Jew and Christian pilgrims going to Jerusalem. Some of these were haggard, wretched-looking beings, with anxious spirits, that seemed to give them no rest. The Mahomedan women were curtained round in an upper bed-chamber-like apartment, and had Nubian guardians; but whenever we looked towards them we could see their bright, dark eyes peering at us from behind the curtains. The weather was fine during the day, and in the earlier part of it we sighted, in the distance, Rosetta, and then Damietta, and saw plainly how the deep blue water of the Mediterranean was discoloured by the out-flowing of the Nile into it at its mouths from the Delta. The evening was serene, and a rosy emerald flush tinged both sea and sky.

*Tues., May* 13.—Arrived at Jaffa, the ancient Joppa, at six o'clock in the morning: were rowed ashore in a small boat, by native boatmen,—Abram, our dragoman, filling the boat with baggage, and with tent, beds, and firelocks. It seemed perilous to pass into the narrow opening of low, craggy rocks amidst the roll and foam of the angry surf that dashed upon them; but we rode safely between the reefs which make the harbour, and then, free from the breakers, floated smoothly to the quay, where we landed on the backs or in the arms of Arabs, amidst deafening voices, which we could not understand, except at the loud and vociferous cry of "backsheesh." Abram soon, by a small coin or two, had all his stores through the "Customs," and cleared our way through a noisy and dense crowd of pilgrims returning from the great feast at Jerusalem, who were eager to get home by the Russian steamer we had left. We were led to the hotel for breakfast; and while horses and mules were obtained for our ride to Jerusalem, I took a guide, and went through the dirty, lane-like, crowded streets of the city, to view the points and places of traditional interest in it. I went to the House of Simon the Tanner by the sea-side, as it is called, and to the dwelling of Tabitha, whom Peter raised to life,—or rather to what they show for these. The town consists chiefly of shops for the sale of old arms, old clothes, tobacco, and various fruits. After viewing the site of Napoleon's bloody massacre in 1799, and the ornamented fountains and gate, I emerged from the city on the land side, where the road and ground around it were crowded with camels, asses, fruit, and dirty Arabs; and passed onwards some quarter of a mile to see the orange and lemon-gardens, so famous in their relation to Jaffa. The air was richly scented with the golden fruit which hung around us; and we were offered a hamper full of large delicious oranges for a shilling's worth of Syrian money. My walk through the city had not at all increased my admiration of it. Jaffa looks well from the water, where its streets of houses rise one over another in terrace-form, from the blue sea at its base to the sloping hill on which it stands, and with its palm and orange-trees at the side; but no sooner do you enter its narrow, filthy streets, and see its motley throng of dirty Arabs, Jews, and pilgrims, than, in remembrance of the first sight of it from the sea, you think of Campbell's line,—

"'Tis distance lends enchantment to the view."

Still, Jaffa is an interesting place. Perhaps, but few of its buildings are more than one hundred years old; so that its houses of apostolic miracles can only represent the sites of the veritable structures belonging to them, if even they do that. But if not so old as some have affirmed,—and if not the place of Noah and his ark,—it is, undoubtedly, one of the oldest seaports known. It was given to the tribe of Dan in the allotments of the promised land. It was the chief port of the Jews to which cedar from Lebanon was brought, for both the first and second temple of the Jews. It was at Joppa Jonah embarked for Tarshish, when he sought to flee from the presence of the Lord, and escape his unwelcome mission to Nineveh. It was there that Peter had his singular vision in a trance, and where he raised Tabitha to life again. And since then it has been the key to the Holy Land for crusaders and conquerors.

We left Jaffa on horseback, at three in the afternoon, to reach Ramleh, said to be the ancient Arimathea, before dark. Abram, our guide and guard, went before, with sword at his side, and a huge firelock in his hand; and our American companion had pistols loaded and primed in his waistband. I and my wife went unarmed, having no fear of danger, and on our slender Arab steeds pranced our way on the road through the gardens—enclosed by prickly pears higher than ourselves on horseback—in the suburbs of the city, and then over the sweet plains of Sharon. My broad, packed-out, Turkish saddle, and heavy angled stirrups, did not contribute to my comfort in riding; but the thought of being in the "Holy Land," and going to "Jerusalem," reconciled me to an uneasy seat, especially as Mrs. Jobson on her English side-saddle, cantered and galloped so comfortably along. The "plain of Sharon," though not yielding to our view any roses, or lilies of the valley, such as furnished emblems for the bards of Judah, was yet rich and beautiful. In this fruitful plain were reapers and gleaners, with camels laden with corn, and sweet lark-like birds singing among the stubble, and in the flowery meadows of intervening lands. The peasantry were somewhat Egyptian in their features and colour, as if they had partaken, in some degree, of the old Philistine blood, from the district lying between their country and Egypt.

But they were better clothed than their neighbours of the Nile; and their striped and many-coloured jackets were a picturesque sight. We met in our way pilgrims on mules, chiefly Greek Christians, returning from the great festival of the holy city; and some of the stout Russian women, who rode astride on huge loads of kit and bedding, and shook heavily at the trot of their burdened steeds, were singular in their appearance. We sought to see, on our left towards the sea, by the use of our hand-glass, the remnants of the cities of the Philistines, such as Ashdod, Gath, Ascalon, and Gaza; but we could sight nothing in that mysterious region, which from childhood had been associated in our minds with Samson and giants, but sand-hills and barren mounds. After some three hours' ride over the gently undulating, enamelled plains, we reached Ramleh, where we were to rest for the night. The town, as seen on approaching it, is pleasantly situated on a gentle elevation, and its white buildings are picturesquely embowered in olive-groves and orchards, with here and there a lofty palm overhanging a mosque or a convent. There is a noble tower on the right, now viewed as a minaret, but which some contend was originally the campanile of a magnificent church, the remains of which are said to be near to it. Certain it is, that this was an important place in the hands of the crusaders; and it was here that they held sumptuous feasts in honour of their patron saints. We rode down a winding road, fenced by hedges of cactus; and at the entrance of the town alighted at the Latin Convent, where we were hospitably received, and waited on at dinner, in their refectory, by friars, each in his brown-hooded dress and waist-rope. They were very obliging; and an Italian, who served Mrs. Jobson and me at table, became almost loving in his demeanour, when I told him that I was a Christian minister who had visited his native country, and seen the Pope. The brethren showed me the chapel of Nicodemus, and said he and Joseph of Arimathea lived there; also another chapel near to it. Both chapels were showily fitted up with presentation-pictures and glittering furniture. But my wife was not allowed to accompany me : these chapels being beyond the precincts of approach allowed in the convent to females. After careful preparation for us by the friar *valet-de-chambre*, in our stone-walled sleeping-room on the ground floor, we retired to rest; and, wearied with excitement and horseback exercise, slept soundly within our mosquito-curtains, until awakened the next morning by the matin-bell and chant of the convent.

*Wed., May* 14.—Left Ramleh on horseback at six in the morning for Jerusalem. We passed through narrow, crooked streets, in which were lounging and sauntering mingled Moslems and Christians, and in which, stretched at full length in the dust and filth, were many hairless, scabby dogs. After emerging from the town, and descending past its burial ground, we rode several miles through plains and fields, with the "mountains of Israel" before us. Lydda, now called Ludd, where Peter, in the name of Christ, raised Æneas from his bed of palsy, and which is the reputed birth-place of England's patron saint, St. George, was seen on our left; with its group of pure white buildings, bordered with sweet green foliage, and nestling on the side of a gently-moulded hill; while beyond it, stretching far away to the sea, swelled Mount Carmel. We soon began to ascend rocky and rugged steeps; and passing at the foot of a desolate-looking village, where we were importuned by clamorous beggars, we wound our way round the village of Lâtrôn, at which, the monks say, the "penitent thief" had his abode, and used to descend upon unwary travellers. It is now a heap of ruins upon the brow of a steep hill. The day became increasingly hot; and after two hours' ride we rested awhile under a broad overshadowing fig-tree, which might have well served as an oratory for Nathanael. Afterwards we rode on for another hour; and then, in a valley among olive-trees, rested again, making the ground our pilgrim's table, on which to take refreshment.

Resuming our travel, we entered more slippery and shelving gorges, or roads, and met many pilgrims of various nations, chiefly Russians and Greeks; but there were some French officers among them in full uniform. The women pilgrims were, as before, astride on mules or donkeys. Towards noon the road began to be all uphill, and was exceedingly broken and difficult: it being chiefly formed along rocky ruts and crevices, intersected by large boulders, and adown which the waters rush in wet seasons. Thus our way was often for a long space over bare and slippery rock, and apparently most perilous. But our horses, though shod over the entire foot, and that without any points, hooks, or heels, were sure in their tread; and we progressed safely. We passed by Beit Nûbah, where Richard Cœur-de-Lion made some brilliant skirmishes without going forth to take Jerusalem; and also Anwâs, which Eusebius and Jerome affirm to be the Emmaus to which the two saddened disciples were walking when the risen Saviour joined Himself to them, and where afterwards

He made Himself known in the breaking of bread. But Anwâs is more than threescore furlongs from Jerusalem, and is too far for the disciples, after their evening meal, to have returned to the city that night, as the Scriptures affirm they did. We also passed by Kuryet, said to be the ancient Kirjath-jearim, though, if so, the ark "brought into the house of Abinadab" must have had a rough and steep ascent. His house, however, Scripture states was "in the hill." And if so, this celebrated robber-village, with its castle-like dwellings and massive gothic church in ruins, was the south-west angle of the territory of Benjamin. The valley of Ajalon was seen on our right, from behind an interposing mountain,—the valley which has been for ever memorialized by the command of Joshua to the moon when he pursued the routed hosts of the five kings. The real Emmaus, it is supposed, must have been in this neighbourhood, and in this direction, also, David's conflict with Goliath of the Philistines; and here, before climbing the steep ascent towards Jerusalem, are to be seen remnants of a Roman bridge, showing that the traveller is in the old highway of this region. Here, to my relief, I obtained an English saddle, brought from the hotel at Jerusalem where we were to be entertained. Neby Samwil appeared on its high, dark, stony peak on our left, as we climbed the rugged steep; and whether the real Mizpeh of the Scriptures or not, no better place could be supposed for a watch-tower, or for a prophetic overseer.

We then reached a rocky plateau, from whence we could look far round, and see the whole mountainous and undulated region. It is difficult, in its uncultivated state, to conceive how such stony heights and depths as these could have been the "pleasant" and "fruitful" land described in Scripture. Yet, upon consideration, it must be seen, that such ground, in its elevations, shelves, and ridges, would be most favourable to vines, figs, pomegranates, and olives; and that when clothed with these in their seasons, the rounded hills and intervening vales would make Judea, both in beauty and produce, a "delightsome land," and the "glory of all lands." Along the road from Jaffa to Jerusalem, at stations of a mile or more apart, stand what are called the "Watch-houses," erected by the Sultan for protection of pilgrims. They are as large as the Martello-towers on our coast between Brighton and Hastings; only, instead of being round, they are square. The soldiers, who sleep and live in them, ride to and fro on horseback, from station to station, like the mounted police in our rural districts. From the last but one of these stations, we had our first sight of the Holy City.

From what we felt we could not wonder that the ancient Crusaders, when they had this sight, threw themselves upon their knees, and wept with emotion. Immediately before us, although more than a mile distant, was the impressive form of the broad, massive tower of Hippicus, whence the lofty embattled wall extended on the right to Mount Zion. Within the wall, and above it, stood up the Armenian Convent and its sable companions, the tall cypress trees. To the right of these, and on the crown of Mount Zion, rose the tower and turret called David's tomb; and beyond a valley, still further right, arose the "Hill of Evil Counsel." The wall, also, extended northward on our left, but it was much hidden from our sight by buildings, and more especially by a very large one in course of erection by the Russians, as their chief ecclesiastical establishment at Jerusalem. A crowded burial-ground was in the descending land immediately to our right; and beyond it stretched the plains and road towards Bethlehem.

We entered the Holy City by the Jaffa gate at half-past five in the evening, and were lodged at Hauser's Hotel in Christian Street, adjoining the Pool of Hezekiah, and directly opposite the once splendid hospital of the Knights of St. John, but which is now a desolate heap of ruins. When we had dined in our stone-vaulted refectory, wearied with our day's excitement and ride, we were glad to retire to bed.

*Thurs., May* 15.—Being unable to sleep for excitement during the night, and impatient to see the Holy City, I went out before breakfast with a Jew guide, to obtain a general view of Jerusalem. Passing northward through the narrow uneven street of our hotel, in which were small shops on either hand, with men of various nations guarding or serving in them; and treading over some two or three hundred yards of the uneven pavement, I reached a covered part, where the Church of the Holy Sepulchre extends itself over the road. I then turned down a narrow way to the right, and, after descending some steps, found myself in the entrance-court of this great church of renown. Its external appearance, with its shattered square tower and swelling stone domes, is solemn and impressive. It is of severe Byzantine style, and its lancet-pointed arches, with their dog-tooth ornament, tell of both labour and cost bestowed upon them. They are broken and mutilated in parts, as if they had been violently assailed with axes and hammers. There are remains of the moulded basements of marble pillars on the low platform from whence you take a view of the front of the building. There are chapels and monastic establishments, left, right, and behind, as you stand facing the church, with mendicants in their tattered dresses crouching against them; and at the entrance door before you, Turkish soldiers are seated on cushions, showing that all is under Moslem guard, and that you cannot enter this Christian temple without Moslem permission.

I was allowed to enter; but not so my Jew guide, who cringed and drew back, telling me with a peculiar shrug and look, that he was not permitted to go in; for they said he belonged to a race who crucified Christ. Turkish soldiers were also within the door lounging on cushions and carpets. I passed them without drawing even a lazy look from them, and beheld everywhere the tawdry display of coloured marbles, gilt ornaments, swinging lamps, and pictures illustrative of Christ's death, burial, and resurrection. The place was scented with incense; for though it was not yet six o'clock in the morning, ardent residents and pilgrims had already been for worship; and in every compartment priests and attendants had been swinging their censers. I felt little of their superstitious ardour, and looked sceptically on the "holy places" before which the several groups were bowing; but yet I could not stand within such walls without peculiar emotion. Intending to return another day, when my wife should view with me this interesting spot,—after hastily pacing my way around the aisles, and through the adjoining chapels,— I passed out, and returned to the road leading northwards from the hotel, joined by my Jew guide. This is the Via Dolorosa, or street along which Christ is said to have borne His cross.

I soon turned eastward down a narrow, irregular street, often broken, and overshadowed at different places by houses built across it. This is the Turks' quarter; and they were seen sitting cross-legged in their small shops, and emerging from low doorways of dwellings which one felt a strong curiosity to enter,— although such a hasty glance as could be gained in passing showed that they were generally abodes of wretchedness. As we descended the rugged and slippery street, my Jew guide pointed out to me, with an incredulous look, the stone projection within its sunken doorway where St. Veronica is said to have wiped the bloody and perspiring face of the thorn-crowned Saviour, and to have received the miraculous impression upon her handkerchief; then a recess in the wall, where the transverse beam of the cross is said to have struck; and the indenture of His hand in the wall where He is said to have fainted and fallen. Of course, these are fictions, because the buildings are modern, comparatively, bearing characteristic features of the Saracenic period; but one could not in a street at Jerusalem hear allusions to the sufferings of the Redeemer without emotion. After a turn or two of the street, we reached the arch of the Ecce Homo—a building thrown across the street, and having a window from which Pilate is said to have shown Christ to the multitude. Still descending, we reach St. Stephen's Gate; and I passed out, eager to have a more extended view of the scene of so many thrilling associations.

We stood on high, broken ground, outside the city, with the eastern wall on our right, and over it the purple dome and gilded crescent of the Mosque of Omar on Mount Moriah,—the site of Solomon's Temple. Before us, in the deep gorge below, lay the valley of Jehoshaphat; and we could discern the line of the dried brook Kidron at the bottom. In the valley, across the brook, stands Absalom's Tomb, and other sepulchres of the Hebrew dead; while all around, in the valley and on the hill, are the graves of Jews, who come from all parts of the world to die in Jerusalem, that their bodies may lie here. To the left, across the brook, and gently rising out of the valley, lay the Garden of Gethsemane, with its ancient olive-trees; and still lower, and more to the left, the Tomb of the Virgin; while over these swelled the Mount of Olives, with the various lines of road across it to Bethany, and crowned with the Church of the Ascension. A little to the right of the Mount of Olives, and more distant, rises the "Mount of Offence;" and in the extreme right, the "Hill of Evil Counsel;" while over all, in front, may be seen the distant mountains of Moab. Not only Mount Olivet itself, but the gorge beneath, and the steep leading up to the eastern wall of Jerusalem, are embossed with hundreds of olive-trees. At the top of the steep, under the city wall, is the Turkish burial-ground, thickly covered with graves and tombs. But one thinks not of the Turks and of their tombs, when gazing upon a scene like this; for here, a Christian feels, are crowded together all the sweetest and holiest associations of his life! There rose the mount up which my Saviour trod to pray in the loneliness of the night. There lay the garden in which, "being in an agony, He prayed more earnestly." Across that hill lay the road leading to the house of His tenderest earthly friendship. There was the dried brook He crossed on the night of his betrayal. It was all real. There could be no deception here. There might be forgeries about spots within the wall of the city, but it could not be so here, and the sight was overpowering! I have stood at the foot of Mont Blanc and gazed with awe at its "sovran" peaks. I have indulged fancy in pictured Venice, and within the spacious ruins of the Colosseum, —and paced the gorgeous aisles of St. Peter's. I have voyaged along the mighty Mississippi, stood in the spray of foaming Niagara, crossed the broad lakes and inland seas of America, and trod the pavement of her rising cities; and I had but lately breathed the air of the newer world of the far south, felt the soothing influence of the sweet natural scenery of Ceylon, witnessed the eastern life of Bombay and Cairo, glanced at the sculptured caves of Elephanta, and felt as if transported to a world more ancient than our own while lying at the foot of those wondrous Pyramids; but I had experienced no feeling like the all-subduing feeling of the morning in which I first saw Olivet and Gethsemane. Every train of hallowed thought seemed to point to that moment; and with mingled sorrow for sin and love to the Saviour, I gazed in over-awed silence upon these holy scenes,—feeling they were really holy in their associations.

I afterwards paced my solemn way by the eastern wall of the city amidst the graves and tombs of the Turks; and passed by the Golden Gate, which is of Roman architecture, and handsome, but which has been walled up for ages. My Jew guide said, it had been walled up at the taking of Jerusalem, and would never be re-opened until his own people were restored. We wound past the south-east angle of the city wall, where are huge stones of ancient masonry, and where projects the broken pillar on which it is said Mahomed shall stand at the last judgment to intercede for the faithful, having the Kidron still below at our left, and the ruined village of Siloam in front; and, climbing over loose rubble on its steep side, reached the site of the city of David, and beheld his tomb.

We re-entered Jerusalem by the Zion Gate, within which, with their fronts turned towards the high wall, were the hovel-looking stone huts of the lazars or lepers. We were now in the Jews' quarter. Here, where Melchisedec, King of Salem, had his abode, was once the favourite residence of David, the magnificent palace of Solomon, and afterwards of Herod; but we had to thread our way through an entangled network of narrow passages and lane-like streets,—the houses looking generally half-ruined, and everything speaking of poverty, suffering, and desolation. It was touching to meet the forms of venerable men in long, flowing garments, and their beards reaching to their girdles; and to see beautiful young girls, fair as lilies, with fine dark eyes and eye-brows, clothed with no richness of garb, yet some of them with exceeding cleanliness, glide out of the dingy houses and under the passages, like things of stealth and scorn, and to remember that here their fathers had once trod in pride and power. The unmistakeable Jewish stamp was upon all the faces we met in this quarter. In the streets of trade, the men were busily employed in all kinds of working occupation, and eagerly solicited me to traffic with them in articles brought from all parts of the world. You felt that the Israelite of the Jews' quarter at Jerusalem and he of

Rosemary Lane at the east of London was the same. Passing next into the better accommodated Turkish quarter, I regained my hotel for a late breakfast.

In the afternoon my wife and I, with our Jew guide, went over the city, to take, in the first instance, a general survey of its plan and topographical relationships. We had previously, of course, examined the various theories of writers upon the relative positions of interesting points in ancient and modern Jerusalem; and, knowing that every foot of ground in and about the city, and almost every stone upon it, had been scrutinized by a thousand keen and controversial eyes, we resolved not to perplex ourselves by the numerous contradictory opinions of predecessors in travel, but to view for ourselves the real Jerusalem in which we were, and to observe how far it answered to our remembrances of reference to it in Scripture.

Beginning with Mount Zion, we saw how high and impregnable it was amidst the hills around it, and that it was naturally chosen by the Jebusites, from whom it was taken by Israel, as their chief fort, or stronghold. Here, upon the brow of this loftiest hill, 2,400 feet above the Mediterranean, and 3,700 feet above the Dead Sea, stood the palace of David, the poet-king, with the Tabernacle of the Lord, while on its slopes around were the abodes of his people, extending to a wall of defence which surrounded it in the depths below. This was the site of the city of David, when that monarch took it and made it his capital in place of Hebron. As he gradually subdued from thence the surrounding tribes, the buildings of the city would extend themselves into the suburbs; and we know that the threshing-floor of Araunah, the Jebusite, was upon Mount Moriah; for it was there the plague was stayed. Thus viewing Mount Zion, as you stand upon its summit, it is not difficult to realize the Scripture declarations of its impregnable security, when surrounded by "walls" and "bulwarks;" and of the beauty of its situation, as "the joy of the whole earth," whither "the tribes went up to worship;" while, in its present condition, the bold and daring prophecies concerning it by Jeremiah and Micah are seen to be literally fulfilled in its being "ploughed as a field."

When Solomon succeeded to the throne, and took possession of Jerusalem, with its fortifications and palaces, his first act was to fulfil the pious purpose of his father David, and to build a House for the Lord. This he did upon Moriah, the hill adjoining, in the most costly and perfect style possible, calling to his aid, as his chief architect, a skilful and highly-accomplished man, who was "son of a woman of the daughters of Dan, and his father a man of Tyre;" so that the gorgeous temple which he built was, no doubt, of Tyrian-Jewish architecture. For this he levelled the rocky summit of Moriah, and made the grand and spacious platform on which the mosque of Omar now stands. During the reign of Solomon, the royal capital, with his kingdom, enlarged and flourished; so that, probably, Acra, immediately north of Mount Zion, as well as Moriah, north-east of it, was enclosed within a second wall; and then between Zion, on the north, and Acra would be the Tyropoeon, or valley,—spanned by a bridge of many arches, extending from the royal palace to the temple,—and from it to the union of the valleys of Jehoshaphat and of the son of Hinnom, at the southeast depth of Zion, ran the "valley of the cheesemongers." The ground, in its elevations and intervening declivities, favours this supposition, which is based upon the records of the Scripture; while on the southeast slopes of Zion, and onwards in the valleys around, are sites and ruins agreeing with historic notices of the orchards, vineyards, and pools of water, with which Solomon adorned and irrigated his capital, in the time when, through lucrative commerce with the East, he enriched Jerusalem until he "made silver to be in it as stones."

Thus far all is clear and satisfactory as to the progressive formation of the city; but in its successive enlargement northwards, there is much uncertainty. Manasseh, we read, "built a wall without the city of David, on the west side of Gihon, even to the entering in at the Fish-gate, and compassed about Ophel, and raised it up a very great height." This was south of Moriah, and was occupied by the *Nethinims*, or servants of the temple; but how the parts north of this mount, and north of Acra, were added, is not known. After the temple had been destroyed by Nebuchadnezzar, and the city laid waste by him, we know that the second temple was built, (no doubt upon the original platform,) amidst mingled rejoicing and weeping,—and after that, in the days of Nehemiah, the city walls were restored; (no doubt upon the old foundations;) but how the city progressed and enlarged unto the time of Herod, who restored it and the temple to more than former magnificence, soon to be followed by burning and devastation, until not one stone was left upon another, is not noted, and cannot now be ascertained. If Josephus is to be credited in his record, that two millions of people were within the city when it was besieged by the army of

Titus, then the circuit of the walls must have been much larger than two miles and a half, which is now their girth; and yet if Calvary was any way near the site of the Holy Sepulchre, and "beyond the gate," then the northern wall at that period could not have extended much beyond Acra, or beyond Hezekiah's Pool, which we should suppose would be within the city. So that when or how Bezetha, or the large northern portion of Jerusalem, was added, with its encircling wall, cannot be known.

Probably, the city now, in its general outline, except at the north-west angle, is as it was in the time of Christ; and the sites of Calvary, Pilate's Judgment-Hall, Herod's Palace, and Via Dolorosa, may have been near to what are named for them. Tradition, though uncertain, yet reaching so far back, is not to be lightly set aside; for within two or three centuries of the events referred to, learned and inquiring Christian teachers would be more likely to learn localities than we who live 1,600 years later. Jerusalem was the birthplace of Christianity, which spread itself from thence in successive circles around, through Judea, Syria, and to the ends of the earth; and, as far as I was able to judge, with the Bible in my hands at the Holy City, the traditions from the early Fathers on the sites and scenes of Scripture events, are, at least, as probable as any modern conjectures.

Some difficulties present themselves; but they may be expected after successive wars and destructions in the long lapse of time which has occurred, and when the vast accumulation of *débris* and ruins has filled up intervening valleys as much as forty feet. The tower of Hippicus, at the Jaffa Gate, with its solid Roman basement, the springing arch-stones of the bridge which led from the temple to Solomon's palace, the bevelled Jewish masonry of huge stones in the lower part of the walls west and east of the enclosure round the temple site, with the aqueducts and pools south of Mount Zion, are points and features of importance in a topographical survey of Jerusalem, and are, undoubtedly, remnants of ancient times, which have been preserved through the wars and destructions of the city during 1,800 years past. We made the circuit of the walls, which are from ten to fifteen feet thick, and from thirty to forty feet high, according to the nature of the ground over which they pass, having battlemented breastworks on the outside, with salient angles and towers at intervals, and running over hills and across valleys in zig-zag lines. The walls are evidently built up of old materials, and vary in their masonry in different parts. They are said to have been constructed by Sultan Suleiman in 1542, but, in all probability, they rest on old foundations. Some portions give evidence of this. From the rampart at the top of this wall, very fine views, both of the city and the surrounding country, are obtained; and it is almost impossible to look round from such a position, and not call to remembrance the gracious promise, that "as the mountains are round about Jerusalem, so the Lord is round about His people."

In the walls of the city (which lieth four-square) there are five gates now open : one on each of the west, north, and south sides, and two in the south wall, crossing Mount Zion. And within the city there are five principal streets, as they may be called : three running south and north, and two west and east. These are narrow, dirty, confined, and arched over in parts, with buildings across them, so that they are dark as well as cumbered with dirt and offal. Small eastern shops and stores line the sides of these, with houses here and there intervening; and persons of all nations throng them, out of a population, perhaps, of 20,000, who, generally speaking, may be said to number, almost equally, one-third each of Mahomedans, Jews, and Christians. Ruin and desolation are everywhere visible; and poverty and wretchedness appear in most of the people. Outside the gates, on every side of the city, sit the lepers, not white and scaly, but dark and diseased, with rotting features and limbs, holding bowls in their fingerless hands to the passers by for alms; while in the cemeteries around the walls are companies of mourners, or "wailers," who make loud lamentations. There is a haughty, masterful bearing among the Turks towards the Jews; and the latter complain pitiably of their oppressed condition in their own city. Jerusalem is, indeed, "trodden down of the Gentiles."

*Frid., May* 17.—Before breakfast I went outside the wall of the city at St. Stephen's Gate, and sketched the scene which had impressed me so deeply the day before. After breakfast we mounted on horses, and, with our Jew guide, descended from the eastern gate a very precipitous road into the vale of Kidron; and then, by a gentle ascent, passed the wall of the Garden of Gethsemane, and wound round the Mount of Olives by the southern road, which leads to Bethany. This is, most probably, one of the roads trodden by Christ in His frequent resort to that place of favoured friendship. The ruined village is pleasantly situated on the eastern slope of the mountain, and to European eyes scarcely contains a house that would be regarded as habitable. Of course, we were shown the house of Martha and Mary, and also the tomb of Lazarus. I sketched these, though really incredulous regarding everything, except the site of the village. The house is far too modern to have been there 1,800 years ago; and the rocky, subterranean vault, with its low doorway, scarcely answers the description, given of it by St. John, who says, "it was a cave, and a stone lay upon it." The few wretched inhabitants of the place seemed to be Arabs; and they gathered around us with looks of wonder, the men, women, and even little children, stretching out their hands, and imploring "backsheesh." As usual, we gave something to the tattered and clamorous beggars around us, not willing to have our remembrance of Bethany at all beclouded by the thought of having refused relief to persons in abject poverty.

Leaving the locality where it is said Christ oft-times resorted with His disciples, with all its hallowed associations, we climbed the Mount of Olives to its summit, where stands an ecclesiastical building, called the "Church of the Ascension." This is shown as the spot where the Saviour ascended, and from whence the cloud received Him out of the sight of His apostles; and there is even shown you His last footprint on earth!— but we did not enter to look. It is hardly probable that Christ ascended from this prominent and exposed spot, which might be seen from all parts of the city. It is more likely that it was from a retired part lower down on the south-east shoulder of the mountain; since the Scripture relates that it was "over against Bethany." We now descended by the middle path, until we reached the place where Jesus is said to have beheld the city, wept over it, and foretold its doom, having on our left the road upon which the exultant multitude spread their garments, and scattered palm-branches before Him, shouting hosannas to His name. The view of Jerusalem from this part is comprehensive and striking; and the temple-site from this descent spreads itself impressively before you. On reaching the depth of the angle, where the steep road from St. Stephen's Gate and the Valley of Kidron meet against the north-west corner of the Garden of Gethsemane, we found the subterranean church and sepulchre of the Virgin open; so, descending its sixty steps, we went into its gloomy, damp vault, and, by the dim, mysterious light of its swinging lamps, viewed at the bottom the reputed tomb of Mary, with its tabernacle, and tawdry altar furniture; and then, on our return, saw, on our left, the chapel and tombs of Joachim and Anna, and on our right that of St. Joseph.

We were glad to emerge into the open daylight; and, looking round upon the steeps and olives of this neighbourhood, reflected that here, without doubt, Christ often retired from the throng and noise of the adjoining city for prayer and communion with the Father, and for private converse with His disciples. We then descended by the Valley of Kidron to Absalom's tomb, with its semi-Egyptian and Roman massive square and inverted "pillar," half buried, as it is, with the stones which the Jews throw at it as they pass. It was over here, no doubt, that David fled from his city on the rebellion of his son and people, and when he went up the Mount of Olives weeping. Behind the large monumental tower for Absalom is the subterranean sepulchre of Jehoshaphat, from which it may be that the valley takes its name. We passed the other impressive sepulchres and tombs adjoining, in the Valley of Jehoshaphat, which are ascribed to St. James and Zechariah. The former is a cave, extending as much as fifty feet back under the mountain, and has a Doric front of pillars and frieze cut out of the solid rock; and the latter is a pyramidical tomb hewn out of the mountain, and left separate from it, with a height of thirty feet or so. These tombs, in their forms and excavations, are said to have some resemblance to the sepulchres and tombs of Petra. The ground in all this part, and on all its slopes and ledges, is covered with the grave-stones of buried Jews.

Pursuing our descent, we had the village of Siloam on the overhanging rocks at our left, and the foot of Mount Zion at our right; and we reached what is called the Fountain of the Virgin, and then, still further on, the picturesque Pool of Siloam, where the waters, flowing through long underground passages from higher sources, still "go softly." There the soil is cultivated and deliciously verdant, so as to support by appearance the tradition that this was the place of the king's gardens. It was in that part of the Valley of Gihon that Solomon was first proclaimed king, and from which Adonijah and his revelling companions, in the city of David above, heard with consternation the shouts of the people. On the left, in the ravine descending to the Dead Sea, is "En Rogel," mentioned in Scripture as the boundary of the tribes of Judah and Benjamin, but now named the "Fountain of Job;" and nearer, in the same direction, is an overshadowing mulberry tree of unusual size, where tradition affirms Isaiah the prophet was sawn asunder. Winding our way westwards round the southern slope of Mount

Zion, in the Valley of the son of Hinnom, we found ourselves in a desolate glen, which, on our left, had stern, rugged rocks and precipices, full of the yawning mouths of caverns, empty and tenantless, and which overhung an impenetrable ravine, or rather a charnel-house. This was "Tophet," where its unquenchable fire, and undying worm, preying upon its multiplied victims to Moloch, made it the type of hell. It was here that Solomon, Ahaz, Manasseh, and others, committed abominations, denounced so fearfully by the prophets, and for which Israel suffered so terribly. Crowning this gloomy glen on our left, is the traditionary "Aceldama," or "Field of Blood," bought by Judas, the traitor, and from which he fell, it is said, into the depths below, when he went out and hung himself. Ascending the valley north-westward, we passed the lower pool of Gihon, with its aqueduct at one end, through which, most probably, water was brought to the temple from Solomon's large pools beyond Bethlehem; and, re-entering Jerusalem at the Jaffa Gate, we dismounted our horses, and walked forth, it being Friday, to see the Jews' "Wailing Place."

It is a short space, like a narrow court-yard, paved with flat stones, but not a thoroughfare, lying under the high wall which forms a part of the western boundary to Omar's mosque, or the temple-site. The huge stones, for about half way up, with their bevelled edges, would seem to be of Jewish masonry, and this is very credibly believed to have been part of the ancient temple-wall. The Jews are not allowed to enter the temple-area, but they are permitted to come here once a week, and wail for the ruined city of their prostrate nation. They do so by reading and repeating, with sobs and tears, passages from the Psalms and Prophets expressive of deep lamentation over the ruin of their holy city, and its holy and beautiful house, in which their fathers praised God. And it was, indeed, a tender and moving sight to see ancient, long-bearded men, and women shrouded in long white robes, enter the area, walk along the sacred wall, kissing its stones, and pouring into its crevices their lamentations and prayers! It was a scene confirmative of the truth of Christianity; for it brought forcibly to mind Christ's own lament over Jerusalem before its fall, and His prophecy on its coming desolation.

Springing from this wall, but nearer to its south-west angle, remains part of an arch of the ancient bridge which spanned the Tyropoeon valley between Moriah and Zion. It is of huge, massive masonry; and some of the stones of the wall against it are as much as twenty and twenty-four feet long, and from five to six feet thick. My guide said it was part of one of several arches which supported the grand causeway that Solomon erected to extend from his palace to the temple, and which when the Queen of Sheba had seen, there was no more spirit in her; but others ascribe the construction of this vast bridge to Herod, when he built his temple; and say, that it was upon it Titus stood when he called upon the Jews, who had fled to the city of Zion, at the burning of their temple, to surrender, without forcing him to further destruction. But, in any case, this fragment is part of one of the arches which supported the extended way from the city of David to the temple, at the time of Christ; and, no doubt, upon it the Saviour often trod, in making that passage over what was then a deep and rugged hollow from Zion to the south porch of the temple. The valley is now much filled up with accumulated rubbish; and round this corner, and along the foundations of the south wall of the temple enclosure, grows an impenetrable thicket of prickly pear; but all the masonry of the lower part of the wall in this part is large and old. Of late it has been discovered that, under the south-east portion of the temple platform, there are vast subterranean vaults, out of which, some suppose, material for the temple was taken; but others view them as having been designed for cisterns and reservoirs, made by Hezekiah and his successors, to supply Jerusalem with water. Another conjecture is that these vaults below the temple area were Solomon's stables for his four thousand horses; and that his palace, as well as that of his father David, was immediately south of the temple. This latter conjecture, however, could hardly be entertained by one who had really visited Jerusalem, and seen the relative position of this eastern hill. Be that as it may, the underground work below the temple area is astonishing in its depth and extent; and passages for blood and water, from sacrifices, have been traced, it is affirmed, extending from the parts where the altars stood, down to the valley of Gihon, which is as much as five hundred feet lower. These theories, however, are conjectural: only it solemnizes and impresses the mind to see and study these extensive works of antiquity in such associations; and, after looking upon these huge ancient stones and fragments, and reflecting upon the vast underground excavations, both here and under the north-eastern part of the city, we returned, full of thought, to our hotel.

The remainder of the day was spent in a visit with

my wife to the church of the Holy Sepulchre,—the building which has cost so much European blood. We had to wait a considerable time at its doors, amidst a motley crowd of sects,—Greek, Latin, and Coptic,—who had come thither to worship, but were not allowed to enter because the Mahomedan worship had not yet closed in the mosque of Omar. The crowd, as it gathered and thronged the doorway, frequently murmured with impatience, and the priests within the church looked through the small square opening in the door, and shook their heads with a sense of mortification; but they had not the means to admit any one of us. I spent the time in sketching the garbs and costumes of the several characters around me. At length the Moslem official stalked across the court towards the church, and ascended a ladder to unlock and unbolt the door,—the fastenings being placed so high, that he could not otherwise reach them. The Turkish soldiers entered first, climbed their cushion-seats as a tailor would climb his shopboard, and there squatted themselves in state, with their turbaned heads, baggy trousers, and glittering swords, as custodians; while we, the multitude, passed in. Our dragoman, who was a Roman Catholic, conducted us round the church, and, together with an assistant whom he called, gave us a volume of information, such as it was worth, concerning the holy spots within the church.

The first object was the "Stone of Unction," upon which Christ's dead body is said to have been anointed for burial. It is a large flat tombstone-like slab of Sienna marble, lying on the floor before you, in the south transept, as you enter the church, having, as its appendages, very large candles and suspended lamps. It is not professed that this is more than a cover of the real stone of anointing, which is said to be immediately below it. Several of the crowd rushed towards this stone as soon as admitted; bowed themselves around it, and commenced repeating their prayers. Turning westwards to its left, we were shown the spot where tradition relates the Virgin Mary stood when the body of Jesus was being anointed. This, too, had lamps burning over it. Then turning to the right, we passed under the western dome, where stands the shrine, said to be raised over the spot within which Christ was entombed. It is a large tabernacle-kind of structure, covered in front with pictures and gold, canopied with a large blue banner, which is ornamented with a white cross and stars. We entered the shrine between lines of giant candlesticks, with candles in them twenty feet high, by a low doorway; and immediately within were shown the stone upon which, we were told, the angel sat when he declared to the women, " He is not here: for He is risen, as He said. Come, see the place where the Lord lay!" This stone is smaller than one would expect to find it, and is enclosed in a font-like pedestal. Pilgrims bend over it, and kiss it most fervently. Through a still straiter door we passed into a narrow cell, in which, on the right side, stands a plain white-veined marble tomb. Over it hang numerous lamps of gold and silver, studded with gems,—the offerings of kings and princes,—reflecting, through their coloured mediums, various lights. This is the Holy *Sepulchre* itself. A strange dreaminess is produced by the varied dim and coloured lights of the lamps, and by the strong perfumes of the incense in the warm balmy atmosphere. Here the pilgrims,—beggars, princes, friars, Greek priests, Armenians, or Copts,—are all one in spirit; and they bow low as they kneel and kiss, with weeping, the marble slab of the tomb, worn as it has been by its myriads of visitors. Beholding the emotion of these pilgrims, I felt at first a feeling resembling shame that I did not bow down with them and show as much apparent affection for my Lord and Saviour; but the whole affair was so tricksy and evidently false, that I could not do it. Behind this shrine, against its western pentagonal wall, in an obscure situation, is the place allotted to the poor Copts for worship. It is small and mean, and they are evidently treated as underlings by the Latins and Greeks. Still further back, and through the western wall of the Rotunda, we were shown a vault which they call the tomb of Joseph of Arimathea; but which appears much too short to hold a human body.

Returning to the front of the shrine, we were led to the gates of the Greek chapel, which is, in fact, the nave of the builing; and is most gorgeously gilded and enriched all over with screens, stalls, and canopied seats for the dignitaries. Numerous lamps, gold and silver, hang suspended from its central lantern, or are swung in clumps from the roof, which are kept ever burning. In the middle of the floor is a marble vase, said to mark the navel or centre of the earth, and to contain the clay from which Adam's body was made. Passing out of the gates of the Greek chapel, we were led into a vestry-like room on the south side, and shown the large sword and brass spurs of the heroic Godfrey, used in the investment of those pilgrims deemed worthy among Roman Catholic nobility of admission to the order of St. John of Jerusalem. Afterwards we were shown various "holy places," such as that where Christ appeared to Mary His mother after the Resurrection, the pillar to which he was bound when He was scourged by Pilate, the prison where He was confined during the interval between His condemnation and crucifixion, and the very impressive crypt, or subterranean chapel at the east, said to have been built by St. Helena, the mother of Constantine, over the spot where she found the real cross. Proceeding round the screen of the Greek chapel, we reached the eastern side of the south transept, at which we first entered the church. Here we ascended some steep steps cut in the rock to what they show as the site of Calvary. It is a curiously arched chapel, lighted with lamps, adorned with pictures, very beautifully paved; and under the altar table there is an orifice, encircled with gold, which is perpetually kept open and often perfumed, and wherein they assert the foot of the cross was placed. They likewise lift up a silver strip of the pavement, right of the altar, and show you beneath it a part of the rock which, they say, was rent as Christ expired. At the side of this chapel is another of meaner furniture, where, they affirm, the cross was laid upon the ground while Jesus was nailed to it; and in the vestibule beneath are the mutilated tombs of Godfrey Bouillon and his brother Baldwin, the crusading kings of Jerusalem. In each of these localities there were devotees kneeling, making genuflexions, kissing the stones, and some of them shedding tears. It is impossible to think of so many "holy places" within the limited space, without suspecting them to be "pious frauds;" yet, while rejecting the multitude of more modern inventions, one cannot but reflect that somewhere within this very enclosure, where Christian pilgrims have come for fifteen centuries, may have transpired the Saviour's crucifixion. It is hard to believe that the primitive Christians, engaged as they were with spiritual matters, and scattered as they were by persecutions, would altogether disregard, or lose the remembrance of the place where Christ was crucified; though doubtless for wise ends, and to save mankind from idolatry and superstition, the exact spots of events connected with the Saviour's life and death, have, for the most part, like the burial-place of Moses, been lost to the knowledge of mankind.

# CHAPTER X.

JOURNEY to Bethlehem—Rachel's Tomb—Salesmen in Bethlehem—Church of the Nativity—Tombs and Shrines—The Plains of Bethlehem—The Garden of Gethsemane—Ancient Olives—Pentecost and a Sacrament with Christian Jews, in Jerusalem—Room of the Passover—Pool of Bethesda—View from the Mount of Olives to the Dead Sea and the Mountains of Moab—Journey to Bethel—Gibeah—Mizpeh—Ramah—The Mosque of Omar and the Tower of Hippicus—Farewell to Jerusalem—Journey back to Jaffa—Voyage Home.

*Sat., May* 18.—UP to an early breakfast, and by six o'clock the iron-shod hoofs of our horses were clattering on the hard, slippery pavement of Jerusalem. We climbed the narrow street and passed out of the Jaffa Gate, for Bethlehem. Turning to the left, we descended into a valley, and after skirting the large lower pool of Gihon, which is hewn out of the solid rock, we passed a long string of alms-houses, erected for poor Jews by Sir Moses Montefiore. Then we rode among pleasant fields in the plain of Rephaim, where David conquered the Philistines, to the Greek Convent of Mar Elias,—where, in contradiction to Scripture, the monks say the prophet Elijah was fed by angels under an *olive* tree when he fled from Jezebel. We then descended by an easy slope to Rachel's Tomb,—a cupola-roofed building which is neither imposing nor of great antiquity; but which, no one seems to doubt, occupies the veritable site where Jacob buried his favourite wife. On the hill before us we could see Bethlehem, standing on the crown of a succession of terraced gardens. Its buildings appeared castellated, as seen from a distance.

Winding by an uneven path of loose stones, we entered Bethlehem, and found it much less imposing and attractive than we expected. The streets were narrow and irregular; the dwellings poor; and within some of them might be seen the people at work upon mother-of-pearl relics, sandal-wood, beads, &c. A crowd was soon around us, offering beads and carvings for sale. The men, women, and boys, were clad in dresses of gay colours, in which red and scarlet prevailed. The inhabitants are Christians. Many of the women were beautiful in feature, dignified in their bearing, and wore crosses and rosaries. The Bethlehemite men, however, while fine both in figure and countenance, are said to be a fierce race. They have a sturdy, fearless look, something like the Highlanders of Scotland; and we found them to be exceedingly clamorous in pushing their sales, and crying for "backsheesh." They followed us to the Convent Church of the Nativity, and at times did not seem merely to entreat alms, but somewhat threateningly to demand them. On entering the church we found the nave large and imposing. It is, undoubtedly, the oldest part of the building, and is said to have been erected by the Empress Helena on the model of an ancient Basilica. The pillars of the nave are of reddish marble, and are, perhaps, older than any other part of the church; having been brought, it is supposed, from another edifice. It is covered with an open roof, which must have been renewed since the church was first built. The building looks dirty, and, in this part of it, seems much neglected.

From the nave we passed into an aisle on the left, and then were conducted into a large room of the convent, cushioned round, as a sort of refectory for pilgrims. It was a day of abstinence; so we were furnished with plain viands, very rudely cooked, and brought by shaven monks in their brown dresses and hoods. They then took us to see the place where Christ was said to be born, which is at the east end of the church, in a cave or recess scooped out of the rock, and reached by descending steps. It is adorned in the Romish way with pictures and tinsel, and is overhung with numerous lamps of gold and silver, reflecting various colours. Opposite this shrine of the Nativity is that of Joseph, the husband of Mary, with similar gaudy adornments. We stood and saw the visitors come and bow; and although we did not bow with them, we could not shake off a feeling of reverence; for we reflected that if the manger in which our Lord was laid were not situated here, it must have been in some spot near at hand.

In this underground region we were also shown the cave and grotto of St. Jerome, in which he is said to have fasted, prayed, and translated the Scriptures into Latin: the translation called the "Vulgate," in common use among Roman Catholics. Near to the gloomy abode and burial-place of the great recluse, there are the tombs and altars of S. S. Paula, his devoted patroness, and of her daughter Eustachia, as also of some saint named "Eusebius," which cannot be the celebrated church historian, though the monks would fain have you believe it is. We left these vaults and passages, with their glimmering lamps, rude altars, and pictures; and emerged from the crypt of the Nativity by a flight of stairs leading into the Greek portion of the church, which was dazzling all over with pictures, gold, and swinging lamps, in their usual way.

From the convent we walked forth eastward to see the Plains of Bethlehem; and felt that here again we were amidst realities. The day was in character with the scene contemplated. The heavens were serenely beautiful, and radiant with pure blue light. No doubt it was surrounded by these mountains, and upon these green and lovely plains, that the shepherds kept watch over their flocks by night, and heard overhead the angels sing the incarnation-hymn. It was here, also, that the son of Jesse kept his father's sheep; and from the caves of the rugged and desolate mountains around came the lion and the bear which he slew before he challenged and slew the uncircumcised Philistine, the shaft of whose spear was like a weaver's beam. From hence he fled to the wilderness of Engedi beyond from the jealous Saul, and sheltered in the cave of Adullam. Here, also, Ruth, the Moabitess, followed the gleaners in the field of Boaz. I sketched the whole scene of beauty and heart-thrilling interest; after which we returned by the Milk Grotto, in which tradition relates that the Virgin and Child were hid from the fury of Herod the royal assassin, before their flight into Egypt; and returned to the convent. After another survey of the church and its crypts, we remounted our horses, and rode back by Rachel's tomb to Jerusalem, full of deep and tender reflections on what we had seen, leaving behind us the "Three Pools of Solomon," and beyond them Hebron, the city of the Patriarchs, and the southern border of the Promised Land.

Finding we had yet some time on our hands, we rode slowly through Jerusalem, then out at St. Stephen's Gate, and descended to the foot of the Mount of Olives, that we might view more deliberately the Garden of Gethsemane. The monks have modernized it by enclosing it with a wall, and by planting it as a "garden;" but when you look upon its ancient olives, their immense boles gnarled, knotted, and twisted, like so many huge enwreathed serpents, they seem so old, that you are ready to believe they overarched the Man of Sorrows in that night of His mysterious agony, when He lay prostrate on the ground, and "sweat, as it were, great drops of blood." You feel sure that if it were not actually here, it was not many paces off, when He cried, "Father, if it be possible, let this cup pass from Me!" and where through the darkness He beheld the gleaming torches and the approach of the base betrayer. It was a spot to awaken feelings which one cannot and would not describe. The monks were reverentially respectful to my wife, and gave her flowers from the garden, and a bit of the branch of one of the olive-trees. After sketching the ancient trees, I went alone in the solemn evening to view and sketch the tombs of St. James and Zechariah in the valley of Kidron, surrounded as they were by the thousands of Jewish graves which I had previously beheld. It was night-fall when I got back to the city; and I was only just in time to pass through the gate before closed at sunset.

*Sun., May* 19.—We attended service at the English Protestant Church, which stands opposite the Tower of Hippicus, on Mount Zion, and not far from the Jaffa

Gate. It is a plain Gothic structure, without any tower, looking in its front like the east end of an English church, with the parapet sloping up to a central point. The congregation was good, and composed largely of converted Jews. In the transept on the right were seated a number of Syrian youths who have been brought to Jerusalem, and are taught in a school situated in the city of David, and which the present Bishop of Jerusalem, Dr. Gobat, who is supported jointly by England and Prussia, founded, and superintends. After the liturgy we had a good plain evangelical sermon by a clergyman, (who preached extemporarily,) on, "Have ye received the Holy Ghost?" it being Whitsunday. We remained, and partook of the Lord's Supper, with the solemnly joyful feeling that we were really "come to Mount Zion," and were holding Christian fellowship with converted Jews. We looked forward to the time when there will be literally one fold under one Shepherd. But even now all sectarian views and feelings were gone, and we experienced one large yearning for the establishment of Christ's kingdom over all the earth.

It being Pentecost, we went from the church to visit the Room where it is said the Saviour kept the Passover with His disciples, and where the Holy Ghost descended upon them in cloven tongues of fire. It is an old, large upper-room at the southern part of the city of David; but, from its early pointed arches, it is evidently a building of only modern antiquity. It *may* stand on the site where Christ took the Last Supper with His disciples; but it cannot be the veritable chamber in which He washed their feet, and spake to them the sweetest words of tenderness and consolation that ever

His voice uttered. From this room there is a descent by steps, under a canopy, to the entrance of the Tomb of David, which is more exclusively guarded and reserved by the Turks from infidel eyes than the mosque of Omar itself. We were not allowed to descend the steps, much less to enter the tomb; and our American friend was pushed away from the very sight of the entrance, somewhat roughly, and with Moslem threats. On our return we entered the church of St. James, connected with the Armenian convent, and which has been highly decorated with presentation pictures and jewelry by wealthy pilgrims. In the evening we again attended Divine service in the English church, and heard one of the missionaries to the Jews preach a good sermon, on "Quench not the Spirit;" but not so plainly evangelical as that we heard in the morning,—and, being only read, not so effective in the delivery.

*Mon., May* 20.—Rose early: went and sketched the "Via Dolorosa, and the "Ecce Homo;" and then turned into a convent, where they show another place, in which they say Christ was scourged, giving me still less confidence in their showings. After breakfast sketched the "Pool of Bethesda," as it is named. It is a kind of huge tank, in a remarkable situation between St. Stephen's Gate and the temple-site; and there is room enough for the five porches to have stood by it; but whether it be the identical piece of water beside which the impotent man sat when Christ bade him take up his bed and walk, is questionable. It is much larger than Hezekiah's Pool, another piece of water which lay next our hotel, in Christian, or Patriarch Street, and which is said to have been provided by the pious king for the supply of Jerusalem; but it is impossible to tell what reliance is to be placed on the tradition. Possibly it is nothing more than a deep fosse which separated the fortress of Antonia from Bezetha. I afterwards called on the Consul, Mr. Finn; and found him exceedingly courteous and obliging. He showed me a fine view of the city from the upper part of his house; and kindly pointed out some of the remarkable sights in Jerusalem. He also promised to send the next day a Janisary, who should conduct me to a spot where I could have a good view of the mosque of Omar and its court.

In the afternoon rode with my wife, and our Jew guide, by the left road over the Mount of Olivet to the other side of its crown; and descending as far as it was thought safe from thieves, we beheld the extensive scene. Bethany was on our right, under the brow of the hill; before us were the broken, rugged hills of the barren wilderness where Christ endured His temptation, —a most desolate-looking region. Far away on our right, over the brown wilderness, lay the "Dead Sea." It was of a heavy leaden colour; and stretching away to the left, but still beyond the "wilderness of Judea," was the winding line of the Jordan, clothed with verdure at its sides and banks. Our guide pointed out to us the serpentine part where the Israelites crossed. Stretching far beyond all, in the soft purple distance, were the mountains of Gilead and Moab, with Nebo amongst them, from which Moses viewed the "goodly land," and on which he died. In the less remote distance, between the line of the Jordan and the barren hills of the wilderness, may be discerned the ruinous heaps of ancient and modern Jericho; and one could now plainly understand how the man who fell among thieves "went down" to Jericho. It is a very dangerous road, along which the traveller needs trusty soldiers to guard him. Some travellers from the North of England, who had gone down thence a few days before, had been robbed and stripped; and a sheik was then in prison, to be confined there until the stolen property was restored. In our foreground was a Turkish burial-ground, with goats in it, feeding under the guardianship of a Syrian shepherd, and with a small mosque to the right upon it. We observed here several lovely flowers and interesting shrubs; and among them a profusion of the prickly green thorn, of which, most probably, the Saviour's plaited crown was made by the soldiers, when they mocked Him and set Him at nought. The sweet, green herbage of the burial-place formed a beautiful contrast to the barren tract beyond, while the shepherd's turban and coloured dress, the black goats, and the mosque, served to give distance to the picture. The vast vault of heaven arched itself in bright translucent blue over the whole. After I had sketched this view, we returned by the middle path over the Mount of Olives, seeing in our way the "Caves of the Prophets," and having from that neighbourhood a full view of the platform on which the temple stood, with the walls and buildings of the city around it.

But what a melancholy usurpation we were witnessing! On that rocky platform Abraham, at the command of God, went forth to offer up his son; and there he received the promise of divine blessing upon himself and upon his seed. There Solomon raised his magnificent temple, and at its opening supplicated Jehovah in that lofty strain, while the incense rose to heaven, and smoke went up from thousands of bullocks and rams, consumed in sacrifice. And there Christ walked and worshipped with His disciples, performed many of His miracles of mercy, and taught the people with words of wisdom, which compelled them to say, "Never man spake like this man!" But there, *now*, the children of Abraham were mere scouted refugees in rags and wretchedness, and the proud, sluggish, and sensual Mahomedan had seized the greater part of the inheritance, while the gilded crescent from the dome of Omar proclaimed it his own. Most likely over this very road on which we stood David fled into the wilderness at Absalom's rebellion; and from this very spot where we have been standing to look upon Jerusalem in its ruin, David's Lord beheld the city, and wept over it.

*Tues., May* 21.—Rode off at early morning with our Jew guide for Bethel, which lies some twelve miles north of Jerusalem. Passing out of the Jaffa Gate we turned to the right, and doubled the north-west of the city-wall, observing how at this higher point, where assailed by invaders, from Nebuchadnezzar to Saladin, the city was most vulnerable: thence descending till we reached the broad Damascus Gate, with its flanking, embattled towers, and many marks of fray and siege,—we struck northward into the road for Bethel. About a mile forward, after viewing what tradition calls the "Grotto of Jeremiah," we reached a singular excavation, called the "Tomb of the Kings," but which is supposed to be the burial-place of the Empress Helena, the mother of Constantine the Great. It is situated at the western side of a large area, or court-yard, sunk in the solid rock, and, like the Tomb of the Prophets, and other burial-vaults about the city, is a series of chambers, with arched recesses at the sides for bodies, something after the manner of the Catacombs at Rome. The front has had a deep and elaborate frieze and cornice, supported by two pillars; and the chambers, or vaults, were reached through a low doorway, closed from observation by a huge rolling-door, which fitted so closely that the place of opening could not be discerned. This tomb of "the rich," whether of Helena or the Kings, strikingly illustrates, in its principal features, the incidental notices given by the Evangelists of the Tomb of Joseph of Arimathea, in which the body of Jesus was laid. Like the new tomb belonging to that rich man, —and like all the ancient tombs of importance at Jerusalem,—it is *hewn out of a rock*. Its sunken area of nearly ninety feet square in front, planted with shrubs and trees, shows how *the sepulchre*, though on Golgotha, the place of skulls, was *in a garden*, where Mary Magdalene mistook the risen Saviour for the gardener. The low doorway, some three feet square, leading to excavated chambers within, explains how John and the women, *stooping down, looked in*, and how Peter and others, *went into the sepulchre*, and saw there the linen clothes lying, and the napkin that was about His head, not lying with them, but wrapped up together in a place by itself; while the ponderous millstone cover to the mouth of the sepulchre, rolling to and fro in a groove, would be sufficient to induce the inquiry by women desirous of entering, *Who shall roll us away the stone from the door of the sepulchre?* Indeed, the truthfulness of the Gospel narrative on this event, as on other events, is singularly evident at Jerusalem.

Soon after, we left the road leading to Anathoth, the birth-place of Jeremiah, and climbed the stone-terraced height of Gibeah, a place associated in our minds with the names of Saul and Samuel from the time we read the historical books of Scripture in our childhood.

Then, on the left, rose Mizpeh, crowning a lofty green hill, and we could imagine the prophet Samuel from thence surveying the country round. Among the hills north of Mizpeh our guide pointed out Gibeon; and we soon met companies of Gibeonites going to Jerusalem with broken wood upon their heads, and asses; for they are still "hewers of wood and drawers of water." We then descended by a zig-zag path into a valley deep and rugged, and had shown to us the scene of Jonathan's adventure with the Philistines, and where his father said he must die for having tasted a little honey out of the rock. We passed Ramah on the crown of a rounded hill amidst trees. It was a pleasant abode for the "school of the prophets," which had the venerable Samuel for its head, and where Saul was once seized with the spirit of prophecy, if that was the real Ramah of Samuel. Skirting the western side of that hill, the rocky, shelving road conducts us to Bethoron, and on to Bethel; and on our way our guide pointed out to us, in the far left, the "hilly country" to which the Virgin ascended on her visit to Elizabeth her cousin, the mother of the Baptist; and also the place where Jesus was missed in His boyhood from the company, and whence Joseph and Mary returned to Jerusalem to seek Him. It was interesting to have even imaginary spots pointed out to us connected with the history of our blessed Lord; but we could not help feeling that they might be only imaginary.

Still pursuing our way northwards on rough and rocky roads, and over hills, on the ledges of which the stone platforms were worn bright by horses' hoofs, we passed Bethoron, and soon reached Bethel. This, also, is a village in ruins. Its scanty inhabitants live in falling hovels; and there are the ruins of a Greek church, near which is a dried basin of a large pool. There are pleasant fields all around; and on the ridge of a high hill beyond stands the remnant of a square tower, called "Jacob's Pillar." It is said to be on this spot that the youthful fugitive patriarch slept on his pillow of stone that memorable night when God appeared to him at the top of the ladder of ascending and descending angels, and promised to be with him, and to give him and his seed that land for an inheritance. We now dismounted, and took a meal from the provisions which we had brought with us, under the broad shade of a fig-tree, in a garden near one of the half-ruined houses of the village. From the flat roof of one of these houses I sketched the surrounding scenes, while the Arabs and their children gathered around us, and cried vociferously their everlasting "backsheesh!"

We returned over the hills and valleys on the way we came, until we nearly reached Jerusalem, when we rode somewhat westwards, and visited what are called the "Tombs of the Judges." These are, perhaps, the most perfect and extensive of the impressive series of excavated tombs which surround the greater part of the city. The whole mountain-range, from the north-west corner of Jerusalem to the village of Siloam, and up the valley of the son of Hinnom, is honeycombed with sepulchres, which often consist of many chambers, extending far into the rock; so that it is said, there are more tombs in the hills around the holy city than there are houses within it. Tradition states, that in these excavations persecuted Christians often took refuge, and had their abodes. After a view from Mount Scopus, where the Roman army under Titus encamped,

—we glanced at the hilly platform from whence the imperial legions made their most successful assault upon the city; but we did not remain long to view it, being fairly wearied out with our ten hours' ride under a Syrian sun.

*Wed., May* 22.—By six in the morning, in fulfilment of the Consul's promise, a janisary came to our hotel to conduct me to the Turkish barracks, which overlook the court-yard of the mosque of Omar, or ancient temple-site. He preceded me through the streets, striking his long silver-topped staff against the pavement, like a drum-major walking before a regimental band; calling the attention of passengers in the street, and the inhabitants of the houses, to the fact that something important was going on. I was somewhat tickled with this parade; but was gratified to find that it secured for me an easy passage through troops, and guards, and sentinels, to the ramparts of the citadel. Here, where Josephus places the proud tower of Antonia, stood, in all probability, the castle and palace of the governor of Jerusalem; and here, most likely, was the judgment-hall in which Jesus was accused by the Jews, and condemned by Pilate. From this point of view, the panorama of the city was more complete than from any other; and from it the temple-site, and the buildings upon it, are beheld to great advantage. You see plainly from hence that the large spacious platform, which is now occupied by the mosque of Omar and its court-yard, has been perfectly levelled by the hand of man in former ages; so as to render it fit for a temple so ample as that of Solomon, with all its necessary adjuncts for the sacrifices of animals, and the dwellings of priests. The mosque itself, which, with its many-coloured marbles and glittering dome of rainbow hues, may lay claim to magnificence, occupies comparatively but a small part of this vast, prepared platform. It stands on the spot where the altar of Jehovah stood, and covers the part of the rock of Mount Moriah which projects upwards above the ground; and through which, it is said, there is a channel perforated down to the vast vaults below, as before noted. These vaults must have had their outlet in the vale of Kidron; for this was the great drain for the blood, offal, and washings of the sacrifices.

The mosque is enclosed at some distance in a square of low Saracenic buildings, which is paved with marble, and entered on each side by high and ornamental gates. On this stand praying-shrines, fountains, and the exquisite Arabic pulpit, so well known. Between this square and the rampart of the citadel is a large space which seems to form a solemn promenade for the Moslems, and into which "infidel dogs," Christian or Jew, are not allowed to enter. There is a small domed erection in it on the left, as you look down from the rampart, which is called "Solomon's Throne;" while on the right, in the distance, are groups of olives and cypresses, with buildings of eastern shapes, and towering above them the tall minaret, from which we heard the muezzin, so often during the day and night, cry, "Allah, Akbar!" and, "Come to prayers!" At the southern extremity, in the middle, is the church-like mosque of El-Aksa, with its beautiful dome. On the right, is a range of cloister-like buildings for dervishes, and Moslem ecclesiastics. The distant landscape is composed of the Mount of Olives on the left, the mountains of Moab in the far centre; before them rises the Mount of Offence;"

and the hill of "Evil Counsel" is on the right; while Mount Zion, and the buildings of the Jews' and Turks' quarters, are seen over the western enclosure. I sketched and coloured these, to make myself familiar with such deeply-interesting objects, as beheld from this elevated position on the roof of the barracks.

The janisary proceeded with me through the streets of the city, to the tower of Hippicus, striking his iron-pointed staff on the pavement very vehemently, and holding his head aloft. This is a broad massive fortification, an undoubted remnant, as we have seen, of the ancient Jerusalem, of the time of Herod; Josephus himself stating that it was spared at the siege, by Titus, A.D. 70. It stands at the boundary of the western wall, near the Jaffa Gate. From the upper part of it I had another extensive view of the city.

Leaving the janisary, I proceeded alone on the road which passes by the Armenian convent, and out at the Zion gate, to the large upper room of the Passover, which I had visited on the preceding Sunday; and, having obtained an entrance, I sat to sketch it. The Arabs, old and young, crowded round me, and with curious looks watched the tracing on paper of the pillars and groined arches of this ancient chamber. They were so familiarly officious in their attempts to help me,— putting their hands quickly into my pockets to reach pencil or penknife, when they thought I wanted it,— and coming so near to my face, that I felt, at times, a little apprehensive as to what they might next do towards a stranger who was entirely in their power. But I persevered with my sketch, new visitors crowding in, and showing equal interest in it,—even Nubian women, as well as Arab men, appearing before me, and placing themselves in certain postures, that I might put them into my picture. But I did not gratify more than one of them, for I had no time to spare; and the one figure was sufficient to give scale to the drawing. On my way back I passed through the Jews' quarter of the city, and saw a marriage procession highly illustrative of the Parable of the Ten Virgins. The evening of our last day in Jerusalem had come. I now returned to the hotel, examined the account presented to me, which I found to be reasonable, and made due preparation for early departure on the morrow.

*Thurs., May* 23.—Our horses were ready, and we left the hotel at five o'clock in the morning. We did not, however, hasten along the road for the first hour, but rather lingered, to take a last look at Jerusalem, and to indulge in reflection on what we had seen, as also in the thought that we might never, in mortal life, see it more. The sun, which had just risen above the Mount of Olives, and threw his soft, gentle light over the upper part of the city, seemed to give additional tenderness to our farewell; while the deep shadow on this side of the embattled walls and towers, and over the road along which we were journeying, seemed to accord with our sadness. Jerusalem looked wonderfully sorrowful to us at that hour. But there gleamed over her hopeful morning rays. After turning to take our last sight of the Holy City, we descended the shelving road in silence,—the thoughts of home gathering in our minds, and mingling with the feeling that we had at last realized our life-dream, and seen the choicest spot to be viewed on earth. We pursued our way back, "up hill and down dale;" for such was the nature of the road, until we rested under a large old fig-tree, in the " heat of the day," to partake our meal. By about six in the evening, we reached Ramleh, embosomed in its verdant and lofty palms and huge cactuses. We remained at the Latin convent for the night, and received most pleasing hospitality from the monks, as before.

*Frid., May* 26.—Left Ramleh early in the morning: our road lying across the beautiful and cultivated valley of Sharon. The Syrian peasants were already in the fields, with their many-coloured dresses, some of them heaping the corn on the backs of camels; for it was still reaping time. The sweet notes of birds were heard on every hand; and sights and sounds combined to remind us that we were in that valley of Sharon whose loveliness was celebrated by Hebrew poets so many centuries ago. We passed by strings of pilgrims on this and the preceding day. They were Russians, Greeks, and some of other nations, slowly returning from the great feast of the Greek Church, which had terminated a short time before we reached Jerusalem. We entered Jaffa on a road enclosed by high cactus hedges, which were in glorious blossom, and by the orange-groves, here so extensive. We did not stay in Jaffa; but made our way through its descending narrow streets to the seaside, quickly passed our examination at the sort of Custom-House, and, by a small boat, were at once taken on board an Austrian steamer, about to sail for Alexandria. We were off in an hour; and, before we started, I sketched Jaffa as we beheld it from the vessel.

Our company on board gave us another glimpse into eastern life. We had several pilgrims on their way to Mecca; a few rich Musselmen, who had each four or five wives; but of these women, as before, we seldom saw more than the glance of their bright eyes from behind the curtains which were drawn across the closet-like places, in which they were secreted, at the sides of the deck. The whole of the middle and fore-deck was crowded with passengers of an inferior grade: some poorer pilgrims on their way to Mecca,—others Jews going to Alexandria or Cairo for trade; and these, with the Jewish women, (several of them very beautiful,) were all huddled together like so many cattle.

*Sat., May 25.*—After a pleasant voyage we reached Alexandria at five in the evening. We landed, and drove to our hotel; found there our Australian birds, which had been pleasant cabin companions to us in our homeward voyage, safe. Then we went to look after our lost luggage; and were told that, after diligent search and inquiry, it was ascertained that it had been sent on to England by a wrong steamer.

*Sun., May 26.*—Attended the English Protestant Church, which is a semi-Gothic and Saracenic structure, not at all pleasing in its mongrel style of half-Christian and half-Moslem architecture. It seems an attempted union and compromise that is neither natural nor desirable.

*Mon., May 27.*—Found it difficult to settle with our dragoman, who, after all the civilities and apparent good-will he had shown us in our travel to Palestine, wanted to overreach us by demands most exorbitantly beyond the original agreement. I had to take him before the English Consul, who declared that I had handsomely dealt with him in my offer and agreement, for £2. 10*s.* per day; so he was compelled to give up his demand. He afterwards came and apologized for the trouble he had given, hoping that I would recommend him to other travellers; but I gave him no promise that was likely to comfort him; nor do I give him any other recommendation than that contained in this recital. The fortnight's pilgrimage to the Holy Land, from Alexandria, cost about £50, as at first estimated; but I learned that, with stricter economy, it might have been made for less.

*Tues., May* 28.—We had a final drive through Alexandria, past Pompey's Pillar, and other objects of interest. By widening our circuit of observation, we found mansions and villas, with their gardens, surpassing what we had seen before. We sailed from Alexandria at five P.M., in the "Elora" steamer, belonging to the Peninsular and Oriental Company.

*Wed., Thurs., Frid., and Sat., May* 29, *to June* 1.—Pleasant sailing. Reached Malta on Saturday morning by five; and after going ashore to see the palace of the Grand Master of the Knights, Armoury, &c., we sailed from Malta by one at noon.

*Sun., June* 2.—Read Liturgy, and preached morning and evening in the saloon of the steamer.

*Mon., and Tues., June* 3 *and* 4.—Pleasant sailing along the Mediterranean, with interesting glimpses of the African coast.

*Wed., June* 5.—Fine bold views of the Spanish coast in the morning,—rich in colour. Two mountains, in the distance, stood up like pyramids. Reached Gibraltar by half-past four, P.M., and left by nine at night; but did not go on shore; because it had been announced that we should sail earlier. It was found, however, that the engine needed some slight repair, so that there was some delay.

*Thurs., Frid., and Sat., June* 6, 7, *and* 8.—Somewhat

rough sailing along the Portuguese and Spanish coasts, until we came to the Bay of Biscay.

*Sun., June* 9.—In the Bay of Biscay: the sea smooth, and the weather fine. Read Liturgy, and preached; thankful to find now, as before, so many desirous of uniting in religious services,—especially of the military class. It was also a pleasing reflection that, on the trial made over nearly the full width of the globe, so much real union exists among true Christians of different denominations.

*Mon., June* 10.—At six in the evening, Plymouth in sight, and ships crowding up the Channel.

*Tues., June* 11.—Passed the "Needles" at six in the morning, entered the Channel between the Isle of Wight and the coast of Hampshire, and felt, after all the lovely scenes we had witnessed, there was nothing so lovely as dear old England. Reached Southampton Pier at nine o'clock; and, on inquiry, found our missing luggage in the Queen's Warehouse, by the water-side. Set off by rail at half-an-hour before noon, and arrived at the Waterloo Station at three in the afternoon, earnestly grateful to the Father of mercies for His signal Providence over us in our long travel, and for His gracious preservation of us from all injuries, in these changeful nine months.

LONDON:
PRINTED BY WILLIAM NICHOLS,
32, LONDON WALL.

# Works by the same Author.

*In One Volume, post 8vo., ornamental cloth, price 7s. 6d.,*

## AMERICA,

AND

## AMERICAN METHODISM.

### WITH A PREFATORY LETTER BY THE REV. JOHN HANNAH, D.D.

ILLUSTRATED FROM ORIGINAL SKETCHES BY THE AUTHOR.

---

"A BEAUTIFUL volume, which we take the earliest opportunity of announcing, and which we hope ere long to commend more effectively by quoting a few of its vivid passages,—descriptions to the 'fidelity' of which, 'as well as to their beauty and force,' Dr. Hannah bears 'willing testimony.'"—*Wesleyan Magazine.*

"MULTITUDES will be happy once more to meet Dr. Jobson, who is a man of a genial spirit, and a highly captivating writer. His large heart finds its way into his work, and breathes strongly through every page of it. A better travelling companion England could not furnish, or a better narrator of passing occurrences...... Rarely have we met a publication of the kind that contained so much quotable matter. Every page presents important facts, and every paragraph is gemmed with beauty...... Admirable everywhere, he particularly excels when touching on Slavery; and his book in this respect cannot fail to be productive of the best effects when it shall have been reproduced among the Americans. The frown and the sorrow of such a man will not go for nothing among that spirited and high-minded people."—*British Standard.*

"THE views of the author, for one who spent so short a time in this country, and nearly all of it occupied in travel, are very correct...... Those who were permitted to converse with Dr. Jobson, and those who listened to his sermons and addresses, express great admiration for him as a Christian gentleman and as a preacher, which estimation will be confirmed by this book."—*Zion's Herald, Boston, United States.*

"DID our space permit, we could interest our readers with a number of well-written descriptions of places and persons that came under the observation of our traveller: that of the Falls of Niagara is specially worthy of notice, and might be read with pleasure even by those who have visited this wonder of our world...... We have much pleasure in commending the book for a wide circulation even in Canada, as, we doubt not, such is the prospect in England."—*Christian Guardian, Toronto, Canada.*

# WORKS BY THE SAME AUTHOR.

"EVERY page gives evidence of the serious spirit of observation which animated the writer, as he passed, with a ranging, ready eye, and an open heart and mind, from city to city, and from state to state, over tracts of country full of the elements of deep interest to a Christian Englishman."—*London Quarterly Review.*

"DR. JOBSON's book combines substance with bright colouring. It is not only a very interesting narrative of voyage and travel, but a highly valuable addition to our staple information in regard to America. It is just such a manual on the subject of American Methodism as was greatly needed in this country, and must be extensively welcomed. And it presents the fairest and fullest view of the relations of Methodism to Slavery in the United States which we have yet seen."—*Watchman.*

"DR. JOBSON possesses many of the requisites necessary for the production of a work like the one he has given us. In the first place he has a mature judgment, a ready and an eloquent pen; and added to this, he has a tact for observing whatever is noteworthy in nature or art, and he has the valuable talent of being able to dash off some of the most admirable scenes, and transfer them to his sketch-book."—*Bradford Observer.*

"WELL worthy of study by all who take an interest in the management of church affairs, and are willing to condescend to take valuable hints, come whence they may."—*Christian Times.*

"ONE of the best and most readable books we have on America: moderate in tone, manly in sentiment, clear and simple in diction, and pervaded throughout with the spirit of genuine philanthropy and piety."—*Christian Family Record.*

"WE may commend this work as useful, informing, and, on the whole, creditable."—*Athenæum.*

---

In crown 8vo., price 4s. embossed and gilt, and 3s. plain,

## THE SERVANT OF HIS GENERATION.

## A TRIBUTE
### TO THE MEMORY OF THE
## REV. JABEZ BUNTING, D.D.:
BEING A SERMON PREACHED ON THE OCCASION OF HIS DEATH, IN EASTBROOK CHAPEL, BRADFORD, YORKSHIRE, JULY 18TH, 1858:

WITH

A SKETCH OF HIS CHARACTER AND SERVICES.

"IT is a faithful, noble, and attractive portraiture."—*London Review.*
"THIS is a graceful monument to one of the masters in the modern Israel."—*Wesleyan Magazine.*

"This publication has been expected with considerable interest by all who knew the friendly relations subsisting between the talented author and the venerable subject of it, and it will not disappoint any reasonable expectations. It is in every sense of the word a beautiful book; beautifully 'got up,' and presenting a beautiful picture of an object that was 'beautiful exceedingly.'"—*Watchman.*

"The subject and the preacher are alike worthy of each other. "We consider the production a masterpiece, superior to everything of the kind that Methodism has yet produced. The two or three panegyrics which have come down to us from ancient times, even as literary compositions, are inferior to it, and the celebrated eulogies of the French Academy are not to be mentioned in the same day. It takes rank with Foster's character of Hall, and Pratt's Dissertation on Cecil."—*British Standard.*

*In crown 8vo., price 5s.,*

# A MOTHER'S PORTRAIT:

### BEING

## A MEMORIAL OF FILIAL AFFECTION.

### WITH

### SKETCHES OF WESLEYAN LIFE AND RELIGIOUS SERVICES.

*Illustrated by Twenty Engravings on Wood by* E. LANDELLS, *from Original Pictures by* J. SMETHAM *and* F. J. JOBSON.

"This book, the production of Mr. Jobson, formerly of Lincoln, is, we predict, destined to become popular. The parts devoted to mother and home are enchanting, from the pure and simple affections stamped on every page." —*Lincoln and Stamford Mercury.*

"The author's design in the preparation of this very beautiful work evidently goes beyond the portraiture of an individual......One of its primary intentions is to recall to the minds and hearts of readers who have enjoyed the same privileges as its author, profitable remembrances of a Methodist home. That this may be accomplished, and at the same time that others who do not belong to our community may have a just conception of what Methodism really is, it will be found that there are here presented living scenes and descriptions of every one of our services......We rejoice that this has been done with equal faithfulness and good taste, in a work which, more than almost any other Wesleyan biography, is likely to pass beyond our own circle......The style of the pen is in keeping with that of the pencil,— indeed, we think, superior to it,—and is that of a clear, unstudied, but never negligent simplicity, perfectly befitting Letters forming a mother's biography."—*Watchman.*

"The subject is good, and the limner's hand skilful. A filial tenderness of touch adds to the effect of his delineation. All is truly *practical*, however; and, large as is our biographical library, we can welcome an accession which promises to be as useful as popular......The social means of grace, as enjoyed among us, are well described. The notices of the progress of Methodism in Lincoln and in the county are full of life: and the sketches of Christian worthies—from the primitive class-leader of the city, to William Dawson, Robert Newton, and John Smith—are truly graphic."—*Wesleyan Magazine.*

"THE substance, plan, and general style of this biography have almost equally delighted us......There is nothing which may be fairly stigmatized as religious cant; genuine, simple, earnest, but sober godliness is exhibited and commended in this volume, and nothing more. We sincerely welcome it as the most interesting piece of Christian biography, dealing with feminine and private excellence, which has appeared for many years past. The least of its merits is the elegant embellishment afforded by numerous spirited vignettes."—*London Quarterly Review.*

"THIS is every way a book of beauty, surpassing everything that has yet issued from the commonwealth of Wesleyan Methodism; beautiful in sentiment, beautiful in style, beautiful in typography, and beautiful in illustration. Mr. Jobson has here performed a great service, not only to his own community, but to the general church."—*Christian Witness.*

"THE author of this beautiful biography was a representative of the British Conference in the late General Conference of the Methodist Episcopal Church. He is an excellent man, and withal an artist; as is seen not only in the superb engravings, which we have faithfully reproduced in this edition of his work, but in the structure of the work itself. It is a perfect gem. It ought to be in every Methodist house in the world."—*Journal of the Methodist Episcopal Church South, U.S. of America.*

---

*In Octavo, price* 5s.,

## CHAPEL AND SCHOOL ARCHITECTURE,

AS APPROPRIATE TO

### The Buildings of Nonconformists,

PARTICULARLY TO THOSE OF THE WESLEYAN METHODISTS.

WITH PRACTICAL DIRECTIONS FOR THE

### ERECTION OF CHAPELS AND SCHOOL-HOUSES.

WITH NUMEROUS PLATES AND ILLUSTRATIONS.

---

"WE are glad to see this elegant volume, which is brought out in fulfilment of a recommendation of the Model-Plan Committee, and of the Conference......There can be little doubt that the labour here expended will be recompensed by a general improvement of our architectural taste."—*Wesleyan Magazine.*

"THERE is no one who has done so much to diffuse among Wesleyans intelligence and good taste in reference to the architecture of sacred edifices as the Rev. F. J. Jobson......His original education and profession, his extensive acquaintance with Wesleyan Chapels, his office for several years as Secretary of the Chapel Building and Model-Plan Committees,—his native tastes and acquired experience, combine to render him our highest authority and best instructor as to Wesleyan Chapel building......As a *Directory* on the subjects on which it treats, it is almost an indispensable volume for every Wesleyan Minister and Trustee. In it they will find full instructions for whatever is to be done in Chapel and School building, from the purchase of their sites to their completion and opening......The illustrations are of great beauty, and exceedingly appropriate and serviceable, and are executed in the best style."—*Watchman.*

"IT sets forth good principles, and will doubtless have a good effect."— —*Builder.*

"MR. JOBSON'S work is of a practical and useful character, and none the less acceptable for the earnestness of its tone."—*Artizan.*

"MR. JOBSON has shown how possible it is to build Chapels and Schools in a style of neatness, and even of elegance, at a less cost than is often incurred for erections singularly devoid of those qualities, and which, in some cases, are as destitute of convenience as of taste. The work is illustrated with drawings of exteriors, and ground plans, both for Chapels and Schools; and though containing much of special interest to Methodists, it contains *more* adapted to do good service in relation to Nonconformist architecture generally."—*British Quarterly.*

"WE recommend all who are about to build to consult this valuable work." —*Evangelical Christendom.*

"WE have great pleasure and confidence in recommending so pleasing and instructive a work to all Nonconformists, as a suggestive guide to the erection of Chapels and Schools."—*National.*

"HIS designs for School-Houses are remarkably chaste and consistent with propriety and taste, and, whether considered as representations of the ground-plans or elevations, together with the furniture and fittings, they will be found extremely serviceable to those parties who are engaged either in the erection or enlargement of buildings for schools."—*Sunday School Teachers' Magazine.*

## WORKS BY THE SAME AUTHOR.

*In crown 8vo., cambric, gilt, price 6s.,*

# AUSTRALIA;

WITH NOTES BY THE WAY, ON EGYPT, CEYLON, BOMBAY, AND THE HOLY LAND.

## WITH A COLOURED ILLUSTRATION OF AUSTRALIAN SCENERY.

### NOTICES OF FIRST EDITION.

"WE have never met with sketches more faithful and more valuable to any class of readers, whether it be the returned colonist, or the future emigrant."—*Australian and New Zealand Gazette.*

"WITH the eye of a painter, and much of the kindred sensibility of a poet, our traveller combines the heart of a Christian and a Minister. Hence the varied hues which shine on his page, lending a fresh interest to all he tells of the island-continent of the south,—of its scenery, climate, produce, and especially of its people."—*Wesleyan Magazine.*

"A BOOK of varied travel, among Methodist and many other scenes, written with great intelligence, and in a uniformly religious spirit."—*Watchman.*

"THE book is unpretentious, but it has more merit than some of less modesty."—*Evangelical Magazine.*

"A VOLUME that teems with samples of power and beauty,......overflowing with important information touching all the colonies, and everything that appertains to them. As relates to the body politic, and the kingdom of Christ at the present moment in those wondrous regions, no publication that has as yet appeared admits of comparison with the work of Dr. Jobson."—*British Standard.*

"DR. JOBSON is a Methodist minister, but has had opportunities beyond most of his brethren in the "home work." They travel only in Britain; he has travelled a good deal abroad, and visited the most distant parts of the earth. He is able, therefore, to bring his knowledge of the world, and his experience of men and things, to bear on a wide sphere. The result has been two good books; of which this second, chiefly relating to Australia, is, we think, not less interesting or valuable than the former, which contained an account of his visit, a few years ago, in company with the Rev. Dr. Hannah, to the General Conference of the Methodist Episcopal Church (North) in the United States."—*London Review.*

LONDON: HAMILTON, ADAMS, AND CO.   SOLD BY JOHN MASON.

www.ingramcontent.com/pod-product-compliance
Lightning Source LLC
Chambersburg PA
CBHW030820230426
43667CB00008B/1296